"I am blessed to have been counseled, mentored and supported by this author. Our journey began with me as a single mother seeking guidance in every area of my life. I now use my new found knowledge to lovingly support my Hospice patients and their families. I will always cherish our work together and the unforgettable and one of a kind wedding ceremony she officiated for my husband and me." ~ Claudette Daguiar

3-31-16

Dear Mary Michelle
you are a gift.
be blessed as you
work with this book!
Love
Grace (author)

The Transforming Power of Affirmative Prayer

It works if you work it!

~~~~~~

Grace Reynolds Victor

BALBOA
PRESS

A DIVISION OF HAY HOUSE

Balboa Press books may be ordered through booksellers or by contacting:

Balboa Press
A Division of Hay House
1663 Liberty Drive
Bloomington, IN 47403
www.balboapress.com
1 (877) 407-4847

Printed in the United States of America.

ISBN: 978-1-4525-6392-3 (sc)
ISBN: 978-1-4525-6394-7 (hc)
ISBN: 978-1-4525-6393-0 (e)

Library of Congress Control Number: 2012922405

Balboa Press rev. date: 11/13/2014

Contents

Chapter 9

Chapter 10

Disclaimer

The information in this book is not to be considered as a substitute for medical, psychological, psychiatric, or any professional diagnosis or treatment. The content of this book does not supersede the guidance or treatment of any health-care professional.

Dedication

I dedicate this book to my family. I also dedicate this book to our beloved Eglah Lewis McBean my mother, and Ian Adrian my grandson who both has made their transition.

I dedicate this book to all who desire to answer the universe's call that we consciously reawaken, evolve and become spiritually transformed. We can clearly see that our world has come to a new order, and many of us have realized that we are all here for God. We are also here to love while expanding in the Christ consciousness, and serving according to our calling. It is my earnest intention that this book serves as a guide in the process of our spiritual evolution.

I also dedicate this book to all those who asked for a follow-up after a workshop I gave; the tools are included here!

I dedicate this book to all those who feel that they are not good enough or that they are better than or less than others.

I dedicate this book to those who are afraid of failure or success.

I dedicate this book to those who desire to forgive and to be forgiven, to love and be loved.

I dedicate this book to the harmoniously whole you that you truly are. I see you rising out from the ashes like the phoenix. I see you enlightened and transformed!

Namaste

In Loving Memory

This dedication also goes from me with love, to my loving mother Eglah Lewis McBean affectionately known as Patsy and Patty, who has made her transition.

Her encouragement to birth this edition was frequent and loving, with a quiet tone of urgency. Completion came shortly after she made her transition. This dedication is a symbol of my unending gratitude and love for her.

My Dear mommy,

The Lord is your shepherd, you do not want; you receive all good things.

You rest in the pasture of love and peace, beside still waters of tranquility.

Your soul is restored and you walk in paths of righteousness glorifying God's name.

Although you walked through the valley of sickness, pain and death, you did not fear. You actually said "I am ready to meet my Lord" You unselfishly told us the exact day! You knew that the Lord was and is forever with you, comforting you.

The Lord prepared a table of healing, victory, joy and peace for you in the presence of your past enemies of sadness, sickness, pain and death. Your head is anointed with the oil of illumination, love and gladness. Your cup of love, joy and healing overflows!

Our Heavenly Father and all creation know that goodness, joy and liberation follow you throughout your eternal reign in paradise; here, you dwell in the house of our Lord praising him forever.

The love you gave us all now defines and lifts you. Your calling as a dedicated mother and a Good Samaritan, who always took in the abused and homeless without cost to them, still fills me with awe and admiration. I told you how grateful I am for your unconditional love and kindness. Again, I thank you; love healed and lifted you! I am grateful and all is well.

I love you now and throughout eternity.

Annin & Boogin (the names you affectionately called me).

Grace Ann Reynolds Victor.

Preface

An Invitation

To every reader:

I can remember just recently smiling to myself and thinking, "*this is great! People are gradually changing their vocabulary.*" I continue to hear words such as *transformation, evolution, surrender,* etc., coming from people from all walks of life. This is good, yes very good. Every occurrence in the universe is a testimony that the universe is evolving. Its inhabitants are being transformed as well. We must not assume that these changes spell doom or gloom. We must understand that this is a spiritual evolution that only serves to bless us into a higher state of God consciousness. This cannot be achieved with our heads in the clouds. We must be right here on this earth, doing God's work, serving all of creation, and obeying the spiritual laws of God through acts of conscious cooperation with God. It can be an adventure of faith if we are willing!

I write this book as an invitation for you to rise up higher in consciousness and to embrace the real you, this self who is always so much more than our finite minds can fathom. I have a burning desire to support my fellow men, and I know that this is one way I can achieve this at this time. This book is not about religious dogma, and you do not have to abandon your particular faith. However with renewed consciousness, for example, when you reread the parable of the prodigal son, every word will burst forth with new meaning. The prodigal you, in your new awareness, will hear and obey the voice of Our Heavenly Father. You will rise up with the intention of becoming your Heavenly Father's child. Your affirmative way of thinking and praying will support you as you leave the land of famine where the ego has taken you. On your way home, the Father makes his way to you as you hold the intention to return to him, because he knows our most secret thoughts and he loves us unconditionally. You will realize that your Heavenly Father has never left you and that you can choose to allow his presence to meet and greet you and to guide you home. Once you make it home, you will not think of eating the pigs' food of guilt and shame because the process of the journey home has transformed you. You will be greeted with a feast of your spiritual inheritance. A golden ring of acceptance and unity will be placed on your finger by your Heavenly Father. He will put a coat of wisdom on you and he will put the shoes of understanding on your feet. You will also realize that no one can save you but yourself, through your obedience of Spiritual laws. Only you can keep your own thoughts and actions affirmative and based on love; you are responsible for your own progress. Change is an inside job; you must choose to allow God's spirit in you to guide and direct you as you elevate your thoughts, renew your mind and consciously transform.

I offer this book as a love offering to Jehovah God and to all of creation, with the intention that it is used as a tool for spiritual transformation. For all of you beloved readers and thinkers, I affirmatively pray.

My Affirmative Prayer for You

Our Heavenly and Almighty Father, I pray in the name of Jesus Christ, who taught us how to pray affirmatively. Gratefully and in your presence, I stand in the gap for my fellow men. I embrace the knowing that all humanity is profoundly supported and revived as they embrace the principles in this book. I am grateful that everyone who reads this book feels the love with which every word was written; they become empowered and awakened from the sleep of mediocrity, fear, and superstition. I understand that through grace, all attain a higher state of consciousness and demonstrate wholeness and completeness now. I rejoice as women, men, and children everywhere now become alive, awake, and aware, bursting forth into their magnificence from glory unto glory! I stand in agreement with St. Paul, who entreated us to be transformed by the renewing of our minds. Let the mind that was in Christ be in all, and let all be subjected to your higher power now. I am grateful that transformation now takes place as this book offers light and order in the dark recesses of our minds. Our Heavenly Father and Lord of the heavenly hosts, all creation now praise you. All is well now and forevermore, and I obediently allow it to be so. For these blessings and so much more to come, I am eternally grateful. Amen.

A Divine Discontent

Several years ago, I decided that a quick fix for my feelings of divine discontent was to affirm, "I am showing up in this world with authenticity, love, and courage in obedience to all that God has prepared for me to do." My doubts weighed more than my courage. In retrospect, I now know that I was not even showing up, much less with courage. Physically, I felt as though I was literally in a life and death situation. Shopping and the white picket fence could not end the feelings of extreme tiredness, sadness and discontent. However, I quickly realized that the universe was responding to my faintest glimpses of intention, often through synchronistic events. One such event came by way of my vegetable garden!

It had been quite a while since I had begun to feel this deep dissatisfaction. I also noticed that when I was still or in the silence,

I felt a quiet joy. I believe this joy is what comforted me and supported my faith in God's grace. I felt trapped as well. I felt that apart from being a wife, mother, daughter, and counselor, there was a big dream that was really God's dream for me. I felt deeply that I was destined to be in service, in the form of spiritual practices.

As a child, along with family members, we experienced prejudices because of religious practices practiced by my grandmother. In one incident, I was afraid. Now I know that I had developed some resistance to fully embracing the spiritual practices that were not the most popular at that time. It was easier to hide and play small even though my desire to expand weighed heavily on me. The truth is that playing small was extremely difficult because it produced an empty, hopeless feeling.

Once the earnest desire was there, the universe conspired to help! I began to notice that at family functions I was often the one asked to offer the prayer. The feedback I received resonated as messages for me ... and yes, I believe that people will show you who you are. I came to the realization that prayers can be a way of service for me. I thought that this might be odd but I could do it as my secret service to God. I also thought that I could visit hospitals and offer prayers to those who would receive them. To me this was a safe place to go; acquaintances would never find out. However, that never materialized. Deep inside I felt I was engaged in a spiritual tug-of-war between the little ego and my real self.

A Lesson in the Garden

One beautiful day, I was tending my vegetable garden when I noticed a large zucchini on a vine, and I felt led to leave it there. A few days later, I realized the vine with the huge zucchini had stopped producing more fruit but still maintained that one huge zucchini. The other vines continued to produce normally.

As I quietly tended the garden, the thought, "what *you focus on grows*," came to me. I realized then why I had felt led to leave the zucchini on the vine; there was a lesson waiting for me, and this squash represented an idea. Because this oversized squash was still attached to the plant, it demanded that the resources of the plant be supplied to it. As a result, the vine's natural focus was on this squash, which demanded its attention and support; there was apparently no resource left to produce new fruit. This is the same pattern in which negative or positive thoughts thrive in our minds, becoming magnified when we give them our focused attention. These thoughts consume us until we have no inner resources available to produce anything else except the thing we are focused on. Whether the thought is positive or negative this principle works the same.

I thought,*" this can be a great lesson for my students; if they focus on learning, they can grow in wisdom and knowledge."* I took my squash to work and shared my experience with my students. Just as I was leaving, a colleague happened to be exiting at the same time. She said softly and deliberately to me, "That squash is newsworthy." I said, "Oh yes?" She replied, "Yes!" I believed her because there was something compelling about how she said it. Shortly after, a local newspaper published an article I wrote about it titled, "Zucchini Zest," with a picture of the squash and me. I thought it had been pretty easy and felt a sense of accomplishment. I also thought I would keep submitting articles.

I continued writing and compiling short inspirational articles but did not submit them to anyone. I however had a firm belief that there was a purpose for my inspiration and urge to write. Much of what I wrote is included in this book and some has been used in workshops, counseling sessions or in conversations with the intention of empowering others. The principle demonstrated by the Zucchini vine stayed with me and is very present in this book, as each reader is asked to focus through Affirmative prayer, affirmation, denial and treatments. **My prayer is that the information in this book inspires its readers to take action as inspired, to become reawakened, to be of loving service, and to live their grandest life. We always deserve the best that life has to offer, no one is excluded as this is our truth!**

Acknowledgments

This section of acknowledgment would not be complete if I did not start at my journey's beginning. I first thank you, Jehovah, for holding this project lovingly in your heart. When I was a child, my grandmother would anoint her grandchildren with oil she blessed. She, along with my mother, taught me to pray. My mother taught me about the nature of God, and I have since known God to be gentler! When I was five years old and complained to my grandmother that I could not open the guava jelly jar, she said to me, *"Come on, you were put here to master things."* I did not ask her what she meant, but as she opened it for me, I understood that mastery meant being able to do things. The word *mastery* reminds me of her after all these years! She loved teaching me songs and stories about Jesus even though she practiced according to several faiths.

Whenever I told my mother that I had a certain need, she would respond, "If you want a guitar, you must buy the guitar's strings first." This was my first lesson about the Law of Attraction. Throughout my childhood years, she has shown me how to forgive and how to be successful. *"Mommy, when you tirelessly and single-handedly take in homeless families without financial compensation from anyone at any time, just as you did throughout my childhood and even today, you continue to teach me the greatest lesson in compassion."* To my late mother, Eglah Avril, and my late grandmother, May Yvonne, thanks, and I love you both.

I acknowledge my husband Gregory; I thank you for your support, patience and for understanding that retreats and workshops away were vital to our loving relationship. I also thank you for understanding that this holy assignment of writing would take me away from the bustle and into the sanctuary of our home quite often. I acknowledge my children, Kenann, Jason, Jamie, and Ashley. You are my greatest teachers. Because of you I have learned about my weaknesses and strengths. I am grateful for the blessing of having you as my children. To my husband and children, you are the catalysts for my spiritual liberation and transformation! I thank you.

I acknowledge my grandchildren, the late Ian Adrian, Ayo Adrienne, Jian Zoe and Alaina Grace. You have taught me about a whole new dimension of love. Beloved Ian, you have made your transition after seven and a half short years. Your life touched many of us, and it continues to do so in the charitable fund called the Ian Thompson-JANYO Fund, which gives to local nonprofits in your name. I will always love you. Ayo Adrienne, Jian Zoe and Alaina Grace, your strength and infectious smiles bring hope to us. I thank you for being joy. I love you.

I acknowledge a wonderful group of visionaries who lit the path at various points of my journey. I have either read your books or attended your workshops, lectures, or retreats. My gratitude goes out to Rev. Dr. Ianyla Vanzant, in whose classes I sat and learned; you one day said that I would do great things, and I believe; Dr. Wayne Dyer, whose book *Power of Intention* I used for self-edification and as a mentoring tool. Tama Kieves, you told me that you loved my prayers, and encouraged me to follow my wildest dreams. Mary A. Thompkin, Rev. Dr. Michael Beckwith, Debbie Ford, Rev. Dr. Barbra King, Marianne Williamson and Paul Ferrini, I was fortunate enough to sit in a classroom where you taught; I thank you. I was blessed to study the works of Ernest Holmes, Raymond Charles Barker, Charles and Myrtle

Fillmore, Dr. Catherine Ponder, Emmet Fox, Mary A. Thompkin, Dr. Robert A Russell, Rev. Dr. Leon Masters, Brother Mandus, Norman Vincent Peale and many others; I thank you all. "I also thank you Miss Oprah Winfrey for allowing yourself to be *love in action*. When you first introduced Gary Zukav on your television show, I felt a deep joy knowing that because of this exposure, the conversation of enlightenment and the practice of Spiritual principles would become more widespread; I also felt a renewed sense of permission and the spirit of boldness to talk more freely of my spiritual beliefs and practices.

I acknowledge Rev. Dr. Dianne Burke, Reverend Joyce Liechenstein, and the staff of the NYC One Spirit Interfaith Seminary. Thank you for creating a priceless program for spiritual study and learning leading to ordination. That experience gently and lovingly touched every facet of my being; for that experience, I am humbly grateful to you all. Claudette, when I mentored you, I discovered that your inspiration, encouragement and willingness to *do the work* in turn inspired me; I acknowledge and thank you. Reverend Abigail, I acknowledge and thank you for often reminding me that I must let everything fall around my writing and never the reverse. Marie Elena, you are an excellent and organized typist, you always found time to do my favorite thing with me, i.e. to crack up laughing! I was fortunate to work with the Balboa Publishing team in bringing this book into tangible form. It is with heartfelt gratitude I say, that I have worked with Balboa's staff members who are truly professional, insightful, supportive and commendable. My questions and concerns were addressed. "To each one of you I am very grateful, thank you."

Chapter 1

The Confirmation

The universe supports us by giving us confirmation! A few days into a work week, a colleague of mine in a serene tone, described her recent rough weekend. She said that she decided to read the town's newspaper to distract her from worrying about her relationship problem. She picked up the local paper and saw the article title, "Zucchini Zest," and thought, "*oh, some silly zucchini story, but I will read it anyway,*" and she did. She described to me how the article brought her to an awareness of her focus. She then decided not to focus on worrying about her relationship. She went on to mention that the article's message made her feel so good that she wanted to see who had written the article. She then checked and realized that it was me.

At this point, we laughed heartily, and she added that the story had really helped her. Her compliments triggered doubts in me. I wondered if I could ever write another article that would have that great of an impact on someone. This seemed too big for me so I allowed doubt to have a party in my head.

Apart from the fears and doubts, I was unsure of how I should serve spiritually. My feelings of discontent grew into anger, boredom, sadness, ambivalence, and extreme tiredness. I experienced a "dark night of the soul." These feelings lasted a whole year. The physical symptoms of this experience grew in intensity. I had to yield, deepening my spiritual practice and following the Spirit's guidance. I felt very peaceful when I wrote, and I decided that writing is a great part of my real service. I decided also that before I wrote anything of a spiritual nature I would write a cookbook. I began the process, and a series of gentle nudges made it clear that it was not the time for a cookbook.

The Dreams

A vivid early morning dream brought much-needed clarity. My grandmother, who had taught me to pray and who had already made her transition, was in this dream. She, along with some women and I, were clad in white from head to toes. She was at the pulpit in the sanctuary in her home, leading a prayer service, as she had actually done when she was alive. She sent three half-used yellow pencils to me by way of one of the "sisters" there. I was about ten to twelve years old in this dream. I received the pencils and began to smile childishly. My grandmother looked at me sternly, letting me know that she was not joking. Although everyone in the room was communicating, no words were exchanged. Upon awakening, I had an awareness that I must also write about inspirational topics like the ones my grandmother used to speak about.

When I had the following day time dream, I also knew that my dark night of the soul experience would begin to end then. I do not sleep during the day, so it was very unusual when I went from alert to intensely sleepy within a few minutes. I initially resisted, but the unusual sleepiness was too intense to withstand. I reluctantly threw myself crosswise on the bed and immediately fell into a deep sleep. I dreamt that I was observing two black lionesses, an adult and a cub. Mental words came to me, explaining the scene. The adult, whose fur was dull and somewhat matted, was faithful. She had worked hard and was worn and tired. She walked slowly with her head down and went toward a corner to rest. The cub had shiny black fur, and she was happy and frisked around with lots of energy. I also understood that since the older lion was tired, she was retiring and the cub had taken over for her. I had a profound awareness, and as the weeks passed I began to feel physically stronger and mentally courageous.

It had been a while since my daughter had given me the book, *One Day My Soul Opened Up*, by Ianyla Vanzant. I remembered scanning it and having little interest in it at the time, so I put it on a shelf. Customarily, I read many inspirational books. One day as I continued to feel stronger, my eyes happened to glance up at this book on the shelf, and my inner voice said, "I must read this book." I knew that I was ready for whatever work this book entailed. I immediately followed through and realized that I loved it; in many instances, it seemed that the author was speaking to me! It was thoughtfully designed to support one's spiritual evolution in the most effective way. I could hardly wait for each new day to complete the required exercises; I committed and did the work!

My soul continued to open up, and I continued to feel stronger on all levels of my being. I was led to several retreat workshops led by gifted visionaries, including Reverend Dr. Vanzant. Since young adulthood as mentioned, I had immersed myself in the writings of Ernest Holmes and Charles Fillmore. Later and as I continued to be open I revisited the writings of Raymond Charles Barker, Emmet Fox, Emily Cady, and Robert A Russell, to name a few, as well as more modern-day visionaries such as Louise Hay, Dr. Wayne Dyer, Eckhart Tolle, Tama Keives, John Randolph Price, Gay Hendricks, Paul Ferrini, Dr. Michael Beckwith, Carolyn Myss, Shakti Gawain, Gary Zukav, Louise Hay and Dr. Leon Masters, to name a few. I continue to allow myself to be mentored by Dr. Dyer through his book *The Power of Intention*.

The Benevolent Laws of God

Affirmative prayer is a practice through which we experience the
working of the Law of Mind. The Spirit of Jehovah in us works
through this law. **We see the demonstration where thoughts
become things**. This has been my experience through the writing
of this book, whether it was a thought I quickly had to write down,
a vivid dream, a page in a book that caught my eye, words that
came to me in silence, something someone said to me or someone
I had to forgive while working on the chapter of forgiveness!
Working with faith, I have never failed to see the Law of Mind
at work.

One such event occurred when I decided to include the account
of my peer and her experience after reading my published article,
"Zucchini Zest." I had not seen her in about five years. I had a
strong desire to ask her permission to include her account of the
experience she had as a result of reading my article. I wondered
where I could find her. Within three days, in just one second of
Divine synchrony, I walked into a clothing store and happened to
look up, while she happened to look out of the fitting room. Our
eyes met. We laughed heartily again, and I asked her permission
to include her account in my book, and she happily replied, "Yes,
and I cannot wait to see it in print!" **When we live and pray
affirmatively and follow God's will for us, the whole universe
conspires to propel us forward, often in a synchronistic
manner. Yes, and even in a fitting room!**

Light along the Way

Throughout the difficult experience of feeling spiritual
discontentment and the fulfilling process of writing this book, I
have proven that as I become obedient to the direction of God's
Spirit within me, all dictates of the little ego become nullified. One
great idea followed another. Knowing that all creation benefits

from God's ideas crowns it all. I admitted to myself and others that I have a natural gift for writing, and since I have embraced the affirmative way of praying, I feel impelled to write about it and teach it to others. The more I write about it, the more enthusiasm overtakes me.

Deciding to write, I clearly knew that the love, beauty, power, and grace of God were too amazing to be kept hidden. All of mankind deserves to be blessed by this wisdom. Feelings of peace and freedom supported my belief in this work. Ideas began to flow through dreams and thoughts that came to me as I drove, exercised, sat on a plane or train, or even waited in a checkout line at a supermarket. I keep myself armed with notepads for these juicy moments of inspiration!

My intention is to use my gifts in service to God and all creation as I fulfill God's dream. **I realized that as creations of God, we are all created to be more and never less and no one is excluded from this gift of grace**. Fear of success and failure had caused me to hide and slip into a box of self-sabotage, which showed up as denial, blame, anger, and excuses. In this box, I learned that when one is not expanding spiritually, he or she can easily be lulled into the sleep of mediocrity. I surrendered to God's call and, though with some resistance, made it out of the box.

Although I have moved into the unknown, I feel a sense of inspiration; moments of awareness are more frequent. I believe God has a sense of humor because at times I have ideas that make me laugh heartily. I am grateful for courage to live from a place that differs from the one my little ego dictated. I know this work supports others as well as me, helping us prove that Jehovah-Jireh is indeed our provider. Serving this way fulfills my heartfelt desire. One of my favorite sayings is, "Writing juices me up!" It also brings me profound joy, which I offer to all.

Chapter 2

The Law of Attraction

"As a man thinks in his heart, so is he" (Prov. 23:7). It is understood that through the law of attraction, the conditions of our affairs and circumstances are attracted to us to accord with the thoughts we hold steady in our consciousness.

The law of attraction also regulates what comes to us or goes from us according to our use of other Spiritual laws such as the laws of faith, forgiveness, gratitude, obedience, love, etc. These laws cannot work automatically; we are the ones who must obey these laws in order for the law of attraction to work on our behalf. In his book *God Works through You*, Robert A. Russell said that **the Law of Mind is the Law by which Spirit acts**, (Pg. 88.) We know that the Spirit of God dwells in and acts through us. I believe the entire purpose of teaching this affirmative way of praying would not be fulfilled if the nature of the Law of Attraction was not explained. **Affirmative prayer, like our thoughts, sets the Law of Attraction into motion; however, the consciousness or condition of mind of the person praying must be of love. Mindlessly repeating affirmations, denials, and treatments would be futile without love as the basis.**

Too many people misunderstand the working of the law of attraction. As a result, they believe they can have a need or want fulfilled by simply and haphazardly visualizing the desired thing dropping into their laps. Nothing could be further from the truth! When Christ taught that we must not worry about what we should eat or drink, etc., he further stated, **"But seek first the Kingdom of God and his righteousness and all these things shall be added to you" (Matt. 6:33).**

We must seek first by going to the deeper Soul level of our beings to know what God wants us to do, have, or become. We can do this through prayer and meditation. Prayer is a two way communication process, therefore after we pray we ought to become still and listen. In this place of stillness, we open our minds, become receptive, and listen to our inner guidance from God's Spirit within us. The more we practice this process, the clearer it becomes.

Any teaching or doctrine that fails to teach that our consciousness must be based on love, forgiveness, faith and thanksgiving, in order for us to make lasting manifestation through the law of attraction, is irresponsible and misleading. This shortcut method does not allow the individual to engage in mental and spiritual preparation and growth. It is the same principle as building a house on sand; the storms and tides of life can quickly erode its inadequate stability. People need to renew, strengthen and condition their minds. They must also do the outer works of faith.

The outer works of faith could involve daily prayers, meditation, cleaning up impulses of discord, doing forgiveness work, releasing fear, living in a state of gratitude, developing one's self-esteem, practicing patience, willing service and love for self and others. The laws of God are immutable! God is just and cannot play favorites. We all must obey these laws if we want to attract our good. When we obey these spiritual laws of God, we support ourselves in developing the consciousness or mental equivalent to the desired thing. This also means that the thought vibration matches the desire and is therefore able to create it. Visualization while having a Christ consciousness of love and forgiveness is vital to having the law of attraction work favorably on our behalf.

Visualization and the Law of Attraction

Visualization is commonly used to enhance the outcome of any situation. This is possible because it entails imaging or seeing the manifestation first in the mind's eye. When tapping into the working of the Law of Attraction through the imagination, the scenery in mind triggers brain responses that help the body to feel as though what is imaged is physically real. The emotions help to seal the desire as accomplished!

We need divine guidance to help us create through imaging. We need guidance to create the mental mold in which the desire will take shape and harden. If the mold is not God ordained, it will not be durable; the ego's winds of doubt will be able to topple it.

Visualizing for a desired thing without first seeking God's will is akin to forcing the hand of God; this way is always futile; then If the desired thing is manifested, it may not last; it may bring misery or attract people with ill will. There have been numerous stories about people who gained sudden or unexpected wealth and then ended up losing it quickly or becoming unhappy because of some circumstance it produced. When the mind or consciousness is not prepared for wealth, perhaps because of habitual poverty which produces a poverty consciousness, these people may have an underlying resistance to wealth. As a result, they can self-sabotage their new wealthy state. People often have an unconscious need to hold on to what is normal, habitual, familiar, and comfortable regardless of whether it's positive or negative and does not support their liberation. They may feel comfortable with having not enough or having just enough. Praying with thanksgiving and allowing God to renew the mind and guide the use of our wealth is the wisest thing to do.

In order to allow the Law of Attraction to work favorably for us, we must first become a vessel worthy of containing the results of

our answered prayers. We must deliberately think the thoughts and do the things that honor God, us, and others. When we enter the silence and seek and receive guidance through our prayers and meditation, we must follow the guidance we receive. We must not make the mistake of thinking that through the law of Attraction only good things come to us. If our consciousness is of ill will or any other negative state, through the Law of Attraction we will manifest a corresponding negative equivalent. *Please slowly reread the previous sentence.* The secret to manifesting and maintaining a God ordained life of grace and ease is to follow the spiritual laws of God first.

Prosperity is our birthright just as much as the gift of choice is our birthright. We can choose to let the Law of Attraction work to attract our good as we let our thoughts, words, and deeds become grounded on the foundation of agape love. We should not seek shortcuts to our success by visualizing it without first doing our spiritual work. In order to have a consciousness of agape love, we must embrace and practice the spiritual laws of love, forgiveness, faith, and thanksgiving. We must also embrace compassion, kindness, and service to ourselves and others. We must surrender anger, fear, greed, jealousy, hate and resentment. Failure to do these things ensures that a person will soon become a house divided against him or herself. This creates situations where this person will experience difficulty manifesting and/or maintaining his or her good.

When you know you have created the fertile mental atmosphere within yourself, the following treatments and affirmation can nourish your consciousness and support the development of the mental equivalent of prosperity. **Always remember that thoughts held in one's mind reproduce their own kind.** Feel complete acceptance for the following practices. **Always be courageous and creative to create more personal prayers.** You may be happily surprised at how creative you already are!

Prayer

Heavenly and Almighty Father, I feel empowered as I praise your holy name! You have provided so wonderfully for all creation. You created us in your image and likeness. I ask that you please grant me a daily supply of wisdom and divine guidance. My desire is that your will be done in and through me. I embrace and accept your will as my will now. Dear father, I ask for specific things and situations such as (**request**) however I am willing to accept whatever you supply. I realize that you will always provide that which makes me whole, and whatever will support the next step of my spiritual evolution. I trust how and when you bless me because you are such a loving God who is always on Divine time. Most loving Father, I now accept your blessings in Jesus' name. I am grateful that you have heard and answered me and that all is well. Amen.

PS. In the above prayer please feel free to specifically name whatever you are asking for. You can add it where the bolded word "request" is placed.

Treatments

- Everything in me supports the manifestation of my desires. My complete being, welcomes the grace of God's Spirit working through me. Nothing can go from me but love, truth, and goodwill. Nothing but good comes back to me. All is well.
- Being in tune with my Infinite God, I am open and receptive to divine ideas. I allow the still, small voice to guide me, and I intuitively know what to say or do. I respond immediately and willingly. I know that as I act, I am allowing the Christ Consciousness to act through me. All my affairs are illumined by the healing light of Christ. For this privilege, I am grateful.

- **D**ivine abundance now manifests in my affairs. It brings me opportunities to do whatever is life giving and uplifting for me and others. I expect, accept, and embrace new ideas and avenues, for self- expression, love, joy and peace. Dream through me Lord, so that I must wake up to do and be what whatever is your will for me. All is well and I am grateful.
- **M**y body is a wonderful creation of God. Every system, organ, cell and function vibrates with the perfect health of God. My body has perfect assimilation and perfect elimination. I declare that my body is God's temple and only Divine life can inhabit it. My consciousness is filled with thoughts of health; I love health, I appreciate health, I am grateful for health.

Affirmations

- **R**ealizing that the Lord is my shepherd, I allow the Lord to counsel and guide me through paths of peace.
- **I** let the will of God be done through me.
- **A**s I allow myself to be divinely guided, I realize that divine order rules my days.
- **I** live and work in atmospheres of calm and peace.
- **D**ivine love prospers me.
- **I** love myself and all my relationships are wonderful.
- **D**ivine health fills my body
- **I** am God's mind expressing in love and gratitude.
- **I** am God's idea of greatness and success.

Denial

- **I** never succumb to the temptation of forcing the hand of God; I always seek God's will before I visualize regarding any need or want.
- **I** do not allow limited thinking or limited beliefs to guide me. I reawaken to a cosmic view of life!

Christ the Master teacher said that he came so that we all can have abundant lives and nothing less. We ought to expect the best in return. Examine your thoughts; are they limiting or are they progressive? Be aware that your thoughts reside in the conscious mind or intellect. The creative subconscious mind is fed by the conscious mind and creates according to what the conscious mind feeds into it. The Apostle Paul also entreated us to be transformed by the renewing of our minds. As we learn to think and pray affirmatively, our minds through Spiritual law must produce after its kind.

We must guard our thoughts with all diligence and think on whatever is pure, lovely, and wholesome. Use affirmations, denials, affirmative prayer and treatments to negate and dismiss thoughts that are not wholesome nor based on love and compassion. We must choose to let our actions become aligned with our affirmative thoughts. This is a surefire way to put the Law of Attraction to work favorably on our behalf. The abundance is already ours; however we have to become the mental equivalent, which is achieved by following Spiritual laws in thoughts, words and deeds. Goodness forever invites us to partake of its bounty; are you willing?

Chapter 3

Our Privilege of Prayer

P rayer is a privilege and a gift from God. In *The Revealing Word*, a dictionary of metaphysical terms by Charles Fillmore, the definition of prayer states, "Prayer is the most highly accelerated mind action known. Prayer is communion between God and Man; this communion takes place in the inner most part of a man's being" (2000, 152). Prayer is the way we communicate with God.

Throughout history, mankind has been known to engage in prayer. It is indeed an ancient practice that took many forms. Whenever new lands were discovered, the natives were found to already have some form of prayer. No one nation can lay claim to the origin of prayer. The innate call to connect with God, our source, is etched in our "Spiritual DNA". Prayer is a universal language of the soul. People have prayed and still do—by using prayer beads, prayer wheels, and headdresses. They have incorporated instruments, music, lights, and scents, raised voices, or clasped hands, and yes, they have also used silence. It doesn't matter what time of day it is or where we are in the universe; there will always be someone praying. The gift of prayer never loses value or power. In the Dictionary of New Thought terms by Ernest Holmes, Prayer is defined as" The act of becoming still and knowing that God The Creative Wisdom and Power, is moving in, upon, and through our affairs" (1991, 115)

As a child, I envisioned God to be a big bearded man who looked like Santa without the red suit. He never smiled, and he sat on a throne while Jesus sat on a chair at his right side. The Holy Ghost/ Spirit was just that; a ghost who was holy. I later came to envision God as a serious man who judges, punishes, and loves us according to what we have done. I also believed he was a wise father who healed and provided for us. I learned that Jesus loved children, and so I loved him too. When my sister and I were four and three years old, respectively, my grandmother taught us to kneel and recite prayers. It seemed my mother and grandmother prayed about everything. Whether it was in gratitude, celebration, or sadness, prayer was a central part of our daily activities. Prayer was also reinforced by the parochial school I attended. My grandmother embraced and practiced according to several faiths.

Once at a Sabbath prayer meeting my grandmother was leading, she explained that when people die, they go to heaven and that their food consists of milk and honey. Several meetings later, I was about age five, I raised my hand and asked what was then to me, a very serious question. I asked if God had a stewpot! Grandma appeared stunned, and I observed her holding back laughter. The idea of milk and honey alone was not settling with me. I preferred rice and vegetables. A few years later, I realized why it became a family joke!

I was about twelve years old when my mother came home one day and announced that the lights from the little white church in our town "called her" every time she passed by. Eventually, she courageously invited herself into the Universal Church of Scientific Truth. There she was introduced to the study of Metaphysics. Soon after, she took me there, and we became members. I immediately began a wonderful and fulfilling spiritual journey. I learned about affirmations, denials, treatments, treasure mapping, and affirmative prayer. I also learned that thoughts are things that have molding power. They are the medium through which the invisible begins to take form. I experienced many demonstrations through affirmative prayer, and I came to realize that there is transforming power in it!

Why Pray?

Throughout the centuries, there have been numerous reports of the truth that prayer works. If we cannot grasp this, we can at least acknowledge that the rituals of lighting a candle, using a sweet scent, and playing music all gently call our whole beings to a sacred order. When we pray, we still our minds, shut out outer distractions, and in the silence connect with God. There are countless accounts of the miraculous ways that prayers have worked on people's behalf. The following account is one such event.

Several years ago, an elder in the church I attended shared with church members printed copies of an email he had received. It read,

> *Have you ever felt the urge to pray for someone and then just put it on a list and said, "I'll pray for him or her later"? Or has anyone ever called you and said, "I need you to pray for me. I have this need?" Read the following story that was sent to me, and may it change the way that you think about prayer and also the way you pray.*

> *You will be blessed by this one:*

> *A missionary on furlough told this true story while visiting his home church in Michigan: "While serving at a small field hospital in Africa, every two weeks I traveled by bicycle through the jungle to a nearby city for supplies. This was a journey of two days and required camping overnight at the halfway point. On one of these journeys, I arrived in the city where I planned to collect money from a bank, purchase medicine and supplies, and then begin my two-day journey back to the field hospital. Upon arrival in the*

city, I observed two men fighting, one of whom had been seriously injured. I treated him for his injures and at the same time talked to him about the Lord Jesus Christ. I then traveled two days, camping overnight, and arrived home without incident.

Two weeks later, I repeated my journey. Upon arriving in the city, I was approached by the young man I had treated. He told me that he had known I carried money and medicine. He said, "Some friends and I followed you into the jungle, knowing you would camp overnight. We planned to kill you and take your money and drugs. But as we were about to move into your camp, we saw that you were surrounded by twenty-six armed guards."

At this I laughed and said that I was certainly all alone in that campsite. The young man pressed the point, however, and said, "No sir, I was not the only person to see the guards. My five friends also saw them, and we all counted them. It was because of those guards that we were afraid and left you alone." At this point in the sermon, one of the men in the congregation jumped to his feet and interrupted the missionary and asked if he could tell him the exact day that this happened. The missionary told the congregation the date and the man who interrupted told him this story: "On the night of your incident in Africa, it was morning here, and I was preparing to play golf. I was about to putt when I felt the urge to pray for you. In fact, the urging of the Lord was so strong that I called men in this church to meet with me here in the sanctuary to pray for you. Would all of those who met with me that day stand up?" The men who had met to pray that day stood up. The missionary wasn't concerned with who they were. He was too busy counting how many men he saw. There were twenty-six! The same amount of guards that the would-be robber reported to have seen.

This, beloveds, clearly illustrates the power of prayer. Psalms 91:11 says, "For He shall give his Angels charge over you, to keep you in all your ways." This time there were twenty-six angels!

Transformation of Consciousness

This is a great time to be alive! It is clear that we are experiencing a transformation within the consciousness of humanity. Some people call it a shift, movement, flowering, awakening, or evolution. These descriptions are all in alignment with each other because they speak to us of positive change, spiritual evolution or a reawakening of our true State of Being. This is an incredibly exciting time in the history of our planet. Right before our eyes we see environmental, social, and economic changes taking place.

We recognize that we are all created in the spiritual image and likeness of Almighty God. This is not a physical image; it is purely a spiritual one. We must be clear about this distinction. The universe beckons each of us to come up higher and stand in our greatness. The old systems can no longer sustain us. We cannot peacefully survive under the domination of the little ego. Economic upheavals and so many other vicissitudes signal a global cry to take notice. We are always evolving; however, at this time in history there is an energetic opening to bring it all together. This opening is facilitated by our wisdom and creativity, which has catapulted technology into a tool that supports oneness of the human understanding, shared global experiences, and the ability to know and love each other better, even across continents!

One of our natural God-given gifts is the power to choose. Each of us is a unique individual with different wants, beliefs, likes, experiences, and needs. **Some of us are unaware that we are evolving unconsciously; as a result, we allow the little ego to dominate, edge God out and keep us small**. Those who are consciously evolving become co-creators with God. They choose spiritual principles to guide them into a life of love, service, and joy. We are called upon to be our brothers' keepers. Those of us who are more conscious and knowledgeable have a spiritual duty to share this transformative information with others. We must use our expanding spiritual awareness to impel ourselves to support this mass reawakening of human consciousness. With greater awareness comes greater responsibility to share it with others. We must also share our presence, time, talents, and other resources.

One key aspect of the evolution of human consciousness is that it first begins in each of us. This is a sacred process that begins at the spiritual level of our beings. Our intentions and the thoughts we hold in our minds set the tone and pace. We may face many challenges, but we must not feel that we are alone. We were given the tools to move through our transformation. Centuries ago, St. Paul wrote, "Do not be conformed to this world, but be transformed by the renewing of your mind" (Rom. 12:2 NKJV). All true change begins within the mind as a thought. Through Divine wisdom, St. Paul understood that the condition of our thoughts determines the condition of our lives. Our thoughts, which form the basis of our prayers, must be wholesome. In this way, the true light of Christ can break through into our souls. We do not have to look with strained vision to realize that the evolution of human consciousness happens simultaneously with a renewed flowering of the practice of prayer. **While prayer supports the renewal of the mind, a person with a renewed mind or an evolved consciousness tends to pray with persistence.**

Creative Power of Our Thoughts

The nature of our thoughts colors our prayer experience. I have had several experiences when this principle was evident. **One experience in particular left its mark on my mind and has forever changed me.** This experience is not uncommon. It shows up daily in our lives, whether we realize it or not. There is constant mind action occurring in us, the nature of which is determined by our thoughts. Have you ever had a needle become stuck in your breast? Or so you thought; then you tried to remove it only to have it sink deeper into your flesh until it disappeared? The pain is excruciating, and the mood becomes one of utter desperation.

I have had such an experience. However, this was a fact only according to my thoughts and feelings; it was not the truth.

Expectation ruled that day. I am forever grateful for this lesson, which demonstrated the power of thought while supporting the truth that God has placed the power of well-being in our minds! *I remember holding a needle to stitch and repair the front of a garment that I had already put on. I was holding the needle slightly above eye level, attempting to thread it, when it fell. I looked carefully on the carpeted floor but couldn't find it. A thought came to me: What if the needle fell in your bra? Then another thought: Yes, that's it. Be careful before it pricks your breast. I frantically grabbed and shook my bra. Then I felt a very sharp pain in my breast. I believed the needle had disappeared into my breast tissue. While the pain persisted, I continued to search. Thoughts of surgery, pain, gloom, and doom—all negatives—flooded my mind.*

In pain, I said to myself, "No, this can't be." Then the following thought came: Keep searching the carpet, and I did. Shortly after that, I found the needle. The experience that followed will be forever etched in my mind. **At the same moment I saw the needle on the carpet, the pain in my breast stopped!** *Stunned, I sat quietly, wondering how that could be. I then had a moment of revelation, and I understood. The truth was that because I had mistakenly thought the needle had become stuck in my breast tissue, my thoughts created the pain. The rationale was that if a needle became stuck in my flesh, I would feel pain. For sure, my thoughts created!*

Beloveds, this is an example of the power of our thoughts. This power does not differentiate good from bad or positive from negative. In that window of denial when I thought, *No, this can't be*, which was compounded by me seeing the needle, my thoughts indicated *no harm*, and the pain immediately stopped. This is a clear demonstration of the power our thoughts have over our lives and our prayers.

In support of a lesson I taught to students about thinking calming thoughts as a way of controlling emotions, I explained how thoughts create. One student boldly reported that she had fallen, hurt her knees, and then felt blood trickling down her leg. She said that when she saw there was no blood, the trickling sensation immediately stopped. Happily, I thanked her for sharing. I was grateful that she had taken the opportunity to share such a valuable lesson with her elementary classmates. These experiences are priceless and help explain how affirmative prayer works. We must remember that our thoughts form our prayers and dictate the nature of our experiences. Our affirmative thoughts and prayers are catalysts for transformation. St. Paul was clear about this when he entreated us to think about whatever is good. Philippians 4:8.

The Lord's Prayer

When we study the lives and practices of spiritual masters and teachers, we understand that prayer has forever been the practice that enhanced their connection to God. The Buddha is said to have become clear only after he sat quietly under the Bodhi tree, after wandering. Jesus often took time out to pray in lonely places. He prayed as he taught and worked miracles. Modern spiritual and religious teachers also teach that prayer is vital to keeping not only individuals, but also organizations alive!

The universe is always responding to us! When the disciples asked Jesus to teach them how to pray, that was no ordinary request. It was the cry of all humanity seeking the pathway along which we can walk in greatness. "Lord, teach us to pray" (Luke 11:1). We can ask the question, "Why didn't Christ, our way-shower, teach his disciples how to pray earlier?" This was a clear demonstration that each of us as individuals must seek this higher calling for ourselves. We have the gift of choice, which is a gift of grace. The disciples chose to ask the Lord to show them how to pray at that appointed time because they were ready then, to receive it. They allowed grace to lead them. It was no coincidence that when Jesus taught them the Lord's Prayer, he entreated them not to make the same mistakes as those who were heaping up empty phrases, thinking God would hear them for their many words. **Jesus was intentional**; he taught them the following pattern for prayer. This pattern became known as the Lord's Prayer:

Our Father in heaven,

Hallowed be thy name.

Your kingdom come,

Your will be done,

On earth as it is in heaven.

Give us this day our daily bread,

And forgive us our debts,

As we forgive our debtors.

And do not lead us into temptation,

But deliver us from the evil one.

For Yours is the kingdom and the power and the glory forever.

Amen. Matt. 6: 9-13

The words *pray in this manner* means we should use this pattern or model as a guide. Upon examining this pattern, we realize that it guides us in the way we are to approach Almighty God and reminds us of our relationship to him. It shows how we should make our requests, what we should request, and how to demonstrate total surrender. For centuries, this pattern for the Lord's Prayer has been recited verbatim. Young children are taught this pattern as the actual words to say. On many tongues, it has become known as the Lord's Prayer. Yet prayers are more than these words put together. Prayer involves a movement of emotions as the intention is held in a person's mind and as he or she prays according to his or her specific need.

Jesus knew that if we repeated the actual words of this pattern, the words would lose depth and would not be specific to our needs most times. For example, we should be able to pray for peace if we need peace and not have to replace the word peace with "daily bread". Jesus cautioned that we should not use vain repetitions. "And when you pray, do not use vain repetitions" (Matt. 6:7). Using the actual words in this pattern as one's prayer has become the vain repetition Jesus warned about. We are all unique individuals with varying needs, which makes it futile to embrace a "cookie-cutter" mode of prayer. At times our needs will be the same, but often they are not. We must be specific in our prayers, as we make our requests to God. The prayers said by biblical figures and Christ the Master teacher were specific; **our prayers must be specific.**

The Christ also described the state in which our minds must be when we pray. "And whatsoever things you ask in prayer, **believing,** you will receive." (Matt. 21:22). This statement also explains why we should pray. We pray to have our needs met. Whether we pray silently or audibly, we must fulfill the framework or pattern of this prayer in order to pray as the master teacher taught. Jesus wasted no time with idle words. Every clause or sentence helps create Divine order in our thinking. We may ask, if God is a God of love, then why can't we just pray in whatever manner we choose? First, we must recognize that Our Father, God, is a God of order. All of God's creations were done in an orderly manner. Living creatures reproduce after their own kind. Disorderly thoughts create disorderly experiences, and orderly thoughts create orderly experiences in our lives. We live in a universe of order. Therefore, in order to create, we must be life affirming and in alignment with Divine order. Chaotic prayers yield chaotic results. Orderly prayers yield orderly results.

The Affirmative Lord's Prayer

We must realize that the framework for the Lord's Prayer is composed of a series of affirmative statements. The actual form and flow is affirmative as well. Let us examine each statement. As we read, please note that we are praying to our Omnipotent, Omniscient, and Omnipresent Almighty God, who is Our Heavenly Father.

Our Father Who Art in Heaven

The master teacher begins with an affirmation of the established relationship between God and mankind—that of parent and child. A parent symbolically creates a child, loves the child unconditionally, and provides for all its needs. The father, or male figure, is physically the stronger protector. There is no stronger bond than the parent-child relationship. Jesus was intentional in saying "Our Father" and not "My Father." Very early on, Jesus conveyed the message that God is the Father of all mankind. Not one person is excluded from the Sonship of Jehovah. This clause also provides an affirmation of the Brotherhood of mankind.

Christ taught that God is in the Heavenly Kingdom and clearly stated that the Kingdom is within us. Answering the Pharisees' question about the coming of the Kingdom of God, Christ responded, "The Kingdom of God does not come with observation; nor will they say see here! Or see there! For the Kingdom of God is within you" (Luke 17:20–21). For this reason, we enter the silence of our inner beings when we consciously make contact and communicate with the Spirit of God within us. We should not hesitate to believe this because God is omnipresent, which means he is evenly present everywhere. To the Samaritan woman, Christ said, "God is a Spirit and those who worship him must worship in Spirit and Truth" (John 4:24). We must get to the heart of the matter and turn within ourselves through our minds, where we can make contact with the Spirit of God. Here we are reminded that since we are created in God's image and likeness, we all are spiritual beings as well.

Hallowed Be Thy Name

The word *hallowed* means holy. The Almighty God is called by many names, all of which are holy. Some of these names are Jehovah, Almighty, Allah, Krishna, Yahweh, Lord, Prince of Peace, Wonderful Counselor, I AM, Abba, Father, etc. The name *I AM* encompasses all of these names because God simply is the alpha and omega, the beginning and the end of all things. He is the most holy and is therefore all in everything that is holy and whole. God is good, and God is all the good there is. Therefore, the name of our Almighty Heavenly Father God is most holy, or hallowed. We must acknowledge this in our prayers.

Your Kingdom Come

The master teacher taught that the Kingdom is not a physical place outside of us. Rather, the Kingdom is our consciousness, conditioned by the state of our minds. Our renewed minds are the catalysts for our transformation. "Be ye transformed by the renewing of your mind" (Rom. 12:2). In this framework, *your kingdom come* is an act of obedience and receptivity. We admit to God that we are allowing our minds to be as Christ's mind. In this Christ consciousness, we allow the Kingdom to freely dwell within us. It is our divine birthright as heirs of God to rule over our consciousness and to have abundant lives. Praying affirmatively with renewed minds supports us in recognizing the Kingdom within us here and now and not in a far-off distance or future.

Your Will Be Done On Earth as It Is in Heaven

As we examine this clause, we might be tempted to feel that we have no choice in our circumstances. Seeing God as a vengeful, judgmental, punitive God who only loves some people can create inner conflict when we say, "Your will be done." We must be clear that God is goodness itself. It is the nature of goodness to desire only goodness, or this would not be the good, Omnipotent God. God desires only good for all of us. Again, if we desire to live abundantly according to God's will for us, we must understand how vital it is to have a spiritually renewed mind. God can only work through us at the level of our consciousness. Our renewed minds, being aligned with the Christ mind, then become one with the Christ mind. *Your will* becomes *my will.* The words, *on earth,* are symbolic of the outward physical realm. Our inner Heavenly Kingdom determines the manifestations in our earthly realm. In a nutshell, we declare, "I align my will with God's will so that through the workings of my mind, my life experiences will be prosperous ones." Yes, it is wise to surrender to God's will as The Christ did even through his crucifixion.

Give Us this Day Our Daily Bread

We must take notice of the authority in the words, *give us.* There is no evidence of begging or beseeching. *This day* denotes praying for what we need at the current moment and on a daily basis. This does not mean means that we can never pray about something which we desire in the future. However, the mandate for the act of daily prayer is quite clear. When the children of Israel were provided with manna to eat, they were warned specifically to take only what they needed for one day. When some of them disobeyed, the extras they took stunk and had worms by the next morning (Exod. 16:20). This lesson applied today symbolizes our need for daily prayer, the constant provision of God, and the fact that our needs constantly change; as a whole, we should focus on the needs we have in the *now.*

Bread is symbolic of whatever our needs are. **Our daily bread does not only mean the food we consume. Our daily bread consists of everything things we need, such as love**, **peace, joy, health, wisdom, money, jobs, food, avenues for service, parking spots, lost objects, relationships, etc**. Our Heavenly Father delights in fulfilling our needs. "It is our Father's good pleasure to give us the Kingdom" (Luke 12:32). We have the power to choose; therefore, we must choose to ask God to fulfill our needs on a daily basis.

Forgive Us Our Debts, as We Forgive Our Debtors

The call for forgiveness is sounded across various faiths. This is in keeping with words of Scripture that explain that if we have grudges toward anyone, we must forgive them before we pray. The master teacher, Christ, taught forgiveness, and St. Paul admonished the renewing of the mind. Not forgiving someone and harboring resentments toward that person fosters a mind cluttered with anger, fear, guilt, and ill will. God can only work for us through us. These negative emotions block the work of God's Spirit in and through us.

In the model for the Lord's Prayer, we read, *forgive us our debts, as we forgive our debtors*. This spiritual law of forgiveness, like all other spiritual laws, is immutable. "God is no respecter of persons," This means that God does not change his laws to suit a particular person. It does not matter who we are, what we have or what wrong was done to us or by us. We will not be forgiven if we do not forgive. Although it can be difficult to forgive, we can ask God's help. In forgiving, we receive the peace of God, which is the manifestation of the forgiveness we receive as a result of our choice to forgive.

The admonition of Paul to the Philippians was that they should think on whatever things are true, noble, pure, lovely, and of good report. Today, this is still relevant to us. St. Paul understood the workings of the human mind and the power of our thoughts. Paul, like Christ, understood the necessity of prayer for our spiritual evolution. To this end, Jesus Christ taught the disciples that they must forgive before they affirmatively pray and get results.

Do Not Lead Us into Temptation but Deliver Us from Evil

Let us come to the understanding now that God does not tempt us or lead us into temptation. The Scripture reads, **"Let no man, when he is tempted say, "I am tempted by God"; for God cannot be tempted by evil, nor does he himself tempt anyone" (James 1:13).** Our thoughts move in our minds before we commit an action. When we are tempted to do wrong, the idea is an impulse of the little ego which is often influenced by evil. As Jesus Christ fasted in the wilderness, he became hungry, and his thought focused at the point of his weakness—hunger. Jesus was tempted to turn stones into bread, which would be good enough to satisfy the physical hunger. He rebuked such thoughts, knowing that breaking his fast would sabotage the work he had to complete for our redemption. This clause in the Lord's Prayer is an earnest request for God to help us guard our thoughts and withstand evil. In this way, we will be able to face temptation without succumbing to it.

The request for deliverance from evil is a natural plea from anyone who is suffering or experiencing fears, terror, or any other evil. **However, this request is not always granted.** Suffering brings lessons necessary for the spiritual evolution and transformation of mankind. In a sorrowful mood in the Garden of Gethsemane, Jesus contemplated the cruelty and suffering of the crucifixion. He prayed, "Abba Father, all things are possible for you. Take this cup away from me; nevertheless, not what I will, but what you will" (Mark 14:36). Evidentially, his request was not in God's will; it was not granted. As mentioned, if it had been, the entire purpose of the crucifixion which was the redemption of our sins would have been prevented. We must pay attention to the fact that Jesus, even in his time of sorrow, declared that God's will must be done. There is a humbling beauty in this clause. Jesus showed his human side by declaring that he was sorrowful. He acknowledged Jehovah's power by saying, "All things are possible for you," and yet he exercised the power of obedience to death by surrendering to God's will.

For Yours Is the Kingdom and the Power and the Glory Forever

Everything that was ever created belongs to our Lord God. The Psalmist David declared, "The earth is the Lord's and all its fullness; the world, and all people who dwell there in" (Ps. 24:1). As we pray, we must recognize this truth: all power and glory belong to God. By ourselves we cannot do anything, own anything, create anything, or be anything. The good works we do are indeed our Heavenly Father working through us; therefore God is glorified through us. "Yours *is the glory*" is constant. The glory belongs to our Almighty God and this cannot be otherwise!

Affirmative Prayer

Our universe is a system of order. Every day an abundance of orderly events occur. When the daytime ends, night time begins. Spring, Summer, Autumn, and Winter always occur in that order. Some regions of the world have a wet, rainy season and then a sunny, dry season in that order. During a recent hurricane, I watched the news for details about the storm. I thought about how orderly it progressed. It lashed out with an orderly fury, swooping and destroying things in its path. Whether the focus was on the destruction the hurricane caused, or the fact that it later became a tropical storm, the truth remains that there was an orderly progression to that seeming chaos.

The orderly progression of nature is testimony of an orderly intelligence that intends and creates. Our prayers, like nature, must have an orderly progression that begins in the mind of the one praying. **This book is written with the intention and design for orderliness. In this way, the reader, who is unfamiliar with this Metaphysical teaching, can systematically follow and learn these principles. Orderliness also creates ease, which in turn allows the mental atmosphere to become conducive to understanding.**

Examining the Affirmative Lord's Prayer, this model begins with us addressing God as Our Heavenly Father. Next appears an acknowledgement of where God is (in heaven). Then we state our intent—that we will do his will. Next we ask for our needs to be met: e.g. daily bread, forgiveness, guidance, deliverance. The prayer ends by appropriating the glory to God as an acknowledgement that he is the cause of our blessings. The presence of unification, submission, orderly progression, and its affirmative nature make this model truly magnificent!

The Nature of Affirmative Prayer

Affirmative prayer is a statement of truth concerning a particular difficulty, need, or event. It can also be said simply as praise, thanksgiving, or surrender. The Lord's Prayer was the pattern used by many ancient prophets and teachers. As mentioned during that profound moment of Jesus's crucifixion, Christ prayerfully asked God to take the cup (suffering) from him but then quickly affirmed, "Not my will but yours be done (Luke 22:42). The psalmist David wrote affirmatively as well. In times of distress e.g. "I will lift up my eyes unto the hills ..." (Ps. 121:1) he wrote words of hope. When he cried out in anguish, he often affirmatively ended with a declaration of the desired results.

Creative Power Lies in Our Words

Affirmative prayer is accomplished using different practices such as affirmations (or decrees), denials, Spiritual mind treatments also known as treatments, or praise. They are different means to one end, which is an answered prayer. These are used according to the nature of the issue and the intention and consciousness of the person praying. All of these beautiful modes of prayer are described in this book.

At creation, Jehovah used a series of statements of decree. He decreed, or affirmed, "Let there be light," and light was created. During this creation period, the desired thing that followed the words *let there be*, came into being. Yes, in the beginning, words were decreed, or affirmed by our wise creator.

In affirmative prayer, we state words in the present tense. To do otherwise leaves the desire to be attained in the future, and never in the now. For example an affirmation for healing must not be "I will be whole" Instead it must be "I am whole." We can only exist in the now. Affirmative prayer is a catalyst for the renewal of the mind. These words are creative and definite. Our words release power into our subconscious minds, where our circumstances are created. Affirmative prayer is not empty robotic babbling; there must be firm thoughts agreeing with our spoken words. In the book *Richer Living*, authors Dr. Ernest Holmes and Raymond Charles Barker explained that in order for prayers to be effectual, they must be affirmative in both the visible and invisible realms (1953). This means that what we think, say, and do must be affirmative and life giving and must match the desire.

Our words have vibratory power and energy, regardless of whether we use them positively or negatively. Even when we are not paying attention (subconsciously thinking or speaking), they produce for us according to how we habitually use them. When we pray affirmatively, the focus is on the desired result, and we speak the words as though the desire has already been fulfilled.

Throughout the ages, the power in the sound of the spoken word has been acknowledged. The acts of chanting, singing, praying, and speaking in unison produced a powerful collective vibration. In the ancient temples of Greece, Persia, India, Egypt, and Atlantis, sound was used as part of spiritual practices. More recently, the Africans who were enslaved in various parts of the world chanted or sang in unison with each other while working in cruel and harsh conditions. Their united sounds strengthened them and empowered them with stamina to withstand their difficulties.

"What thought has done, thought can undo" (Holmes. 1991, p151)

Affirmative prayers stretch our minds because we have to firmly hold in our minds a vision of the answer even though we have not yet physically observed it. This form of prayer was not used at creation and then forgotten. It was taught and used in ancient mystery schools, and because of its power, it was selfishly kept secret from others. At this moment, our thoughts and words continue to be the catalysts of creation. What we hold in our thoughts will be reflected in our lives; as we think, so will we be. For these reasons, our words and thoughts are vital to affirmative prayer.

This form of prayer is also called Scientific Prayer because it is innately comprised of spiritual principles and truths. This pattern does not always agree with intellectual reasoning. It aligns with the deeper absolute, which is always the universal truth of the matter. For example, affirming that a need is met when in fact a person has not even glimpsed the means to meet this need sounds absurd. However, the spiritual truth is that all we will ever need was provided before we were conceived in our mothers' wombs and even before the foundation of the world! We know that nothing can be taken from or added to the universe; knowing this supports us in accepting this truth.

Principles of Affirmative Prayer

The following five principles give affirmative prayer its authentic wholeness:

1. *Recognition*

Following this principle, God is recognized as a particular quality, usually a quality in relation to the need. For example, if someone is praying affirmatively about a decision he or she has to make, then he or she may recognize God as wisdom; for example in the actual prayer, the one praying may say, "Dear Jehovah, I recognize you as the wisdom I seek" If someone is seeking healing, he or she may recognize God as wholeness. If there is no specific need and someone is saying a prayer of thanksgiving, he or she may recognize God as the great I AM, El Shaddai (the God of more than enough), abundance, or peace, etc.

2. *Unification*

Following this principle, we acknowledge that we are created in the image and likeness of God. In Genesis 1:27 we read, "So God created man in his own image; in the image of God. He created him; male and female he created them." We therefore possess the same spiritual qualities of God. Seeking the manifestation of peace, health, guidance, and harmony, we can prayerfully affirm, "I am peace," "I am wholeness," "I am Divine intelligence," or "I am Divine love," respectively. We decree that we are the quality that is the very answer to the need. Remember that the Kingdom of God is within us, so we can declare the quality we desire, in our unifying statement by acknowledging that we are already it.

3. *Realization*

Following this principle, the truth of the matter is always realized. Realization begins in the mind before it can be experienced in tangible form. For example, a person experiencing conflict with others can say the following affirmation; "In this moment there is a sweet peace among us." An appropriate denial could be, "There is no conflict among us, the harmony of God now fills our hearts and minds; I am so grateful." A person with a health challenge can say a denial such as, "There is no sickness in my body. Every cell, organ, system, and function in my body is perfect with the perfection of God. I am grateful." An affirmation could be, "I now enjoy perfect health; the cells of my body rejoice in ease and gratitude!" These statements of Realization are the outer works. The inner work must be a deep and firm conviction that these words of decree are the truth and cannot be otherwise. We can boldly come to these realizations because the truth is that everything good is already provided for us. However, we must choose to call them forth as acts of faith.

4. *Thanksgiving*

Having realized the truth of the situation, we embrace this principle and affirmatively offer gratitude to God, our provider. Through the law of attraction, thanksgiving creates more good for which we can be grateful. At this time, we also act as though we have already had our needs met in the physical. For example, someone praying about a career or a job can affirm, "I believe that the law of good supplies all our needs. The door to right work opens before me, and I gratefully and joyfully enter."

Someone who prays about a relationship by speaking as though it has already manifested can give thanks, affirming, "I am grateful for my relationship. My partner and I love, respect, support, and wonderfully complement each other. We enjoy each other. Our hearts' desires are established and I am grateful." We must always be clear that a state of gratitude is a spiritual mandate for answered prayers.

5. *Release*

Following this principle, the prayer is released. This means that everything about the matter at hand, down to its minutest detail, is entrusted to God. This matter is never revisited in the same mood. The mood is now lifted above the level of the problem and becomes one of "knowing," which is an unshakable belief that all is well. St. Paul wrote that we must pray without ceasing; however after releasing, when we pray again about the same issue, the prayer must then become a prayer of thanksgiving. It is vital that once the prayer is released, all thoughts, words, and actions remain affirmative and in alignment with the manifestation of the desire. A mind that wavers brings little results. The mind must be kept firm and positive through diligence.

Beloved, prayer is an individual experience. The act of prayer itself supports us in becoming aware of which form of prayer most often aligns with how we relate to the world. For example, some people favor silent prayer. However, one must at times exercise the power of words through audible prayer. **The above steps need not be followed in that order.** As we allow ourselves to be guided by the Spirit of God within us, we may at times be guided to begin with thanksgiving as a testimony of our faith! To pray affirmatively is to think creatively with expectancy and gratitude. The energy of expectation heightens our awareness of an Almighty God who seeks only to bring us good. We feel more worthy of this good, which is ours by divine right. Only then are we ready to receive our many blessings. The entire universe is ready to support us!

The Silence

You will realize that this book often mentions the necessity of entering the silence, but what is this silence?

Since ancient times, religious and spiritual groups have recognized the silence. In Fillmore's Revealing Word Metaphysical dictionary, the Silence is defined as a state of consciousness entered into for the purpose of putting man in touch with the Divine Mind, so that the soul may listen to the "still small voice." The deep truth of who we are is spiritual. We are created in the spiritual image and likeness of God. **Because God is a spirit, we are asked to worship him in spirit and in truth. We are told to seek the Kingdom of God, which is within us.**

In order to enter the Kingdom, we must quiet our minds. This is achieved by stilling our bodies and closing our eyes in an effort to shut out any distracting sights and sounds. Those that master this practice may easily enter this silence with their eyes opened. In this moment, we want to be present with and for Almighty God. We meet God in the silence within us, through our quieted minds. This is necessary because the work of creativity occurs in the silence. For this reason, the silence is sometimes called the Creative Silence. **Going within is the way to communicate with God. In the silence we can tap in to the inspiration that is already within us!**

Several requirements must be met in order for the silence to be a creative space:

- We must surrender the stray thoughts and emotional responses caused by our awareness of, and interactions with the environment.
- We must have a firm, unwavering knowledge that we are making direct contact with God.
- We must have the faith or belief that God will fulfill the need in the way that is best for us and according to his will.
- We must have a loving, forgiving and receptive mind.
- We must be in a state of patience and gratitude.

The silence is far more than just becoming quiet. This is the place where we experience the subjective as tangible and where we harness the feeling of the way we would feel when we tangibly have acquired whatever we desire. It is a place where the mind of God thinks through our minds. All is positive and life affirming in the silence. This is a place of love where God speaks to us through our divinely inspired thoughts and realizations.

The silence is for everyone and it has always been, and will ever be a place where only goodness can exist. No matter whom we are or what we have done, we can choose to enter the silence. In the silence there is peace. There is no harm, no judgment, no condemnation, illness, hatred or drama. In this place we can step out of the little ego mind, because there is no place in the silence for it to be. In fact, feeling that one cannot reach the silence may signify that the little ego is in the way.

Preparation for Entering the Silence

Breathing stimulates and sharpens our perception because of its calming effects; it also helps to still our thoughts. Take a few slow breaths or as many as you need to begin to feel calm. You can with closed eyes, envision a peaceful scene as you do so. This can be a calm lake, a beautiful garden, an expansion of land or water, a ball of light, or a quiet place in your home or yard. Direct your thoughts to each body part and stay gently focused on each one until it relaxes. Feeling relaxed in each part, think of the image you have of God. This may be a light or open space or the word *Jehovah* or *love*, etc. Allow a feeling of sweet peace to wash over you as you enter this silence with joy. Allow yourself to feel loved because you are God's Beloved child and you are truly deeply and unconditionally loved. You are safe here in God's presence within your soul.

Know that all is well and rest in this silence for a while. Be open and receptive to Divine guidance and be sure to follow guidance received. One would normally feel impelled to act when the guidance is from God. When you are ready to leave the silence, take a refreshing and deep breath. Say or think words of gratitude to your Heavenly Father for the privilege of this creative silence and for the guidance you received. You can always come back to this creative silence when guided to; this is your place of silence that always welcomes you.

Patience is necessary when entering the silence. This is because the chatter of mundane thoughts often begins to swirl around in our minds. Troubling and worry thoughts, fearful thoughts of failure, success, joys, and thoughts of a host of various issues usually surface. One cannot normally cease from thinking; however negative thoughts can be replaced with positive ones. In the silence we often can recognize what our shadows are. We can obscure our shadows from others but not from ourselves. **It is counterproductive to push away interfering thoughts, because to do so requires our attention to them. What we give our attention to becomes magnified and can set up a counterforce; for this reason what we resist persist. Instead of pushing away, gently release the worrisome thoughts**. The person, who usually meditates, is more likely to begin to pray or meditate without any or much mental interference; practice supports perfection. In quiet and confidence comes our strength.

The way we perceive guidance can be as unique as each snowflake. For example, in my experience as I release undesired thoughts, I hold in the center of my mind, the thought of Our Heavenly father, or the Christ, a glowing light radiating at the center of my body which symbolizes the Christ light, or of myself looking out to the sea in gratitude etc. I allow stray thoughts to dissipate. A certain thought would remain, a new thought may surface or I would "hear" a certain name, phrase, song, sentence or other guidance come into my awareness. I would proceed to pray and accept guidance surrounding this information. In this instance, this information would form the focus of my prayer or mediation and I often gather new insights in this process. When I feel impelled to stay with a particular thought, insight or idea, then I know that at that moment my prayers should be guided to address that information. If this information is not something that I am currently dealing with, very soon that becomes the case.

We are each unique; one may choose to pray about a specific need or issue at hand, or about some negative belief, miscreation or emotion which is usually fed by the little negative ego and which can wreak havoc on one's self-worth and wellbeing. No issue is too small to pray about. The question may be asked, "How can we be certain that the guidance received was divine guidance? One can examine this information to see if it aligns with the Laws of Jehovah God. If it does not it is clearly not of God and must be peacefully dismissed. Patience is necessary as we remain open to receive guidance.

The following is an example of a prayer one can use after they have entered the silence and before engaging in (as an example) a business transaction. This can be changed to suit one's specific need.

Dear Jehovah,

You are our rock of all ages. My Heavenly Father, I seek your grace today, knowing that you always supply my needs according to your will. I ask your guidance as I complete my purchases today. In the name of Christ, I ask that you move on the hearts and minds of all involved. Bless us all with the spirit of honesty and integrity. Please show us how to be, what to say, what to look for and what is best for all involved. We are receptive and we allow the Light of your Spirit to illuminate every facet of this transaction. Dear Lord, I thank you for hearing and answering me now and always.

Acts of Meditation and Affirmation

In "The Revealing Word," a dictionary of Metaphysical terms by Charles Fillmore, meditation is defined as "continuous and contemplative thought; to dwell mentally on anything; realizing the reality of the absolute; a steady effort of the mind to know God; man's spiritual approach to God."(1991, pg. 131)

In the Scripture, we are told to meditate on God's word day and night. Meditation is a mandate of God, yet it has its doubters and naysayers. Some people believe meditation is something sinister or spooky. In the Old Testament, God gave the following commission to Joshua: *"This book of the law shall not depart from your mouth, but you shall meditate in it day and night, that you may observe to do according to all that is written in it. For then you will make your way prosperous, and then you will have good success" (Josh. 1:8). We are instructed to incorporate biblical teachings into our lifestyles in order to create and manifest true success in our lives.*

When we enter the silence, we focus on our joys and observe any difficulties at hand. We can also enter the silence and meditate on God and his grace and mercy toward us; Meditation is an action of the mind. One might ask, "How can meditation be an action of the mind when there is, for example, walking meditation?" Using the example of walking meditation, when the meditator walks, he or she mentally focuses on each step. He or she also focuses on the sensation as the heel, ball of the foot, and toes touch the ground. This trains the mind to focus on a single item at a time. Each item can be a feeling, principle, scene, thought, scent, taste, or texture. This serves to train the wandering mind to focus. This is what Jesus meant when he said, "The lamp of the body is the eye. If therefore your eye is single, your whole body shall be full of light" (Matt 6:22). This means we can receive Divine guidance, or light, as result of meditating or focusing only upon God/ Good; keeping a singled eye beaming on God/Good. Meditation teaches us to have a "single" eye or unwavering focus.

Contemplating or meditating on the word of God, an idea, or a feeling helps us receive the light of clarity concerning

the condition or thing that we wish to attain. Scientists have realized that meditating and taking slow, deep breaths helps lower blood pressure, releases stress, and promotes general wellness. Meditation renews the mind and supports us in receiving inspiration. Meditation therefore, nurtures us physically, mentally and spiritually!

Meditation is an active process. We may or may not physically move when we meditate, however, there is always mental movement that creates. Every article we create was first conceived as a thought. The core of meditation is mental action. For example, when we focus on thoughts of worry, we are meditating on that worry, and this creates more of its kind. The process of creating through meditation does not discriminate between something favorable or unfavorable. In order to receive our good, we must meditate on what is good, as stated above. (See Josh. 1:8). **I would be remiss if I did not also mention that our consciousness must be based on love if we desire to create anything good, through meditation and Affirmative prayer.**

Challenges with Affirmative Prayer----Understanding Sabotage

In as much as affirmative prayer works, it is not unusual for someone to become frustrated with his or her prayer practice. Such a person might be confused when he or she feels worse just after praying. It should be of great comfort to realize that frustration with one's prayer practice can be an underlying spiritual stirring of the desire for a more vibrant practice. Frustrations can arise for many reasons; however, there are always lessons to be learned. These lessons create the path to our transformation when we allow and use them to support us. This path becomes our road to freedom.

The Ego

In the play of life, ego matters. Why does ego matter? It matters because it can dictate the condition of our consciousness, or awareness. We must remember that **the ego is a thought form which we create. It operates by profoundly accepting certain beliefs and then acts from those premises**. The general thinking is that ego is a bad thing; however this is not the truth. To bring some clarity, our Little ego self (little i) is said to be a bad master but a good servant. We must take dominion over this ego and let it work for us only to e.g. remind us to groom ourselves.

On the other hand, **our Spiritual ego or our higher (I AM) self, seeks to raise us ever higher and operates from the basis of agape, or brotherly, love. The Little ego, or lower self, operates from the basis of control, self-centeredness, or "separateness from others." John Randolph Price author of "Empowerment" referenced the separation of the dot from the body of the little i as symbolic of separation. This Little ego also thrives on believing that it is better than others and that it is always right. In a strange twist, this ego loves being a victim and not being "good enough" It sabotages the work that would liberate it. This is another way of controlling others who rush in with pity.** Wars, hatred, jealousy, strife, and stress are other ways through which the little ego controls. As the saying goes, it Edges God Out (EGO).

When someone prays, he or she seeks communion with God and in essence surrenders conditions and outcomes to him. The Little ego sees this surrender as the death of itself. Its goal is to stay alive, be independent, and wallow in doubt, fear, excuses, blaming, lies and self-sabotage. For example, someone may begin to doubt that prayer works while unconsciously accepting the little ego's lie that prayer is for the weak or that it means a loss of control. The result may be that this person begins to pray in a lackluster manner, due to an unconscious impulse of this ego to maintain control;

the emotional tone of prayer often becomes absent. Such a person may explain, "I am too busy to really sit down to pray," or "I will begin my prayer practice in the near future."

Many of us who are driven by the little ego may wear masks of bravery to hide any feelings of guilt or vulnerability or the shadow parts of ourselves. When one believes that praying admits that there are feelings of guilt or vulnerability, they are more likely to hide or suppress the need to pray, all to this ego's ease and delight.

Though subtle, another way of sabotaging our prayers is by prematurely telling others what we are praying for. If a person's blessings, whatever form they take, have not yet been solidified in his or her consciousness and he or she broadcasts them to someone with opposing views, things could turn out negatively. The negative energy of the opposing thought can contradict or weaken the energy of the idea, which is only in its baby stage. **Even animals protect their babies from the elements and from predators by sitting over them. We too ought to sit with our demonstrations, achievements, or blessings until they are fully established, and before we expose them to others.**

Once when Jesus performed a miracle by healing a leper, he told him, "Tell no one, but go and show yourself to the priest" (Luke 5:13). **Jesus the Christ understood and taught this principle.** A priest has spiritual authority; he or she performs ceremonies and blessings. The significance for us today is that we should initially tell only those who will bless our success, even if only with their thoughts. When we patiently allow the blessing to become solid and in a manifested form, no one can infuse doubt in our minds and the little ego or limited way of thinking will not be able to deceive us into believing that prayer does not work.

It is challenging for many of us to accept our oneness with God, meaning that the one spirit in us is God's Spirit. This is pretty empowering to know; however, it can become challenging to believe. God's word says, "We are created in his image and likeness" (Gen. 1:27), and "Our bodies are temples of God's Spirit and that we have dominion over our circumstances" (Gen. 2:28). We often forget the words of Jesus the Christ: "I have come that they may have life, and that they may have it more abundantly." John 10:10

Recently on a radio broadcast, a show that is aired throughout many countries, the teacher explained that in God's sight we are as filthy rags that deserve no mercy. He also said we ought to beg God. This is totally different from the concept of being created in God's image and likeness and the truth that Christ died as a ransom for our sins (missing the mark). In the affirmative pattern of praying, which Christ taught, begging is not a part of the mood. That sort of teaching often, through our thoughts, becomes imprinted in our subconscious minds. Efforts to prove the teaching otherwise often encounters resistance. This resistance shows up in us as low self-esteem, lack of spiritual self-esteem, detachment from God or anything spiritual, a feeling of being stuck, a feeling of being unworthy to pray, frustration, and anger, etc.

We ought to stand firm in our awareness that God lovingly created us with the freedom to choose, while also giving us the gift of prayer. We are free to surrender any thoughts, miscreation, beliefs, or behaviors that do not serve our higher selves. We must tame the little ego and let it serve the Spiritual ego. We can allow it to help us in our activities of daily living, such as how we show up in the world and with our general mannerisms etc.

We must embrace the truth through spiritual wisdom and acceptance. The truth is that **God is the only power there is and God is a power for good, always seeking to bring more good into our lives. This belief must be the state of our consciousness**. We must be very vigilant of our thoughts, always keeping them in an affirmative state.

Finding Peace through our quiet mind.

Our mind is the medium through which we successfully work and allow our Heavenly Father to work in the silence. When the mind is disturbed it causes the body to become disturbed and vice versa. This creates a cycle of unrest. Any discord can mesmerize the mind and form a hindrance to prayer much to the little ego's delight. The following process can also support one in communicating with Almighty God.

Process

Sit or recline in a quiet comfortable place. Consciously think of your breathing as you take slow deep breaths. Feel the air as it enters and exits your nostrils. As you inhale quietly say or think, "I breathe in peace and the healing, revitalizing breath of God." As you exhale quietly say or think, "I breathe out worry, stress, limitation, doubt and fears." Pay attention to the feelings in every part of your body. Be aware of sensations of the head, face, neck, shoulder, back, abdomen and feet. These areas of the body tend to become more constricted in times of stress, worry, anger, or fear. Feel these body parts become soft and relaxed.

Feeling relaxed, quietly say or think in communication with your Heavenly Father, "Almighty Father, you breathe your breath of life in me and I became a living soul. This breath now soothes me and gives me peace in my mind, and body; I am relaxed in your love. I surrender all sorrow, anger, regrets, fears and doubts. I invite you to fill me with wisdom. Loving Father, I am listening."

Preferably with eyes closed and if you so choose quietly say or think, "Peace... be still." Feel a profound peace and gratitude envelop your body. Think on thoughts of Almighty God's unconditional love for you. Become aware of your own God essence as a child of Our Heavenly Father and fully surrender. Now silently pray...

Prayer

Heavenly Father, I feel a deep abiding peace. I know that you find expression in and through me right here and now. I allow you to find your rightful place at the center of my being as I transform and support others in doing so. Backed by your wise presence, I take dominion over every circumstance in my life. I align myself with you and co-create a life of peace and joy. As a co-creator with you, my desires are fulfilled according to your will; your will is my will. I accept the truth that your dream for me is always bigger than I can imagine. Here I am, willing, ready and open as I accept my good... (Pause) Through my Christ consciousness I say, "Thank you Almighty Father for hearing me always and for hearing me now."

Affirmations

I live in peace, joy and a perpetual state of gratitude.

Divine Intelligence guides me into paths of peace, happiness, love, joy and perfect life. In surrender I allow myself to be guided. With zeal and gratitude, I share these gifts with others.

Peace like a river, peace like a river, I have peace like a river!

Denial

Nothing can confound the peace of Christ in me. I am the manifestation of peace and all is well.

No one and nothing can disturb the calm peace of my soul. I have an elevated consciousness!

Treatment

I am at peace, knowing that I am always held in the soft caring embrace of my Heavenly Father. As I recognize this presence within, I allow the thoughts of all worries, stressors and unwanted circumstances to fade away into their native nothingness. The love and the peace that surpasses all human understanding are with me here and now; I am grateful.

Chapter 4: Spiritual Practices

Dismantling Prayer's Challenges

Beloveds, your births heralded blessings just because you showed up on this planet. You were created to be creative and always expanding in consciousness. We are destined for greatness and lives of love, peace, and joy. We all deserve prosperity. These gifts are our birthright; God is no respecter of persons which means that he has no favorites; no one can ever be excluded from these blessings.

We might doubt our greatness. Perhaps we became afraid of it. There is no need to accept any lie we made up or was told about ourselves. The truth is that we can do greater things than Jesus the Christ did; he assured us of this. But just as Christ did, we must also maintain a connection to God through our affirmative prayers. Its benefits are unlimited! When we dedicate ourselves to this practice of being in the presence of God, we are in fact exercising our spiritual muscles, which can only develop with use! **Practice supports us first in seeing the glass half full instead of half empty. As our faith expands, we see the glass full and never empty, despite any appearance to the contrary!**

There is a quality of clarity that comes into our awareness as we continue our Affirmative prayer practices. We tend to live more in the present moment. We experience joy and peace *now*. We smile more often because the Spiritual ego, or higher self, now guides us. We also realize that divine order rules our days, and synchronistic events become quite normal. Will we encounter challenges from here on? Quite likely; life presents us with challenges and challengers who become our great teachers. However, through these times, our Affirmative prayer practice ignites a light that shines on our ways; we realize the lesson and purpose for every event, whether it is sad, happy, or both.

> **No person and nothing can change the truth that Almighty God is a power for good, seeking to bring us only good. We cannot change the truth that when we surrender our cares, our experience is that Jesus' yoke is easy and his burden becomes light. (Matt 11:30) We cannot rewrite the affirmative statement. "You will also declare a thing, and it will be established for you; so light will shine on your ways" (Job 22:28). We cannot change the truth that God responds to us as we respond to him. However, we can change our understanding and our awareness as we embrace these spiritual truths. Are you willing? The universe beckons!**

Spiritual Practices

After realizing that the ego is only a thought form, we must condition our consciousness, through our minds, to be the catalyst for change. In his book *This Thing called You*, Holmes wrote, "What thought has done, thought can undo" (1948). Thought is creative, and is the groundwork for manifesting. The creation of affirmative prayers, spiritual mind treatments, affirmations, denials, and meditation have their origins in our minds. They must be formulated first in our minds with an earnest intention to remove any mental hindrances to our prayers. The person saying them must bring an intentional emotional component to this practice. If we mindlessly engage in these practices, the process is futile.

The following treatments, affirmations, and denials can be life changing and practical in strengthening our prayer practices.

Treatments

- There is a power for good in this universe, and it seeks only to bring me good. This power is God, the Good, Omnipotent, and Everlasting. I believe I deserve this good, and I am ready to receive it now. I believe in the transforming power of my Affirmative prayers, and that I am in contact with my Almighty God each time I pray. I open my mind and clear away the clutter of false beliefs. For too long, I have believed that I am unworthy of receiving anything good. I now surrender the lies I have learned since my childhood. I surrender all error thoughts, falsities, and decisions that support any belief of unworthiness. I now recognize them for what they are; nothing! The transmuting power of Christ now transmutes them back into the nothingness from whence they came. I deliberately allow this to be so, and so it is, now and forevermore. I am grateful.

- I know that my Heavenly Father knew me before I was conceived in my mother's womb. I know that I am created in the spiritual image and likeness of God. I know that my body is a temple of the Holy Spirit of God. This Spirit within me is poised, confident, and secure. I allow this Spirit to pray, love, and live through me. I show up in this world with the confidence that God always hears and answers my prayers. I align myself with the Spirit and surrender any belief that no longer serves to help me prosper. I open my spiritual ears and let the Spirit whisper to me, telling me how to be of service in this universe. The perfect law of God is now operating in my life and the lives of my fellow men, and I am forever grateful. All is well.

Affirmations

- I live in a harmonious world. Everything in my life and affairs works in harmony with God's will for me.
- I am worthy of all that is good. I enthusiastically receive my good; I am so grateful.
- The intelligence of the Spirit fills my mind. I know what I must know, and I do what I must do on divine time and in divine order.
- I am filled with the light of God. I see all mankind filled with this light of God. Together, we illuminate our world.
- There is a vibrant power for good in this universe. I know it works for me and all others.
- Right here and now, I am immersed in the presence of God.
- In this holy moment of now and in this holy place where I stand, God supplies my daily bread.

Denials

- There is no fear in me; I am courageous, confident, and strong.
- No error or thought of lack can confound me. I dismiss such thoughts as false. I am always lovingly provided for by the great I AM.
- No false belief can block my prayers. God always answers my prayers.
- My prayers are not futile. I am worthy, so worthy to commune with God who always hears me, and I gratefully do so.

Let us now look at affirmation, treatments, and denials in greater detail.

Affirmation

The use of affirmations has been recorded since the event of creation. When God said, "Let there be," those affirmative words were followed by an object that was created. Those words were the catalyst for creation. This preceded the affirmative Lord's Prayer taught by Christ. **To *affirm* means to declare positively and to make firm. When we say an affirmation, we are in essence using the power of the spoken word in a positive declaration that makes firm the manifestation of our desires. Affirming is a practice that forms bedrock for transformation of our consciousness. As we have determined, the Lord's Prayer is consisted of a series of affirmations.**

Affirmations are also often called decrees because when one affirms, that person is in essence decreeing or pronouncing the evidence of his or her needs fulfilled. An affirmation is a statement of truth. In the Scripture, as Job was experiencing troubles, he stated, "You will also decree a thing and it will be established for you; so light will shine on your ways" (Job 22:28). The psalmist David affirmed, "The Lord is my shepherd, I shall not want" (Ps. 23:1). He was sure he could not come to the state where he would want for his good because, "The Lord is his shepherd."

Affirmations must contain the tone of our moods, beliefs, and intentions. We echo them through our powerfully charged words. As we say them we impress them on our subconscious minds. We must **feel** as if our desires have already been attained; this creates an emotional connection between us and the desire. We must be clear as we focus on what we want. This is crucial because the subconscious mind is neutral and will cause the manifestation of what we focus on, whether favorable or unfavorable.

Affirmations are of course affirmative. The words are set in present tense. If past or future tenses are used, and they rarely are, they serve to demonstrate an occurrence of the past that has caused a current situation. This is also a demonstration of the Law of Cause and Effect. For example, see Psalm 121:1–2:

> I will lift up my eyes to the hills [Future]
>
> From whence came my help? [Past]
>
> My help comes from the Lord, who made heaven and earth. [Present]

An affirmation is usually a simple yet powerful and concise statement. It should be said with a firm feeling of possibility, faith, and gratitude. To do otherwise is to speak in vain. Affirmations have been embraced by other faiths throughout the centuries. The ancients believed in the power of affirmation. **Solomon said "Death and life are in the power of the tongue" (Prov. 18:21). Scientists have discovered that the energetic frequencies of identical words are different when phrased positively versus negatively. Vibrations of our words move into the atmosphere, creating conditions that match them energetically. In the same manner, our affirmations create the conditions we decree. The following are some examples of affirmations:**

- I was created through God's impulse of love; therefore, I am love.
- I surrender the burden of mediocrity and embrace my true purpose now.
- I am healed and made whole and perfect now.
- Wonderful avenues of good now open for me; I am grateful.
- The light and love of God now surround me. I am wonderfully blessed.

Denials

In the *Webster's New World Dictionary and Thesaurus*, the word *denial* is defined as a "repudiation, disclaimer, refusal to recognize, renunciation, dismissal, the cold shoulder, the brush off." A denial is an ancient mode of praying that renounces or dismisses the difficulty directly. It may seem that there is no reason for denials when we can simply claim what we want. However, there are some instances in which a denial is appropriate in order to strengthen faith or bring about positive change in one's affairs.

We live in a world where on any given day we can experience a myriad of issues. This may begin as soon as we recognize ourselves as individuals. At this tender age through our experiences, we develop our unique personalities. Our experiences often affect our ways of approaching prayer. Personality is vital to how we conduct our lives and respond to our world. Some people grow up in homes where they experience much negative conversation. Negativity becomes internalized over the years and subsequently forms the tone of these persons' consciousness; they are more inclined to focus on what is lacking rather than on the good that is present. They see the glass half empty.

It is true that the thing upon which we focus grows; this can make it seem like denials would be counterproductive. Nothing could be further from the truth. Furthermore, it can be deleterious to subscribe to one particular way of praying. A person who more often benefits from denials can at times have a prayer need that is better fulfilled by an affirmation! When we are open to the Spirit of God that dwells within us we are guided to pray adequately. Simple prayers, affirmations, treatments, or denials—supported by a consciousness of faith—are equally potent. **Denials support the attainment of freedom from the stronghold of a negative consciousness.**

Our words have life and energy whether we use them for affirmation or denial. Our intentions and consciousness always support our prayers. With practice, we each will intuitively feel confirmation when we have prayed in the appropriate manner.

Let's examine the following example: While growing up, a person often heard his parents say, "We are saving money for hard times." This person is more likely to develop a consciousness that expects him to fall on hard times. Later in life, through a self-fulfilling prophecy he is faced with lack of money and hard times. A useful denial would be the following:

Denial

There are no hard times in my experience. I have enough money to use, to share, and to spare at all times. I love money, and money loves me. I am worthy to receive money. Money freely and constantly flows to me from expected and unexpected channels. I am so grateful.

Notice that there was no focusing or lingering at the first sentence, only a brief statement to confront then negate the condition of lack. The focus becomes the evidence of money freely and constantly flowing toward the person. Remember, we focus on whatever we desire to see increased. Nature abhors a vacuum, so immediately after a statement of "no" or negation is uttered, the consciousness must be voluntarily filled with a positive replacement (as demonstrated above). If not, it will soon be filled involuntarily and more often with a negative thought all over again.

Denials also serve to dissolve or renounce fear, lack of faith, stress, sickness, addiction, low self-esteem, relationship issues, or any appearance of evil. They renounce or release any negativity held in the consciousness. For example, for an appearance of illness, the following **statement of denial** can be used:

There is no sickness in my body. I am well and whole.

To heal relationships, a **statement of denial** could be the following:

> I dispel all animosity from my experience. My relationships are loving and peaceful. I am a friend to all people, and all people are friendly to me.

For an **addiction** to a harmful substance, a person could make the following **statement of denial.**

> No substance can render my mind or body addicted to it. I take dominion over my mind and body. I take into my body the nourishment that is healthy and life-giving. I practice only healthy behaviors. I praise and bless my wonderful mind and body. I accept and bless my body as the temple of my Almighty God and so it is.

For obsession or a negative or **compulsive behavior**, a person could express the following **statement of denial**:

> There is no obsession in my mind or body. I am free to think and act in healthy ways. I am free to think and behave in ways that honor the divinity in me and others. My mind and body are in alignment with perfect action. Gratefully, I accept and embrace this perfection now.

Someone with a **lack** of substance such as money, a place to live, food, etc., could make the following **statement of denial:**

> There is no lack of any good thing in this universe. I see beautiful and comfortable homes everywhere. The stores are brimming with food. Money circulates everywhere. This is all I see, and it is real. Lack is an illusion, and I release it from my consciousness. I now open myself and allow the Spirit of God within me to reveal to me the channels through which my good comes. Acknowledging our Heavenly Father as the source of all good, I am obedient to all that I am guided to do. Grateful that my needs are met, I release all fear of lack, and I rejoice!

It can seem rather untrue or silly to say "grateful that my needs are met" when you do not have the money or home or food. However, because change always begins within the mind, we seek to first change the mental picture through our creative words. We replace our words with new, positive, and life affirming ones.

Denials help to reeducate our minds by confronting the difficulty head-on. Believing in the negative situations for most of our lives causes this way of thinking to be at the forefront of our minds. By denying the appearance of whatever is undesirable, we briefly move to its level, firmly deny it, and quickly replace it. We move quickly to avoid becoming immersed again in that old negative energy.

Spiritual Mind Treatment

Specific forms of prayer are used according to the needs of the person praying. A *spiritual mind treatment*, also referred to as a *treatment*, is one of these forms of Affirmative prayer. Like an affirmation, it is positive, current, definite, and clear. It helps condition the mind of the person saying it. As we consider the mind-body connection that has always existed, we must realize that a spiritual mind treatment can only but enhance the functions of mind and body. This is a priceless tool for transforming a situation because of its effectiveness in changing one's mind. Change begins within. One can change their situation by changing the beliefs about it. **We must become aware of our unconscious thoughts; the ones that run our lives. Spiritual mind treatments support the changing of our beliefs.**

Although a spiritual mind treatment is simple, it is not merely mouthing words; it involves our feelings along with our words of faith. Our emotions are gifts from God; our emotional conviction attests to our faith and our belief in the creative power of our words. This is absolutely necessary when giving a spiritual mind treatment. A treatment is not a petition; it is a statement of realization and power that allows us to exercise our gift of dominion over our circumstances. Since our words are creative, we must be definite about our prayers and desires when creating and using these treatments. When we combine our words with a conscious realization of creative power, making our requests known, we attract that for which we speak or something better and in accordance with God's will.

In a spiritual mind treatment there is no forcing, begging, or hypnotism. There must be faith and conviction. We must also have a definite intention. We then act with conscious cooperation and direction, making affirmative statements that give voice to our thoughts, feelings, beliefs and desire.

We must believe the good which we seek is already manifested. This acceptance is absolutely necessary. Anyone can create a spiritual mind treatment and use it successfully. The main prerequisites are to seek God's guidance and to have a consciousness of unconditional love, faith, and forgiveness. See the following two spiritual mind treatments as examples.

Co-Creating with God

Treatment

I know that the presence and power of God are around me and that they move through me. I am an individualization of the presence of God. I know God must work for me, through me, therefore I willingly and joyfully create an internal and external atmosphere through my thoughts, words, and deeds. This allows God to manifest good through me, for me and others. Knowing that God always provides and never fails, I humbly say "thank you, Almighty God."

Seeking Guidance for Service

Treatment

I now embrace the Spirit of God within me. I know this Spirit is closer to me than my own heartbeat. I accept that new and wonderful experiences are now happening to me, and I gratefully let them happen. New avenues to serve now open for me. I remember to help those who are in need by helping them reveal their own inner strengths and splendor. I offer love, joy, and peace to whomever I contact. I am grateful for the privilege of supporting others. All is well; I let it be so, and so it is.

Always feel free to create your own treatments, as the Spirit of God within you guides you. Don't be surprised if you feel guided to create a treatment that seems irrelevant. Very soon you may have the experience that matches up with the content of that particular treatment. **The universe often responds even before we ask!**

Become an Open Vessel!

In order for the light that guides to flow through us, we must become trusting, open and receptive. All the wisdom we desire is already available to us. No one is excluded…no one. We must consciously cooperate with the Spirit of God in us and allow it to guide our Spiritual practices. I fondly say that Spirit loves us into compliance no matter how resistant we are or how challenging a learning experience may seem. Beloved, Spirit is beckoning you whether you feel broken or whole, rich or poor, worthy or unworthy. Our heavenly Father does not play favorites. Our Master teacher the Christ said that he (God) is "Our Heavenly Father" not my, not your, not their Heavenly Father; The Almighty God is *Our-Heavenly- Father*!

The following Treatment can support the development of openness and receptivity

Treatment

I know that the Spirit of God in me now guides me. I surrender any fear, doubt or complacency and allow myself to be divinely guided. I know that I am a Spiritual idea in the mind of God; therefore my Spiritual practice is guided into alignment with God's ideas. I open my mouth in prayer and with praises. I act with love and compassion and I think with the same mind that was in Christ Jesus. My earnest intention is always to support the building up my fellowmen as well as myself. When I speak the word of truth for myself the Universe responds. When I speak the words of truth for others the Universe responds. I am receptive to and embrace all practices that serve God and lift up all creation. For the wisdom and privilege to do so I am eternally grateful. I am at peace and all is well.

Chapter 5

Transforming Power in the Name of Jesus Christ

Apart from teaching the disciples how to pray affirmatively, Christ also promised that if we asked God for anything in his name, he will do it: "If you ask anything in my name, I will do it." (John 14:14).

The foundation of Jesus' thoughts and actions was love and forgiveness. This was clearly demonstrated at his crucifixion. During his three years of ministry he showed compassion for those in distress and taught lessons that supported the people in realizing their individual worth. He pointed out that Our Heavenly Father God loves the tiny sparrow very much; yet still he loves the person who does his will so much more than those sparrows. He further explained that for such persons, God even knows the number of hairs on their heads! (Luke 12; 6, 7)

Jesus demonstrated that there is no need for our spiritual lives to be burdensome. On a Sabbath day when the disciples were hungry, they disregarded the law of the Sabbath, went into the cornfield and plucked corn and ate. The Pharisees told Jesus that his disciples were doing what was unlawful on the Sabbath. Jesus responded by asking them if they had not read what David did when he was hungry. He explained that when David and those who were with him were hungry, they went into the temple and ate the temple showbread. It was unlawful for anyone except the priests to eat this bread. He also brought to their attention, the fact that on the Sabbath, the priests profaned the Sabbath and were blameless (Matt 12:1-5) Jesus also healed a man's withered hand on the Sabbath day. Before the healing, and in answering those who asked him if this was lawful, Jesus asked which one of them would have a sheep fall into a pit on the Sabbath and would not lift it out? He told them that it was lawful to do what is good on the Sabbath. Jesus was demonstrating that these rules were put in place by the religious system and not by God. (Matt 12:9-13) In those instances he was exposing the hypocrisy in those man made laws. The laws of God for the Sabbath were simple; as a matter of truth, Jesus Christ explained that he is Lord of the Sabbath. **The Sabbath was made for man and not man for the Sabbath**. Jesus Christ also demonstrated that he read the bible in the format it took in Biblical times. Yes, Jesus read the same Old Testament doctrine that we read today!

Jesus wasted no time on idle words. He taught what was absolutely necessary. When we examine the miracles of Jesus, we realize that he was the person called upon to perform healings. However, he never took credit for it and said that it is the father who worked in him. He always called on his Heavenly Father God through prayer, for the manifestation of all miracles. Jesus's role was the intercessor. Today, whether we pray for ourselves or practice intercessory prayers for others, Jesus continues to be our intercessor when we ask God for anything in his name.

Scientists have discovered that out of all the great teachers who lived on this earth, the name of Jesus Christ has the highest calibration of power. No other name on earth has ever had such transformative power. Names are made with words, and words have power, but that is not the only reason Jesus's name has such matchless power. We must recall that an angel of God told Jesus's mother, the Virgin Mary, that she would give birth and the child's name would be Jesus. Knowing all these truths, we can fathom that this would be no ordinary or powerless name.

Throughout history, no other name has stood for such mighty works. The healings, miracles, lessons, and acts of love, faith, gratitude, and forgiveness are remarkable. Jesus held children in high regard and demonstrated that he made time for them. He lived a life of being nonjudgmental and humble; allowing a woman to anoint his feet with fragrant oil and to wipe them with her hair. This is remarkable because at that time women were seen as inferior, yet Jesus allowed women to support him in his ministry; Jesus intentionally rebelled against prejudice and discrimination. He disregarded the customs of his times since they created social boundaries. There was separation between Jews and Gentiles, rich and poor, male and female, righteous and sinner. Jesus broke bread with all people and always saw the divinity in everyone. He demonstrated compassion instead of judgment. He allowed others to help him carry out his work, setting an example for us to do the same. He demonstrated his humanity when his friend Lazarus died; he felt sadness and wept, giving both males and females permission to cry as a natural way to soothe their emotions. Through his resurrecting power and his compassion, he brought Lazarus back to life. This also demonstrated his deep love for his friends. In Matthew 22: 37-40: he entreated us to love the Lord with all our heart, soul and mind as the first commandment. The second like it is "You shall love your neighbor as yourself."

We know of his obedience in making his earthly life a living example to us. Jesus showed us how to resist temptation and how to follow God's will as he did, even in the darkest hour of the crucifixion. While dying in agony, he intentionally assigned a disciple to care for his mother Mary who followed him to the crucifixion site. He taught us to love and to be obedient to our parents; He obeyed his Mother's command to turn water into wine which was also his first miracle! This also helps us to understand the power of a mother and that we must care for our parents and them for us. There was a display of his supernatural power at his death. The veil of the temple was miraculously torn in two. There was an earthquake, graves were torn open, and souls were resurrected (Matt. 27:51). After Jesus' death as a ransom for the sins of mankind, he was resurrected and ascended to heaven. Jesus had the profound and undefiled belief that as a seed of the woman his body was the temple of God; his body never decayed after the crucifixion. **Throughout Jesus Christ's ministry, he empowered people. With humility, he said that we will do the works he did and even greater works we will do.**

Christ showed us how to stay connected to God. These acts of Jesus, the man himself, showed that he was the embodiment of pure goodness. He was interested in our prayer practices and wanted our lives to become transformed; therefore, **he taught us how to pray affirmatively using the model of The Lord's prayer. Affirmative prayer serves as a steady anchor for us as we transform**. For these reasons and so many more, the name of Jesus Christ will never lose its power.

This of course does not mean that we neither had nor have any other great teachers. St. Paul taught tirelessly about love and obedience to Christ. King David, the psalmist, showed the power of redemption. Paramahansa Yogananda taught about peace. Mohandas K. Gandhi, Dr. Martin Luther King Jr., Bishop Desmond Tutu, Rosa Parks, the Dali Llama, Thich Nhat Hanh, and many others stood for peace and justice. Nelson Mandela, who was imprisoned for twenty seven years in South Africa under the Apartheid regime and who later became South Africa's president, taught and demonstrated forgiveness and reconciliation. There are men and women, who will never be known in a public way, yet they strive for peace in their homes, at work, and in the holy instances of the opportunities they seize.

When we take a deep look at the act of praying in the name of Jesus, we can glean the wisdom of who we really are. St Paul wrote, "I have been crucified with Christ; it is no longer I who live, but Christ lives in me." (Gal 2:20) When we pray in the name of Jesus Christ we are indeed praying from the core of our real Christ selves! We must embrace our Christ selves and pray from this point of reference and authority. We can only experience good by praying in Jesus Christ's name; he advocates and petitions our Heavenly father for us as we evolve spiritually. We can attain our Christhood as children of God, and then when we pray, we are praying through our enlightened Christ consciousness through where there is absolutely no block to our prayers. Jesus Christ remains the teacher whose name stands for the mightiest of all good works. **Again, he promised that if we ask Almighty God for anything in his name, he will do it.**

Waiting for Answers

I have listened to people who said they have prayed hard for a certain outcome, and I am sure many of us have listened to people relate these concerns as well. Praying "hard" is really unnecessary; it sets up a resistance in one's mind. It indicates that the thing or condition that is prayed for is difficult to attain. Whether one prayed "hard" or without strain, whether the prayer was simple or advanced, there will be times when it seems that prayers are not answered. Some people feel simple prayers are not productive, and because of this, they might pray with a consciousness of doubt.

The focus then is to confidently and earnestly say simple prayers as little children do, especially if we are not yet familiar with the more advanced ways of praying. The more advanced methods of affirmative prayers are spiritual mind treatments, affirmations, denials, visualization, and meditation as explained in this book. The universe responds to us; when the time is appropriate for someone to embrace the more advanced ways of praying, the teacher will appear and this cannot be otherwise. In reading this book and practicing these methods one can become knowledgeable of these methods. When people are spiritually receptive, they often get the desire to embrace advanced ways of praying at the right time. They are usually led to open the appropriate books on prayers and other spiritual practices, or they may be led to attend workshops, classes, and gatherings where they learn these methods. Yes, the universe knows our wants and when to supply them.

Some people waiting for answers after they have prayed might explain that they used only the advanced way of praying. Whether prayers are engaged in a simple or advanced method, we are dealing with the spiritual laws of God, which when followed support us in creating what we pray for or whatever is most appropriate for us. This law must await our alignment with it. To do otherwise is to block its creativity in our prayers. As we examine some of the following ways we often block our prayers, some may sound familiar!

Patience

One of the most common blocks to prayers is impatience; patience is the virtue that helps build our faith and stamina. We are truly blessed with wonderful examples in nature, yet we often fail to make the connection! I can remember a scene that I was not fond of as a young child. Our family raised livestock, and my mother never failed to show much excitement when she heard peeping sounds coming from the hatching eggs. These sounds can be heard before the chick breaks through its shell. Several times I noticed that my mother, in her excitement and impatience would gently pick off a piece of the shell from the eggs within which the peeping noises came from. Her belief was that she was helping them. When the hatching happened overnight while we were asleep, of course we missed hearing the peeping sounds, and those chickens had the blessing of breaking through their shells on their own. When

I was about five years old, I made a connection; most of the chicks that died soon after hatching or either survived but struggled for about two days, were the ones Mommy "helped" by partially removing their shells. I remember always helplessly watching her and thinking, "she *shouldn't do that!*" She needed to wait.

As I got older, I learned that in order for butterflies to survive, they must be allowed to struggle as they leave their cocoons. The struggling motion causes vital fluid to be pumped into parts of their wings, strengthening them and enabling them to fly. I then realized that the chicks needed the opportunity to peck and push through their shells to build stamina and strength to survive as well. Often in life, we fail to realize that after we affirmatively pray, we must allow ourselves to patiently wait in faith. **It is true that we often struggle with our feelings and perhaps situations as we wait. However, it is in this gap between asking and receiving where we may struggle and where our stamina and strength of character is built.**

"But those who wait upon the Lord shall renew their strength." *(Isa.40:31)*

When things are manifested earlier than normal, whether it was forced or it happened on its own, there's always more care needed to maintain it. For example, premature babies often require a significant amount of extra care. There is cause for worry; some might die, and a few might have a disability or limitation of some sort. (Thankfully most survive and enjoy healthy lives.) This same pattern repeats itself when we manifest things earlier than we should. When the woman's body is not ready to deliver and labor is induced, there can be more pain and complications. When we try to force the hand of God, we often create drama and pain in our lives. What we manifest might cause us worries as we try to hold on to something that is not fully developed and which we are not ready for, or are capable of maintaining. Beloveds, please embrace patience, for it is your testimony of faith.

The Gift of Waiting

Looking in the Scripture, we see examples of people waiting for an appointed time before they can see the manifestation of some event or condition. When the Virgin Mary was pregnant with Jesus Christ, Joseph was told not to touch her in an intimate way until Jesus was born. He had to wait. When Joshua led the army to destroy Jericho, they were victorious because of their patience to obey his specific instructions with precision. See Joshua 6:3-20. Jesus Christ waited forty days in the wilderness to complete his spiritual assignment. He faced hunger and temptation, yet he waited patiently and proved his Divinity to all mankind.

Doubts

When it seems prayers are not being answered, we must examine the thoughts in our minds to see if they are thoughts of hope or doubt. If we doubt, we will harbor thoughts of fear; these thoughts at times mesmerize us into complacency and failure. In the scriptural account of Job, who suffered great losses in his life, he declared that the thing he feared most had come upon him. His fear caused him to focus on what he did not want and this is exactly what he manifested. Do not fight those negative thoughts; just change them by thinking about something else such as the wisdom and faithfulness of Jehovah. Think of the positives in your life. Think of the good things you have done as well as the good that others have done. Remind yourself that you are the wonderful creation of a God who loves you unconditionally. Sometimes negative thoughts seem to enter our minds with such rapidity that we forget to pray. This is why it is good to have an active prayer practice; this "builds our Spiritual muscles" and can also support the habit of seeking God first instead of seeking him after much unnecessary worrying.

Outlining

Another behavior that causes blocks to our prayers is the act of outlining. The need to control often shows up as outlining and is one of the little ego's modes of operation. It is wise to ask our Almighty God for what we desire; however, when we ask we must be careful not to try to control the way we believe God should supply it. Very often God supplies our manifestation in a grander way than our finite minds can fathom. When we outline, we can limit our blessings or block our prayers by asking for less than we deserve or for things we are not ready to have. In preparing to receive something, we must feel and believe that we are worthy of it. Our belief, which must be in alignment with our desires, sets up the motivational pull that opens us to ideas of how to create and maintain our blessings. **When our firm belief aligns with the desire, we are said to have the Mental Equivalent.** Without the belief and acceptance that we are worthy, we may self-sabotage in an unconscious attempt to live up to this unbelief, thereby blocking our good.

Preparation

We must be prepared to receive and hold on to the substances of our manifestations. When we prepare, we must do our inner and outer work; this is how we put our faith into practice. We first must have in our thoughts what we want to create. We pray and ask God for guidance concerning this specific thing. For example, if someone wants to manifest a romantic relationship leading to marriage or simply long-term companionship, the first step is to seek God's will. To do this, the person can get into the silence and pray about the desire. This person must also be receptive to whatever guidance is received.

"Seek ye first the kingdom and all things will be added to you" (Matt. 6:33).

One must always be aware that God cannot answer prayers that do not benefit all concerned. Prayers that are created with an intention to benefit only the person praying are creations of the Little selfish ego. This prayer would be amiss because its success will be blocked. Whenever guidance is received, it is imperative that we follow it accordingly. One person may be guided to show self-love so that the mate he or she manifests will act lovingly toward him or her as a result of the Law of Attraction. This person must show love to themselves as a statement that he or she is worthy and ready to receive love and that he or she knows how to practice and maintain it. If someone does not have love for themselves, it would be difficult for them to attract it from someone else. Guidance may indicate that he or she must take care of his or her spiritual, mental, emotional, or physical selves; then this is what that person should do to develop self-love and a sense of worthiness. (See Chapters 6 and 7 for these practices.) He or she may then be guided to visit a certain place at a certain time where they can meet the divinely ordained person.

The outer works must match up with the desire. The ultimate intention however, must be that both people benefit and are happy in the relationship.

Being Realistic

We must be reasonable in all things. If the thing we prayed for is unrealistic, it may seem that our prayers are not being answered. For example, a person should not apply for a loan to get a house or a car without having a job or some means of repaying it and expect to get the loan. One can, however, pray concerning avenues that can open up to make this possible. Then he or she can follow guidance received in prayer, faithfully and with patience. In other instances such as after praying for a home or a family, he or she may wait actively by looking at model homes, reading articles or books about families, preparing mentally and financially for a family, or one can choose to see a fertility specialist if there is difficulty in this area, to rule out a problem or to remedy some area that may need it etc.

One should not pray for health while neglecting the health of the body, or behaving in self-harming ways and expect to manifest the healthy condition they prayed for. Instead one can pray for guidance, motivation, and wisdom regarding personal health care. Our thoughts and actions must be in alignment with our prayers and desires. Spiritual laws govern every facet of our lives, and we must obey them along our path to transformation. **These laws of God are always life affirming and were created so that we would never have to live wondering nor wandering like lost sheep.** The universe loves us and beckons us to use these laws!

Act As If

When we act as if the particular desired condition exists, we put the Law of Attraction to work. This law works in a neutral manner, meaning it does not discriminate whether we manifest something favorable or unfavorable. By acting as if we have already manifested something, we capture the feeling we believe we would have when we receive it. We are also conditioning the emotions to be able to handle it when it arrives. We allow the feeling to bring the object or situation into manifestation. Harnessing the feelings is very important. Since scientists proved that we can choose our moods, we can deliberately choose to create how we feel. This does not discount the fact that in times of e.g. tragedy, this can be extremely difficult to do. This step can open the way for us to confidently speak or act just as how we would speak or act had we already seen or manifested our desires. Our attitude opens the way for our prayers to be answered. It is counterproductive to pray for something and then keep rehashing our lack of it. It is God's will that we prosper; therefore, we ought to cease focusing on lack and instead focus on prosperity.

One day during my early teenage years, I remember speaking to my mother about something I wanted. Her words to me were, "If you want a guitar, you must buy the guitar's strings first." Since I wasn't speaking to her about a guitar, I immediately realized she was telling me that I must act in preparation and expectation in accordance with my desire. This was my first lesson to "act as if!" Although from this vantage point, we can also visualize what we want and then "act as if," **when we are not following the spiritual laws of love, forgiveness, faith, gratitude, etc., we can visualize and "act as if" as much as we want, yet still it will be difficult to manifest our desires**. Visualization works through one's mind and consciousness, which is where we create an image of the desired thing. Our consciousness is a powerful thing that we cannot deceive. Our desire must be birthed out of an impulse of love and nurtured in *a love Consciousness* as we follow spiritual laws, in order for our prayers and visualization to be successful.

A State of Gratitude

Being in the state of gratitude creates in us the mental equivalent to having our prayers answered, and our desires fulfilled while it makes us whole. Gratitude affirms faith and trust. Faith and trust prevent fear and hopelessness. Recognized from this vantage point, gratitude is not merely saying thanks; it is an inner affirmation of faith and trust. Gratitude is a catalyst for co-creating with God. As we wait for our desires to manifest, we can engage in some practices that support us. The following practices can be helpful in fostering faith and trust and patience.

Affirmations
- Today I surrender worrying and allow God's light to dawn on my experiences.
- There is nothing to be afraid of; God's loving and watchful eyes are on all my affairs.

75

- This world is a peaceful place. I am at peace with all people, and all people are at peace with me.
- I enjoy my work; it provides a great opportunity to be of service to God, myself and others.
- Divine health flows through my body. I am whole and well.
- I let go and let God. In quiet and confidence comes my strength.

Treatments

- Today I surrender all my concerns to God. I have complete confidence that my needs are now being met on Divine time and in Divine order. I open myself to Divine creativity and am eager and willing to consciously create with my Heavenly Father. The pure energy of life is available to me, and I now immerse myself in it! Knowing that this is the truth, I declare that all is well. I allow it to be so, and so it is forevermore.
- I am in the Father, and the Father is in me. I spread my wings of faith and fly on winds of love. In this holy moment, I choose to think of higher thoughts that bless every person of whom I think. I see peace everywhere for everyone. Knowing that this universe works for everyone, I confidently rejoice!

Denial

I no longer walk in fear. I embrace courage, power, love, and my sound mind.

Prayer

Almighty Father, I recognize my oneness with you. I recognize that your most Holy Spirit dwells within me. I know that this Spirit goes before me and makes my way perfect, clear, and straight. I pray these words with confidence, knowing that the Spirit speaks through me in this holy moment. At times I worry and then pray. In the name of Jesus, I ask for and accept your forgiveness. Please forgive my forgetfulness; it is my intention to walk according to divine guidance. Thank you Almighty God, for hearing me now and for always hearing me. Amen.

Praying with Others

"Again I say to you that if two of you agree on earth concerning anything that you ask, it will be done for them by my father in heaven. For where two or three are gathered together in my name, I am there in the midst of them" (Matt. 18:19–20).

Our master teacher Jesus Christ demonstrated by example, that there is a collective energy which works for the good of all, when we come together in unity. He chose twelve disciples to support his good works. At times and for various reasons, many of us feel we must go through adverse circumstances alone. The following are some common reasons that can prevent someone from asking for or accepting help:

- Based on the little ego's reasoning, a person can decide that someone would not want to help him or her, so it would be useless asking for help. This person might conjure up the explanation that he or she doesn't want to bother others because it is not right or fair to do so.
- Some people feel that asking for help is a sign of weakness or ignorance, so they refuse to ask for help.
- Some people prefer to credit their achievements to themselves alone.
- Some people are afraid to let people know about their vulnerability for fear of repercussions.
- Some people choose to protect their privacy because unfortunately, some people gossip about others.

- Some people are steep into the judging, blaming, and taking on the victim's role. They usually help others but have difficulty receiving support or saying no when they should. This can also be a result of unconscious beliefs of unworthiness.

Everyone deserves to be supported through his or her challenges and, yes, even in their happy times! St. Paul often challenged people to love and support each other. He wrote, **"Bear ye one another's burdens, and so fulfill the law of Christ. (Galatians 6:2).** We are also told not to forget to assemble together: **"Let us consider one another, in order to stir up love and good works"** (Heb. 10:24–25).

With this spiritual mandate, it is imperative that we have at least one other person with whom we pray and discuss our good works. We should choose a frequency that is reasonable: once daily or once weekly, and whenever a need arises between those times. These sessions can be used for praying for world peace, prosperity, and healing of the body, mind, relationships, or other affairs. Prayers of praise and thanksgiving to God can sometimes be the only act when a group congregates. It is not necessary to have a request; at times the group can gather just to say prayers of praise. Some groups have live phone conferences, such as mastermind groups where each participant holds a vision for each other and prays about it.

Jesus demonstrated the need for twelve disciples. Likewise, we need the support of each other. Jesus met and prayed with the disciples in the upper room, where they received the power of the Holy Spirit. When we pray with and for each other, we are in truth, lifting and affirming each other. We also employ the power of cooperation, which fosters power, unity and success. Everyone brings his or her own ideas, feelings, desires, and energy. This is a microcosm of how the collective consciousness of the human race works on our behalf. **Any act that is a spiritual mandate, when done with a right intention, prospers us.**

Holding the Space for Each Other

If someone is too distraught, worried, or upset to effectively gather his or her thoughts, members of the prayer group or a partner can help them to calmly focus and become receptive. In this way, praying for others also helps someone to take the entire focus off their own self as they pray for others. This builds self-esteem in each member because it creates a sense of purpose in everyone.

The primary goal of each member of a prayer group or a prayer partnership is to hold a sacred space of faith, trust and support for each other. This is done by firmly holding in consciousness the absolute truth of any situation at hand. For example, if during a session someone reveals a challenge in a particular relationship, the other members quietly and actively listen while simultaneously holding the thought that the absolute truth about this relationship is peace, love, and understanding. During this time, they remain receptive; they then accept the inner guidance for the most appropriate way to support the member who is experiencing the challenge.

There is no mandate for how one should physically position themself. However, sitting with one's feet on the floor, eyes closed, and palms upturned and resting gently on the lap has been found to foster receptivity and openness. Naturally, the fingers would not lay flat open; concentrating to keep them this way can obstruct the mental flow.

Another benefit of praying for others is that through the Law of Attraction, the good we call forth for others also blesses us. Jesus admonished us to even pray for those who harm us. We can never help others without helping ourselves, and that is a spiritual law. I often teach this to students and ask them at the end of the lesson, "What happens when you help others?" They respond, "I also help myself."

Forming a Prayer Group

Forming prayer groups or praying with a partner is a simple procedure, yet it requires patience, discipline and rules. Once the members are determined, the following should be considered and addressed.

- Will the meetings be held in a person's home or office, a church building, another meeting place, or by way of Internet or phone? If the group members decide to hold the meetings in someone's home, it would be nice to rotate the homes, so no one feels he or she always has to host, or this can create resentment. Meeting in person achieves a more intimate feel. Phone conferencing or meeting through the Internet by video chatting and listening via the computer are not as intimate. However, this convenience can add longevity to the group.

- There must be an agreement that issues discussed during the meetings will be held in confidence, unless outside help is necessary for a potentially life-threatening and serious situation or one needing professional help. Everyone must understand that they will be treated respectfully by one another. Everyone should be expected and allowed to participate. A great exercise to start off an initial meeting is for each group member to be told by the other members, "We know you are here to be seen and heard; we see and hear you." The person who was just told this should then join with the other group members to say those exact words to another person. This process should be repeated until everyone is addressed. In this way, each person feels the sense of love and equality that is present. This process was very empowering to me personally.

- Everyone must practice active listening and not interrupt others. No one should say anything sarcastic, unkind or demeaning to anyone before, during, or

after he or she speaks; this should never be tolerated.
If someone values, trusts and honor another enough to
share his or her story with them, the least the listener
ought to do is to respectfully acknowledge the person
who is sharing.

- The group should choose a set amount of time that each
  member gets to share his or her information. Gently
  remind someone if they seem to overlook the time.
  Some people are naturally more talkative than others;
  however, everyone must be heard and supported. Group
  members must also understand that some situations will
  warrant a longer duration than others. Compassion,
  understanding, patience, respect and love are absolutely
  necessary for the effectiveness of any prayer group
  or prayer partner arrangement. **Be mindful so that
  everyone in the group feels that he or she is heard.**
  Once, I was a member of a mastermind group that
  was held by way of phone conferencing. One or two
  persons constantly dominated the sessions. To me it
  began to feel dry, boring, lopsided, and unproductive.
  This group quickly fizzled out of existence. Everyone
  should be heard!

Some people prefer a single prayer partner, and that is good as
well. Once we are receptive, we will be inspired about everything
concerning the nature of our prayer practice. Participants should
be on friendly terms with each other. If there is any unfriendliness
it should be mediated quickly. Trust and respect for self and others
must be demonstrated. Members of the group must hold fast to
the rule that a prayer group is not a group for constant whining or
complaining. **A problem cannot be solved if the consciousness
of the one praying is not raised above the level of the problem.
Schedule an occasional group meeting at which everyone speak
only of the positives in their experiences. Verbally reinforce
each one as they offer their testimony.**

Prayer for Groups or Partnerships

All-knowing and Almighty Father, we gather on one accord and pray in the name of Jesus Christ. We know your divine intelligence fills each of us. There is a holy presence within us that knows, and we are one with it. As we state our desires, we let every doubt be converted into trust. We allow our fears to be converted into love and courage. We pray and listen to the Holy Spirit's guidance, and we are impelled to obey. We rest our desires and thoughts in the wonderful possibilities that are already ours. We thank you that as we pray you hear us. For the gift and privilege of this group, for each other and for your guidance and blessings upon us, we humbly say "thank you, Father" all is well.

Affirmations

- We are filled with the wisdom of God. It now flows into our world through our thoughts and actions. Peace, harmony, and order now fill our world.
- There is one power from which all good emerges, that is God, the Good and Omnipotent. Good flows unhindered through our beings, infusing us with willingness and commitment to support each other. We now lovingly support each other and we are grateful.
- Lessons from the past have brought us to this moment. We choose to feel joy now, and we know that joy, through grace comes in this eternal now. Praised be our Heavenly Father.

Treatments

The presence of God guides us and lifts us as we serve each other. We join each other in our brilliance and let our Christ light illumine every thought and every act. We resolve to see through the consciousness of perfection and align all that we are and all that we do with the will of God. With compassion, we keep our consciousness open and receptive as we serve each other and the universe. We are grateful for each other and for the growth our relationship brings. We release these words deep into the heart of God, knowing that all is well. We are so grateful; to Almighty God be the Glory!

We rely on the power that is greater than we are. We identify ourselves as vessels of Divine love and wisdom. Together we form a force for good. We do not yield to discord or confusion. We let go of anything in us that denies the Power that is greater than we are. We surrender with complete faith and conviction. We expect and accept that all our needs are met through grace and that everything we do according to God's will prospers. We allow this to be so for ourselves and everyone. We are forever grateful for this provision of grace. All is well.

Note... Please be mindful enough to keep the little ego from running the group, or it can soon become a venue for pity parties and negativity. *The little ego always seeks to Ease God Out!* Members ought to lift each other with love, wisdom, power and authority. As we embrace our daily Spiritual practices, seeking the daily bread of wisdom etc. one can realize that others are blessed by our presence. This is a significant and holy manifestation in Spiritual growth and transformation. However, in order to accomplish this we are mandated to act from love. You can do it...you have the power!

Chapter 6

Fortifying Ourselves

When we embrace the blessed and fulfilling work of praying with and for each other, we can take on the energy of the challenges other members of the group are experiencing. **After the Christ ministered, he often found a lonely place to go where he could pray, meditate, and replenish his energy.** We expend energy when we deal with our own and other people's issues. People who work in the helping professions and have direct contact with the people they help are particularly vulnerable to becoming emotionally and energetically drained. Christ, with all his power, felt energy leave his body as he did his spiritual work. When the woman who had the issue of blood discreetly touched the hem of his garment with her desire to be healed, Jesus felt it so powerfully that even with crowds of people touching him, he was able to distinguish her touch for healing. Jesus asked his disciples, "Who touched my clothes?" When considering the crowd, this question must have seemed absurd. Jesus explained that he felt virtue leave his body. This was the vibration of the healing energy, emitted in response to this woman's firm faith (Mark 6:25–34).

Integrating the Four Aspects of Ourselves

When we are in the service of supporting others or ourselves through prayer, we ought to fortify ourselves. We exist through four levels of awareness, and each should be whole and stable. Our existence is governed by the spiritual laws of God. The law of nature is God's law. It does not matter who we are, what we own, whether we are rich or poor, what our ethnicity is, or whether we do good or evil. If we are not caring for ourselves, there will be dire consequences. **Jesus Christ was tempted to violate every aspect of his being. He was able to withstand temptation simply because he was fortified on the spiritual, mental, emotional, and physical levels** of his awareness, which are also the levels we exist on. This also empowered him to maintain his perfection. People, who work in the fields of counseling, health care, teaching, ministry, etc., can become absorbed in the negativity and details of the issues of the people they are helping. Those who are hypersensitive can also show the same symptoms as those for whom they are praying or helping in other ways. We can also absorb negative as well as positive energy from those closest to us.

As we embrace an affirmative way of living, we must remember that we function on four levels of existence. When we seek healing or answers to our prayers, this truth must be at the forefront of our awareness. These four aspects form the vehicles through which spiritual laws operate. We must embrace these aspects of ourselves and open them to the free flow of God's Spirit within us. This is the realization that helps us understand ourselves better and also to understand that each aspect is necessary to the whole person. We must seek to integrate these aspects of ourselves.

Careful study of the doctrines of the Holy Bible and books of various faith traditions in terms of healing and transformation reveals that much emphasis is placed on these four aspects. The following sections address each aspect and offer practical ways to support their healing and integration. When they are fully integrated, they support each other and create balance in the individual. This work of integration is very much like praying without ceasing or asking our Heavenly Father on a daily basis for our daily bread. Our experiences, whether joyful or sorrowful, can at times knock us off balance. Of course, this is determined by how we accept and deal with those issues. **We must consciously intend to be about the continual spiritual business of integration. It is our life-long practice and requires persistence.**

Our Spiritual Aspect

Our spiritual aspect is our divine unchanging core. Almighty God as a spirit created us in his image and likeness; therefore, we are spiritual beings. **Our spiritual aspect is rooted in our consciousness of our connection to and oneness with God.** We know that the Spirit of God dwells within us and that there is much more goodness about us than our finite minds can fathom.

Our spiritual aspect demands that our divine purpose be fulfilled. When this is lacking, we experience feelings of emptiness, hopelessness, anxiety, sickness, anger, selfishness, and despair. We may engage in destructive behaviors. In groups, actions as dictated by many social ills become the norm. We are asked to seek first the Kingdom of Heaven before all good things can be given to us. The spiritual aspect serves as the grounding place for the work of transformation to begin, and as well as an anchor for the emotional, mental, and physical aspects of ourselves.

Developing the Spiritual Aspect

Daily meditation and prayer are mandated as taught by way of the model of the Lord's Prayer. They are tools through which we seek the Kingdom and develop our Spiritual aspect. These are the means by which we communicate with our Almighty God. In essence, we are also conditioning our consciousness with spiritual strength in order to establish spiritual control over our lives as promised in Exodus 31:3: "And I have filled him with the spirit of God in wisdom, in understanding, in knowledge and in all manner of workmanship."

Being in service to others is another way of developing spiritually. Looking at the ministry of Jesus Christ and the lives of many Spiritual teachers, we often observe them in service to others. Practicing self-love and care helps us to develop spiritually. Sharing our gifts and talents, teaching others, and practicing kindness, forgiveness, love, and gratitude are also ways that develop and fortify the spiritual aspect of our beings. (See chapter 7 for more ways to love one's self and others.)

The following prayers support the development of our spiritual aspect:

Almighty Creator, you created me in your spiritual image and likeness. This does not mean that I will live without challenges, but by your grace, I shall overcome them. I ask through the Christ Mind in me that you help me to be aware of my gifts of wisdom, peace, spiritual power, and divine love. Help me to use these gifts to further your will, honor you and to bless myself and others as I serve with humility and joy. I thank you for hearing and answering me now. Amen.

Wonderful and Everlasting Father I glorify your most holy name. I come to you as an empty vessel seeking to be filled with the wisdom to create a vibrant Spiritual practice. As I ask in the name of Jesus Christ my redeemer, I know that my search is over. I now follow the guidance of the Divine presence that is forever with me. I know you promised that you will always hear us and that you will never leave nor forsake us. I place my hands in yours and I allow you to lead me now to the ideas, people, places and events that only serve to add richness and life to my spiritual practice. Please lead me to those that I am assigned to help; I am willing and ready. I watch with holy expectancy as all unfolds in Divine synchrony. I glorify your matchless name and I say, "thank you Heavenly Father."

Now remain silent and receptive for a while. Listen to the still, small voice within and follow its guidance, by taking the inspired actions which support the development of your Spiritual aspect.

Our Mental Aspect

Our mental aspect consists of our mind and thoughts. In our minds, we store information we have received since childhood as well as current information. This information does not only consist of what we have heard; it consists of what we have seen, felt, smelled, tasted, etc. When we gather information, we form beliefs and conclusions about ourselves, others, and our world. These become our core beliefs, which we allow to guide us through life.

For example, the scourges of hateful acts committed against others often result from the core belief that some people are better than others. Fear of failure or success can result from the observation that some people are ridiculed when they fail while others are ridiculed when they succeed. Some people are successful because they always heard that they could succeed or because they deliberately refuse to accept negative, defeating messages that could have stagnated them; yet others allow negative messages to color their thoughts and eventually paralyze them into complacency and mediocrity. Thoughts are things that are out-pictured in the condition of our lives.

Great relationships have been torn apart because of core beliefs that dictated roles. For example, when most women did not work outside the home, it was expected that they carry out the domestic duties and care for family members. Today, statistics show that in forty percent of households, women are the main bread winner. This is up from eleven percent in the 1960's; often these women are still expected to carry out the domestic duties and care for their families by themselves. They may receive less income than a male counterpart for the same work! I believe that husbands and other males in the home should equally carry these responsibilities in these circumstances. These inequities negatively affect families. Relationships can become more harmonious when the core beliefs about the role of the sexes reflect an equal standing for everyone.

I've heard of so many instances when someone was told by a parent or someone with authority in his or her life that he or she would "amount to nothing." When this message becomes someone's core belief, (e.g for some people during the slavery era) the individual at times lives up to that expectation. Such person may also self-sabotage just before they accomplish something good. They exist, expecting and accepting a life of mediocrity. Such person may fear success, failure or both. To anyone with this challenge, the time has come for you to clean the negativity and cobwebs from your mind. Our mental faculty is a gift that will support a life of ease when it is empowered to do so through our thoughts and beliefs. I agree with St Paul who entreated us to become transformed by the renewing of our minds. The following practice is offered for the support of healing at the mental level.

Fortifying the Mental Aspect...practice

1. Ease into the silence. Through your loving Christ consciousness, simply pray for guidance. Accept guidance and follow through.

1. Start the visualization process. First recognize your thoughts and let go of the troubling ones. Be open to spiritual solutions to any problem. Relax and know that God is with you and loves you more than you can imagine. With your eyes closed, see yourself sitting in a beautiful, peaceful place, talking to a wise person. You may choose Jesus, Almighty God, a person you trust

or a friend. Tell this person of your needs, fears, hopes, and dreams. Confess to them that you have surrendered the core belief that kept you stuck in mediocrity. See the word *mediocrity* slowly float away in a bubble that gets smaller and smaller until it is reduced to nothing. Listen to what this person says to you. Thank this person for his or her presence and for hearing you. Feel in your body that you have surrendered. Come to the acceptance that God has answered your prayers. Be grateful to Jehovah God. You have been heard!

2. Take all necessary steps to support yourself. For example, take classes or learn a new hobby or skill, venture out into a new career and leave any situation or experience that does not serve a divine purpose for you. Practice things that can enhance your life, even those which you may be afraid to do. Love yourself so profoundly that all you do is life affirming for you and others. Engage in activities that stretch your imagination and renew your mind. You truly deserve only the best that life can offer; dare to accept it now!

3. **This treatment can be useful as well**

> I know that that the Spirit of my Lord is forever with me. It surrounds, enfolds, and fills me with its love. It is closer to me than my own heartbeat. I now surrender every problem, thought of worry, fear and doubt to this Spirit and I allow it to instruct my will and my emotions. I deny any idea which indicates that I am poor, sick, not good enough, or less than others. I am surrounded by people who love and support my spiritual evolution. I enjoy great friendship. I enjoy right work, love, ease, grace, wholeness and

beauty in my life. I serve in this universe with unconditional love and generosity. My life is wonderful and I am grateful.

Denial

There are no negative thoughts in my mind that can constrict my positive progress. There is only room in my mind for thoughts of good for me and all others.

Affirmations

I am the thinker in my own life. I allow my positive thoughts to penetrate and eradicate any unhealthy thought that may be lurking in the recesses of my mind. I obey Spiritual laws and commit the acts of faith that heal my life. I feel deep joy in my soul... Dear Heavenly Father, I thank you.

I express my freedom to think in magnificent and affirmative ways. I choose to think rightly of all creation. I see all people as equal, as this is the ultimate truth. I hold all people lovingly in my thoughts.

Our Emotional Aspect

There is a specific purpose for every aspect of our existence. Throughout different faith traditions, we are told to have compassion and empathy for one another. Christ wept when his friend Lazarus died and expressed sorrow shortly before his brutal crucifixion. Our emotions serve to make us aware of what is favorable or unfavorable, pleasant or unpleasant, good or bad. Our emotions are a divine gift. It is an aspect through which the love of God is revealed.

Our emotions were therefore not created to be something we shut down. They are an inner guidance system to which we must pay attention. The minister of the church I attended as an adolescent never allowed dead bodies into the church during the funeral service. The coffin or casket rested closed on the basement level while the funeral service went on upstairs. When anyone cried, he briefly stopped his sermon to say, "Stop that!" He explained that the body was full of germs and that the spirit had gone on to evolve, so there was no reason to cry. In another more recent instance, when a woman did not cry at her son's funeral, she was described as classy.

Let us face it; unpleasant events usually cause sad feelings, while pleasant events usually cause happy feelings. These judgments cause many to habitually suppress or avoid unfavorable feelings or any actions leading up to them. Many have fears they will not overcome because they are afraid to move through them. Some people mask their anger because it is said to be a bad thing. My younger students at times say it is not okay to be angry. When I explain that anger can be a friend which tells them something in their environment may not be good for them, they look at me with wide eyes. After a lesson on anger and how to appropriately express it, I can see the relieved looks on their young faces. Feelings of joy, hunger, boredom, excitement, frustration, anxiety, resentment, peace and happiness all have a place in our experiences. They are the catalysts as well as the rewards for our actions. The fact that repressed emotions cause diseases tells us that our emotions were never created to be repressed.

We must however ensure that our emotions are triggering appropriate responses and that we do not allow negative ones to control our lives. We also have to address our emotional needs with the response that is life affirming. For example, if we feel stress and decide to relieve it with some form of harmful drug, then our action is not life affirming and certainly not based on love. We must learn to communicate our feelings effectively. **We must seek to face and heal the effects of any emotional wound that lingers in us so that we can become lovingly united with our vulnerable self.**

Fortifying Our Emotional Aspect...practice

1. Get into the silence, pray about the emotion of concern, and then listen and follow guidance.

2. Learn to respect your feelings. For example, if you are tired and somebody asks you to do an errand, be honest and loving to yourself. If you are too tired to go, say so. We are told to love our neighbors as ourselves but never more than ourselves. Support yourself through assertiveness.

3. Find outlets for pent-up emotions. Jogging, walking, talking, advocacy, writing, yoga, dancing, and drawing are great activities. Exercising and deep breathing are other useful ways to release built-up emotions. Crying helps with the release of painful emotions; "Jesus wept"

4. See chapter 8 on forgiveness for other activities that help to relieve pent-up emotions. Be careful to begin with the scanning process.

5. See chapter 6 on Love and commit to using those ideas of ways to practice self-love. These should be committed to and done as a way of life.

Treatment

There is peace at the center of everything and I allow this peace to color my emotions. I allow wisdom to guide my emotions. I invite the Spirit of God in me to be a constant presence in my awareness, as I allow my emotions to guide me to the right actions that glorify Almighty God and serve all creation.

Denial

My emotions do not negatively impact my life. They support me in knowing how I affect others and how others affect me.

Affirmation

Knowing that the Lord is forever with me, I feel a calm assurance. I allow my calm emotions to govern how I act and react in this world. For the wisdom to do so, I am grateful.

Our Physical Aspect

Our physical aspect is our most visible aspect. It is no more or less important than the others. We experience it as our bodies. Our bodies are the vehicle through which the effects of the other aspects are manifested. Throughout history, there has been an emphasis on the body. Women were described as weaker vessels. They were considered unclean during times of menstruation, and generally beautiful. Men were described as physically stronger. The body was generally described as having a sinful nature and inherently inferior to the other aspects of our being. These messages we made up about our bodies are indeed mixed, inconsistent, and inaccurate.

The life-giving and life-affirming functions of the body are often overlooked. While discussing the book *I Like Me* by Carlson, Nancy L, 1988) some of my students exclaimed that they did not like their feet because feet were stinky. We traced a school day in their lives, and we noted each time they changed activities or locations. With guidance, they ended by thanking their feet amidst giggles. I often with humor reminded them that not one of them left home without their heads or their feet!

When something is disapproved of, our first response may be to get rid of it, change it, or at least control it. When we disapprove of our bodies, we often make conscious and often unconscious efforts to change them. The body might be abused in various ways. Not able to completely get rid of the body, some people undergo drastic surgery to change it. Some starve their bodies and have died doing so. Some ingest substances that are harmful and may be addictive. Some people allow others to physically abuse them.

Changes can be necessary to keep a person healthy, and though some of them may be drastic, they should by no means be ignored or avoided; not all changes made to the body are unwise, however appropriate professional help should be sought. Choose health!

Fortifying the Physical Aspect

1. Be willing to understand and accept that your body is wonderfully created.

2. Use prayer and meditation to calm, balance and relax the body. Listen for and follow your intuitive guidance.

3. Be aware of feelings in the body and follow up with necessary care, such as medical, physical, etc.

4. Get exercise, rest and partake of healthy amounts of food, and water. (See the section on self-love in the next chapter for more ideas.)

5. Acknowledge the pleasures you enjoy through the sense organs and be grateful daily that you can receive pleasure through these senses. Verbally thank each part

of your body for enabling you to serve God and all creation.

6. Pay attention to what your body is saying to you through its symptoms. Understand that specific needs in your life can trigger the corresponding ailments. For example a headache may be the result of worrying, fear, self-criticism or it can be that you are hungry. Louise Hay's book "Heal Your Body" discusses mental causes for physical illness and the Metaphysical way to overcome them. (See Reference)

Beloveds, please remember that the body is God's vehicle. The hands and feet serve to bring divine love into action. All action to serve must begin in the mind. As we serve willingly, we cannot help but feel a sense of fulfillment, joy, love, and peace; this engages our emotions. Serving willingly out of the impulse of love is our spiritual practice. Take time to notice how each level is supported by the other. This is indicative of the truth that the different levels of our existence must work together to form the harmoniously whole person.

As we fortify these four aspects, we will realize that our whole outlook on life changes. We feel mentally, physically, and emotionally stronger because we are no longer a house divided against itself. This also allows harmony to begin with us. Prayer is absolutely necessary as we work on each aspect. We cannot do this alone; however, we can do all things through Christ, who strengthens us.

A Prayer

Creator of all mankind and Heavenly Father, I praise your holy name, Jehovah. In your perfection you created all things perfect. I ask that you help me to continually be aware of how I treat my body. Help me to correct any belief or behavior that does not support the health and integrity of my body. My intention Lord is that I always honor you by loving and respecting your temple, my body. Your life in me is strength and vitality; for this privilege I am humbly grateful.

A treatment

I was created to have an abundant life and that includes perfect health. I accept myself as healthy and filled with the life of God. I think health and I embrace every idea of health, therefore my body responds in life affirming ways. God's action in me is health; every cell, fiber, organ, system and function vibrates with the health of God. I am strong, able and am full of vitality. My whole being responds to these words which are true about me. God is my health and in my gratitude, I Allow it be so now and forevermore.

A Denial

There is no illness in my body; the perfect health of God is my health.

Affirmations

My body is a temple of the perfect Living God; I claim and accept perfect health now.

God's Love courses through my body like as cleansing stream. Anything that can cause illness is now washed away from my body and I rejoice!

The Christ presence in me fortifies me with Divine energy. I accomplish my work with ease.

My health is perfect as my Heavenly Father is perfect, and I am grateful!

Oneness with God

When we each are no longer "a house divided against its self," our spiritual, mental, emotional and physical aspects of our being equally support each other. We can then know through our consciousness, what it means to experience "The Father and I are one." Of course we are not the Almighty God; however, the Spirit of God dwells in each of us; and there is only one Spirit. Jesus, as he experienced his illumination, exclaimed, "The Father and I are One!" In this experience he became profoundly aware of his Oneness with Almighty God. This does not mean that we are Jesus Christ either; However when we are transformed, we gain the same Christ consciousness or illumination that Jesus achieved. Jesus was his earthly name and Christ was the Spiritual state he attained. The God mind that was in Jesus Christ is the same mind that we can allow in us. We ought to allow this mind to think through us and to guide us in even the minutest of ways. As children of God we are inherently one with God.

It can be challenging to integrate ourselves. There can be self-sabotage that shows up as not having enough time, energy, money, friends or other support and slippage. We must move through these blocks with affirmative prayer, willingness, persistence and confidence. The little ego would rather see us scattered wearing the victim's hat. Put it on notice; The Spiritual ego is in charge! Like our body parts, each aspect of our being is vital to us in living out our true purpose. Doing our Spiritual work affords us wisdom, fortitude and the manifestation of transformation! Are you willing? The universe beckons!

Chapter 7

Love—Spiritual Law

The presence of brotherly love is absolutely vital to having our prayers answered. It is our birthright to live lives of abundance. Christ our way-shower came so that we can have abundant lives. His ultimate mission served to teach mankind just how to do so. Every spiritual law of God was demonstrated by Jesus Christ. This is not to deny that other teachers also taught us to follow the laws of God. Jesus's three-year ministry encompassed many miracles and teachings. His crucifixion was his sacrifice for the redemption of our sins/missing the mark. His triumphant resurrection was the ultimate teaching of love! The time was birthed for new laws; the spiritual reawakening of mankind demanded that the new sacrificial lambs must be us, as we surrender to God's will and follow Spiritual principles. The older Laws supported an "eye for an eye." Jesus taught mankind the newer laws of grace, which mandated forgiveness and the new commandment of Brotherly love..

As the human race attained a higher consciousness, the laws of "an eye for an eye and a tooth for a tooth" could no longer maintain order. A new order was required even though the Ten Commandments had already been instituted. Although they are at times interpreted differently, the Ten Commandments are the foundation for major religious and spiritual organizations. They were reinforced by Jesus when he held his Sermon on the Mount. He expounded on the way we should think and act to elevate our consciousness. These commandments are embraced by Hebrew scholars. In Buddhism, the eight steps that form the path to enlightenment are similar to the principles of some of the commandments. We can also glean wisdom of the sacredness of all creation from many indigenous tribes and their practices. Their practices imply that everything and everyone is sacred and must be treated as such.

When ancient customs demanded a sacrifice as an honor to God, the animal chosen was the best of the herd or flock and therefore the most suitable. In Christian teachings, Jesus Christ, the begotten son of Jehovah, was the ultimate sacrifice on our behalf. He was most suitable because he was sinless and blameless; he loves us. He did it because of his desire to obey our Heavenly Father Jehovah and his great love and compassion for himself and us. Our sacrificial work entails obeying the Ten Commandments as our way of obeying spiritual laws. We are also blessed with the gift of prayer and meditation as a way to communicate with God. However, when we do not obey the spiritual laws as set forth by the Ten Commandments, we erect a block to having our prayers heard and answered. Throughout Jesus's ministry, he emphasized the laws and spoke extensively about them. He also demonstrated the use of such laws. He taught that love, forgiveness, faith, and gratitude through thanksgiving were spiritual practices necessary for fruitful prayers. This chapter on love and following chapters will provide explorations of these spiritual laws.

Christ's Demonstration of Love

After the Passover feast, Christ humbly washed the feet of his beloved disciples as a symbol of humility, for his love for them and as a lesson for them and us to love and serve each other with humility (John 13:5–12). He was sorrowful about his impending crucifixion, yet he made it a point to institute a new commandment of love. The biblical account reads, "A new commandment I give to you, that you love one another; as I have loved you, that you also love one another" (John 13:34).

There are countless quotes written in religious and spiritual doctrines and spoken by numerous teachers of spirituality and religion. Some of these include:

- "Beloved, if God so loved us we ought to love one another" (John 4:7).
- "Owe no one anything except to love one another. For he that loves another, has fulfilled the law" (Rom. 13:8).
- "And if you keep all these commandments and do them, which I command you today, to love the Lord your God, and to walk always in his ways…" (Deut. 19:9).
- "[Love] is a deep sense of the underlying unity and beauty of all life, the goodness running through everything, the giving-ness of life to everything" (Holmes 1953).

In his poem "Give All to Love," Ralph Waldo Emerson wrote the following about love:

> "Tis a great master
>
> Let it have scope
>
> Follow it utterly
>
> Hope beyond hope"

The Essential writings of Ralph Waldo Emerson, (Emerson 2000 pg. 697) **I do believe that when we allow love to be our master, our service becomes the greatest work of all**. Mother Theresa said that in our lives people will hate us but we must, love them anyway. Dr. Martin Luther King Jr., Mohandas Gandhi, Desmond Tutu, and our modern Popes have all asked us to live according to the dictates of love.

We must make a clear distinction of the nature and quality of love, especially because love is necessary for a successful prayer practice.

As we can glean from the wisdom of biblical quotes, the absence of brotherly love in us sets up a block to answered prayers. Eros or sexual love however, has its vital place in relationships. Agape love is free, unconditional, unending, and without sexual implications; it was revealed through Jesus Christ. Eros can be governed by the Little ego and can be conditional; it can be selfish, domineering and used as a means to victimize. The spiritual ego governs agape, or brotherly, love. This is the love that makes an opening for us; it is the love that the Christ and other teachers ask us to embrace.

We understand that God is love, and therefore love is of God. We also know that we can contact God through prayer and meditation. It is in divine order that we approach God through our consciousness of love. To do otherwise is to pray amiss and render our prayers futile.

The benevolence of God is unlimited. His love is Omnipotent, Omnipresent, and Divine. As creations of God, we embrace our oneness with God and our fellow men through agape love. This law of love cannot be altered; we must let love be revealed in and through us.

To understand the connection between love and affirmative prayers for transforming any situation, we must understand that we are always working with spiritual laws. **Every spiritual law remains inactive in our affairs until we employ it through love**. Whether they are the laws of faith, supply, obedience, attraction, cause and effect, forgiveness, or increase, to name a few, we must approach their use through our consciousness of agape love.

When we examine Christ's ministry, we come to know that agape love takes precedence over every other principle because it is the catalyst that spurs the desire to obey other spiritual laws. This holds true today, as love is the essential expression for life to continue on this planet. Love, as the great harmonizer, not only draws people together but synchronizes the manifestation of our daily bread of ideas, time, health, food, money, or whatever is most appropriate for us.

When it seems prayers go unanswered, it is most useful to examine the consciousness of the one praying. I used the word *seems* because sometimes the answers show up in ways we do not recognize, expect, or appreciate. Sometimes the yes or no answer we prefer is not appropriate for our spiritual transformation or for the spiritual transformation of others for whom we might be praying. It can also mean that the one praying has not developed a mental equivalent that matches the desire. What is true, however, is that God can only work for us, through us; we must become vessels through which God can work; vessels that can also contain our good. St. Paul, who taught that a renewed mind supports our transformation, also implored his audience to live a life of love. Dr. Wayne Dyer, in his book *The Power of Intention* (2004), wrote that love is one of the faces of intention. He further explained that we were intended (by God) out of love; If we are to intend, (set creativity to work for us), we must have love for all of creation. The energy of unconditional love is a force that sets creativity in motion for anyone who puts it to work for themself. No one can be excluded.

God's Gift of Love

Love is the all-encompassing gift from our Almighty God. With our other God-given gifts like creativity and freedom of choice, we can express love in innumerable beautiful ways. Love is fondly described as an action word. When we say we love someone or something or that someone or something loves us or others, there must be some mental movement of wholesome thoughts directed toward the object of this love. This precedes the physical movement. The mental movement is a stirring of energy that is not very foreign to us; we can feel it as it is broadcast out into the atmosphere. For example, the energy of hateful thoughts is dull, slow, heavy and sluggish. It depresses, weakens and destroys. The energy of loving thoughts is bright, quick, light, and uplifting; it strengthens, soothes and gives life. The proof lies in our own feelings when we are in these states. Think carefully about your feelings when you have a hateful or loving thought; you aren't alone with those results!

Love heals any situation to which it is applied, whether it is for our health, relationships, finances, vocations, or other issues. Love ultimately transforms the situation making it whole, because it can only attract more love to itself. When there's love, there's harmony. Let's suppose that we all love ourselves, each other, and all other creations. We would subsequently attract that love back to us from each other and all other creations. We would exist in an atmosphere of love and harmony, where we would also realize our oneness with all creation. Love as a harmonizer can stop nations from rising against nations. Love moves beyond material boundaries, dissolving barriers erected in the name of "otherness" and as a dictate of the little personal ego.

The founder of Science of Mind teachings, Ernest Holmes, said that love is already complete in us. We understand that we are created in the image and likeness of God, that God is love, and that our bodies are God's temples. We then can confidently say that our bodies are temples of the Spirit of love. We also read in the Bible that we were created with the Spirit of love, courage and, a sound mind. There is therefore no need for us to search outside ourselves for love. Christ taught us to love each other because he knew we were already equipped with the power to love. Our ultimate calling is to release this love to our Heavenly Father, ourselves, and all of creation. When we release this love, it becomes very evident. Our thoughts and intentions broadcast themselves often louder than our words can. **According to the law of attraction, our circumstances must reflect our most** dominant thoughts. When we embrace love, our presence reflects peace, calm, beauty, and self-confidence. People are healed and comforted by our presence. Beloveds let us walk this pathway of agape love; this is also vital in order to establish a Powerful Affirmative prayer practice that works when you work it!

Self-Love

Withholding love from ourselves is equally detrimental to us as withholding it from others. A lack of self-love triggers anger and self-hatred. This sets up blocks to our prayers' effectiveness. We cannot give genuine love when we do not have it for ourselves in the first place. Also, as a part of our spiritual evolution and transformation, **we are called upon to be of loving service in this world**. We have to speak directly to God from our hearts to understand how we must uniquely serve. We must be aligned with our source of wisdom, which is God/love, in order to communicate with him. There are no shortcuts to aligning ourselves to truth. The only path is through love.

The practices in the remaining parts of this chapter support us in practicing self-love.

Loving and Blessing God

Before beginning any practice demonstrating love, we must acknowledge God with praise, prayers, and thanksgiving. The following are examples; however, each of us is gifted with our own unique sense of creativity, so it can be empowering and rather fulfilling to create your own. These practices are for the benefit of both males and females.

PS. Loving and blessing God serves to elevate the one praying. God is good itself and cannot change or be changed.

Affirmations of Praise, Love and Gratitude

1. Almighty God of love, I thank and bless you for creating me in your image and likeness. I praise your wisdom and power!

2. Almighty God, I love and bless you for loving me; you are the Truth of my being.

3. Loving Father, I love the truth that you love me unconditionally; blessed be your name!

4. Almighty Father, I honor you; all glory is yours. You are the great Almighty! God!

5. Thank you, Jehovah, for creating me out of your sweet impulse of love

6. Thank you, wonderful God; I praise your omnipotence. I praise your omniscience. I thank you for your omnipresence as you embrace me, even now.

It is empowering to say the above affirmations with loving feelings of gratitude and adoration. Our feelings confirm the mood and condition of our consciousness. Choose one or more and say them whenever you feel led to. Now proceed with the practices of self-love as described in this chapter.

Prayer of Praise

Whatever we praise, we raise. Praising God for the good things in our lives becomes a powerful act of self-love. This is because we love ourselves by calling forth, raising, and attracting more good in our own lives. Say the following prayer of praise with deep feeling:

Prayer

Everlasting Father, most Holy God, in the name of the Christ I come into your presence with praises. I recognize my oneness with you and that I am wonderfully made. I know that you are goodness itself; you are the love I seek. out of this love you created me, therefore I am also love. I praise you!

I praise you, great Jehovah, for the good you continuously do through me. I praise you for the vibrant life and health expressed through my mind and body; I praise you! I praise you for the gifts of wisdom, knowledge, and understanding. As I understand your laws, I use them to your glory and honor; I praise you!

I praise you for my gifts, talents, and my unique calling. With love and understanding, I use them to further your work here and now. With my gifts and talents, I love, bless, and support my fellow men so that through my works you are glorified. I praise you!

I praise you, mighty Jehovah, for your protection of my mind, body, and affairs. I praise you for creating me as a magnificent being. To you, loving Father is the glory! I praise you!

Know Yourself

In order to truly love ourselves, it can be helpful to understand why we are the way we are. This does not have to be negative or positive; it is a neutral exploration. Being in a quiet place where we can think clearly is best. Here we can discover any shadow parts of ourselves that may be dictating our thoughts and actions and that might have set up barriers to our wholeness. We can also recognize our unique gifts and the grace of God working magnificently in our lives.

Note, anyone who is undergoing mental health challenges, is receiving treatment or counseling, or has anger issues

should consult a mental health service provider or religious or spiritual advisor before doing the following exercise.

In this exercise, you will be guided to become aware of the various parts of yourself, some of which you might have ignored, suppressed, hide, denied, or perhaps shown to the world.

As feelings of anger, sadness, and unforgiveness surface, you must breathe deeply. Set an intention to breathe in peace and to breathe out any negative emotion. This helps you relax as you face these emotions. This exercise also conditions any negative emotion to become less potent when remembered in the future. With time and earnest forgiveness work, these negative emotions may never show up again even though the memories may surface.

Know Yourself--exercise

Think of your experiences from childhood. Is there an experience that caused you to believe you are better than others, less than others or maybe not good enough? Did you experience something that caused you to believe you are ugly or beautiful, intelligent or unintelligent? Did you allow friends to get away with being bossy toward you? Are you bossy? What type of interactions caused joy or instilled fear in you? Were you a people pleaser? Did you come from a dysfunctional family and if so, do you blame yourself for any part of the dysfunction? Were you a parentified child? Were you in an abusive relationship, being abused by an adult, child, or both? What messages did you receive about God, money, work, or people who are different than you based on race or color or class or any other aspect?

What about today? Do you have relationships with people including family members who support, honor or affirm you? Do you enjoy your vocation? Why or why not? Do you have friends you like and can depend on? Can you be depended on? Do you take time out for prayer, inspirational readings, meditation, rest, fun and recreation or exercise? Are you compassionate towards yourself or others? Do you eat healthy? Do you feel like a victim? Do you feel shame, guilt, or constant anger? Do you embrace the practice of forgiveness for yourself or others? Do you trust others? Are you trusted? Do you volunteer and find ways to be in loving service in this world? Are you affiliated with any group or organization that edifies, validates, and uplifts you? Are you satisfied with your current state of affairs? In what part of your body do you feel uncomfortable as you contemplate any of the above questions?

The answers to the above questions can help us to acknowledge and build on the aspects in our lives that are supporting our transformation. They can also help us uncover the shadow parts of our personalities and can be salient in pointing us in the direction of appropriate healing intervention on our behalf. **Contemplating these questions can be empowering if we use this process to bring us much needed clarity.** Practicing the self-help techniques in this book and other books, some of which I listed in the reference and additional resources lists at the back of this book, as well as seeking professional intervention are very empowering steps toward healing and loving one's self.

We can use the following affirmative practices to support us as we seek to know ourselves.

Prayer

Almighty Father and most loving God, I know you are the essence of wisdom and that you created me as a wise and worthy being. As I quiet my mind, I ask that you speak to me. I willingly listen to the still, small voice of your Spirit within me. Please show me any part of myself that I block, deny, or shut down; show me my strengths so that I can use them for your glory. I open myself to the guidance of Spirit as I embrace every part that is revealed. I ask and allow your healing love to flow through them, washing away any aspect that is not life affirming. With wisdom and through your guidance, Lord, I move forward as my united self. In my Christ consciousness, I say "thank you, Heavenly Father."

Treatment

I know that the Divine Spirit of God fills me. I am never limited by any past or present circumstance. I have complete confidence that my Heavenly Father is now operating in my affairs through the Divine Spirit. There is a manifestation of beauty and harmony in my affairs and I allow myself to acknowledge and experience it daily. For these blessings I am grateful.

Affirmation

I let go of any label, belief or agreement that does not uphold my Divinity. I always embrace everything that affirms my Divinity and the truth of who I am.

Denial

There is absolutely nothing in me that can doubt that the power of Almighty God's Spirit is working in my life here and now. Divine wisdom empowers and informs me!

Nurture Yourself

Once we become aware of any old issues, causes for anger, or old hurts, we can begin to give ourselves the same tender treatment we would give to a newborn baby with all its innocence. Again, we must honor the airline safety rule and put the oxygen mask of compassion on ourselves first if we desire to help others. There must be an inner and outer preservation of ourselves; we must nurture our bodies while filling our thoughts with goodness about ourselves.

When dealing with a newborn, we have to be very patient, tender, loving, and kind. We ought to be the same way with ourselves. Whether male or female, young or elderly, we must make it a priority to treat ourselves with reverence and kindness. As we nurture ourselves, it is good to begin with concrete steps such as getting physical exercise, eating healthy foods, getting adequate rest, taking time out for enjoyment, a massage, a manicure, a pedicure, health checkups, etc. People are who are hungry or tired can have difficulties thinking, praying and studying. We can nurture our spirits through our spiritual practices. We can take classes to increase our knowledge if necessary. We can read books that will inspire and build us up.

If we realize that we are following a negative family pattern (since most people are innately loyal to family patterns), we can make wiser choices and seek help. We can decide that when it comes to generational dysfunction, it stops with us! Joining groups that promote the growth of the whole person is an excellent idea. These groups usually offer support in areas such as parenting skills, employment readiness training, test preparation, self-esteem building, vocational training, mental health counseling, grief counseling, and rehabilitation for abuse of various substances. Change does not occur overnight, and we deserve all the patience we can offer ourselves. The following tools can offer much-needed spiritual support as we nurture ourselves. Stretch yourself and create more that are even more personal to you.

Prayer

My Heavenly Father, I praise your wisdom. You have shown me the areas of my life that must be healed and nurtured. I ask in the name of Jesus Christ that you show me how. Please hold me up as I allow you to bless me with the wisdom, patience, and the support to do whatever is in accord with your will. I gratefully choose to nurture myself and allow my healing to be completed. I release everything to you, knowing that in your loving mind I am whole. I thank you for helping me now. I let it be so, and so it is always.

Treatment

I boldly claim and exercise my right to be my authentic self. I joyfully allow others to be themselves. Whomever God has ordained for me to nurture and guide, I nurture and guide with love, respect and patience and I also include myself. I seek and obey the guidance of God's Spirit in me as I nurture us. I embrace the spirit of wisdom, compassion, peace, gentleness, and love, and I let it expand through my actions. I now welcome and embrace my authenticity. Sensing comfort at the depths of my soul, I know that all is well and I am grateful.

Affirmation

I create the space in my life for beauty, ease and grace. All is well and I am grateful.

I treat myself gently and with compassion. I surrender any habit or situation that does not honor my divinity and I allow love and wisdom to dictate my actions.

Denial

No negative pattern of thinking can confound me. I cultivate only thoughts that move me forward to my spiritual destiny.

Trust Yourself

Spiritual teacher and founder of Science of Mind Dr. Ernest Holmes said that principle is never bound by precedent. Through agape love and forgiveness, we can redirect our thoughts, words, and actions to the truth of God's perfection in us and as us. Isn't this what all the great teachers taught? And isn't this the idea of redemption being possible? When we show love to ourselves, we do not have to wait for a religious or spiritual teacher, mother, father, sibling, child or anyone to redeem us. Through the power of unconditional love and forgiveness for ourselves and others, and as the Christ secured for us through his death and resurrection, we allow the process of redemption to occur in our lives. We have removed the energetic block that kept us bound.

We must believe and trust that we are worthy of redemption, that the abundant life belongs to us as well. The little selfish ego may scream, "I am not good enough!" or "Look what they did to me!" or "Look what I did!" We must hold on to the truth that it is Christ the Nazarene who showed us the way we now follow, one that is guided by unconditional love and forgiveness. Sometimes the screams come from loved ones and acquaintances who, like the prodigal older brother, resent our freedom and our wisdom to trust enough to awaken and forgive ourselves. They may tell you, "But look what you did." We know it is their little egos who want us always feeling guilty and defeated so that they can wield a so-called power over us and maintain the ego's victim mentality. Beloveds, step boldly away from this toxic energy. Their skeletons might scare you! But we must remember that even Christ had no need to tell us that he was a victim or that he was better than anyone. In fact, he said that we will do greater works than he did because he had to leave. His ministry, in the format it took at that time, was fulfilled. Trust yourself that what Jesus Christ said is also true for you and about you.

When we trust ourselves, it gives birth to self-confidence. When we are confident, we don't feel the need to linger in the past or the future. We learn to be present, flexible, yielding, and calm through what is happening in the holy moment of now. Trusting our inner guide as we affirmatively pray, we are impelled to follow Spirit's directions. We subsequently feel guided, supported, more grounded, and stable. With constant prayers, we begin the empowering cycle of always trusting and knowing. The following Affirmative prayers support us in establishing and maintaining trust.

Prayer

Wonderful Heavenly Father, your name is most holy. I place my trust in you and I allow your will to be my will. Acting according to your will, I trust every step I take. I know that the universe conspires to support me in every way. I gratefully move forward in Divine time and order. I let go of any fear that anyone can withhold my good from me. I trust that everything is working together for the benefit of all creation and I ask you to forgive me for not trusting earlier; I simply forgot that I am created in your image and likeness. I thank you Father for showing me an excellent way. I know that all is harmoniously whole and I am grateful.

Treatment

I know that the creative process is always at work in my experiences. Whatever I need, wherever I go, whatever I must do or say, the divine Spirit is always there willingly and readily providing for me. This I trust is the truth of my being and it cannot be otherwise. In my wonderful state of gratitude, I rejoice!

Affirmation

I am Jehovah's wonderful creation; I manifest the perfect gifts of God

Denial

Nothing can block the never ending flow of Good in my life. Almighty God always provides for my needs.

Respect Yourself

When we nurture a baby with tender love, patience, and compassion, we trust that it will grow bigger. We usually don't beg the cells of its body to grow. We let nature take its course. We have respect for this human being. If we think this child is not being respected, we most often deliberately demand respect on the child's behalf. We know that as a creation of God, this child deserves respect.

Every person deserves to respect themself and others and to be respected by others. We ought to be deliberate in ensuring our own respect from ourselves and others. We must use simple wisdom to remove ourselves and stay away from people who disrespect us. We ought to stay away from anyone who abuses us verbally, physically, sexually, mentally, or emotionally or who makes us feel bad about ourselves in any way. This can be complicated at times, especially when family members are involved. Regardless of who is involved, we must always use prayer and other spiritual practices. We must also work with others for a resolution, and seek our religious or spiritual advisors, counselors, acquaintances, or any authority that can help. Seeking a win-win resolution is always best; all sides benefit. (See chapter 8 on forgiveness.)

We show others by our words, our actions, what we allow, and how much we respect ourselves. For example, it is not unusual to hear someone say, "Oh, I am so stupid. I forgot that person's name." The truth is that there is nothing stupid about forgetting a name. We have to be careful of our words because they can attract with mathematical precision! I have seen people make cruel jokes about themselves so that others would laugh. These people believed that the way to make others like them was to make them laugh, even if it came at the expense of their own dignity. Whether we speak to or about ourselves respectfully or disrespectfully or treat ourselves respectfully or disrespectfully, we employ the Law of Cause and Effect; we teach others to treat us the way we treat ourselves. Also, through the law of Attraction we create situations that correspond with how we talk about ourselves; the Scripture reads, **"Death and life are in the power of the tongue."** (Prov. 19:21)

What we think about ourselves helps shape how we relate to ourselves and others. It also shapes how others relate to us. We ought to habitually think about ourselves with uplifting and kind thoughts. It is true that as a man thinks in his heart, so is he. Our powerful thoughts, apart from controlling our feelings and actions, broadcast their energy out into the atmosphere. We must be mindful of our habitual thoughts if we desire to attract respect in our lives. Our thoughts do not discriminate between good and bad; they create according to the dominant state of our thinking.

The work we do, whether we are inside or outside the home, represents our attention and energy, which are both very sacred and valuable. As a mark of self-respect, we ought to make sure we are adequately compensated for our services. We must be assertive in asking for whatever good we deserve. This also encourages others to respect the value of the work we do. When we give our services for free against our true desire, or charge below cost, our work loses its intrinsic value as the recipients place less value on it. Tama Kieves, author of *This Time I Dance!: Creating the Work You Love*, once reminded me that when I do not ask for fair compensation for my services, it can ultimately affect how others view the work of my peers as well.

The following practices can support the work of building self-respect

Treatment

I am established in the power of The Spirit of God. I show up in this world with self-respect, wisdom, love, power and authority. As I embark on this awesome spiritual journey, my hands are in the hands of my spiritual brother Jesus Christ, our way shower. My sight is focused on my divine purpose and I allow myself to fulfill my spiritual destiny. All is well!

Affirmation

Whatever I have done or not done cannot define me. I am a magnificent Spiritual being who continually evolves higher in consciousness. There is no condemnation coming to or going from me. I identify myself with everything that upholds respect for me and others.

Denial

Nothing can obstruct my spiritual path. I am firmly established in the love of Jehovah. I have dominion over my circumstances and I am grateful.

See Yourself

Our self-image is a powerful determinant of the quality of our self-esteem. An image in our mind has to have thoughts to qualify it. The messages we receive about the image of ourselves is also accepted at the subconscious level of our minds, where the directive to act in a certain ways originates. With the wisdom and understanding that we are created in the image and likeness of God, we must see ourselves as worthy of all good. We must see ourselves as worthy of unconditional love no matter what. Many of us see ourselves as unworthy based on things beyond our control, such as being born into a particular ethnicity or class, being born as either male or female (some cultures place preference on boys), experiencing other discrimination, being raised in a dysfunctional family, or being abused in any way. We must separate ourselves from our circumstances. We may make mistakes along the way, but we are not those mistakes. It becomes almost impossible to love ourselves if we harbor guilt, shame, and blame.

We must find self-acceptance within ourselves and begin to see ourselves and our lives from the perspective of the big picture.

We must step back, take a look at whom or what is dictating our lives and readily dismiss any negative way that we have been judged. We also must become aware of our strengths as this often determines our calling; we must build on our strengths. We must become aware of our weaknesses then fortify these areas. We can then move forward through our spiritual practices, education, and self-care and in any other way that our healing requires. Then we can begin to see ourselves through the eyes of our divinity. Only then will we be able to deliberately co-create with God.

The following exercises can support our development of a healthy self-image.

Treatment

I know that love renews, overcomes and harmonizes. I allow love to fill my vision as I see myself through the eyes of Christ. I allow love to lead me and I see myself as a being whose presence brings comfort. I see myself through the eyes of the peace that surpasses human understanding. I offer this peace to all.

Denial

Nothing can keep me from the love of God. I am a place where love is made available to me and others. I am valuable in this world and I have my unique gifts which I offer in loving service. I am thankful for this holy privilege of being called to serve.

Affirmations

I know that I am divine in nature. Knowing that my divinity is Jehovah's gift to me, I cherish everything my divinity affords me. I am grateful for my divinity. The divinity in me greets the divinity in others.

I choose to see myself as a divine being who shows up in this world with wisdom, beauty and a zest for living. I am loving, kind and compassionate. The life of Spirit flows through me and I am perfect as my Heavenly Father is perfect.

Honor Yourself

We must acknowledge the work we have accomplished and the guidance we have received. This work never ends; each new day requires a new loaf of bread in the form of new courage, new ideas, food, peace, friendship, strength to forgive, rest, and the like.

As we honor ourselves, we live with authenticity, which is based on our inner truth. Often, however, one of our most difficult challenges is to respect our true feelings. All too often in a misguided effort to be polite, some people refuse to say yes or no when they appropriately should. For example, many women who work outside the home are expected to provide most of the care for their family members and households, and their husbands choose to relax after work. Some women talk of the frustration, anger, and resentment it causes, yet they refuse to address it.

Some Excuses many of us make in these types of situations might be such as saying that (1) to get something done well one has to do it them self or (2) Staying quiet about the situation keeps the peace. I understand that men face these types of situations as well. I believe that most of us, both men and women, have experienced a similar situation at least once. These situations also occur in the workplace, where we might find ourselves having to unfairly do more of the work. Often when we do not address these situations in our homes or private lives, we see the pattern repeated at work or places we go. What an intelligent universe we live in! It has a way of presenting us with the challenges and experiences we need in order to inspire us to ultimately love, be loved and move forward. When we honor ourselves by standing up for ourselves, we make this possible.

Society often rewards us for stuffing our feelings under the carpet, where everyone—including us—can step on them. We hear, "Big boys/big girls don't cry." My take on that is simple: Jesus wept! Isn't he our way-shower? He did not hesitate to show the human aspect joined with the divine. We must honor ourselves by developing the courage to ask for help when we need it. The little ego may say, "You get all the glory when you do it alone" or "You will appear intelligent or in control." Nature does not flourish that way. Just observe the symbiotic relationships of ecosystems and food chains. In the creation story, we read that Adam needed Eve. Jesus needed twelve disciples, and Almighty God needs our bodies through which to manifest good works; we need each other. We must learn to be assertive as an act of loving and honoring ourselves. We must also teach this to our children.

Learn to forgive yourself for times when you did not honor yourself or others. **Diligently engage in practices that are self-honoring. You can also complete exercises for self-forgiveness.** Be grateful that you are now aware and awake to the truth of this mandate, as well as to the ways to honor yourself. We can also complete exercises for showing gratitude for the courage to undertake this bold step. As we honor ourselves, we honor all of creation. We too must embrace our new awareness with our Divine self. To honor ourselves is to honor God.

Practices

It is always beneficial to begin any spiritual practice in the silence through prayer or meditation. In this way we surrender and allow ourselves to be spiritually guided and supported. We can follow up with other practices like the following:

Treatment

I am mindful of the truth that I am created out of love. I know myself as a worthy child of the universe. I see myself surrounded by love, and I allow this love to lead me. I feel myself loving me and all creation; I feel all creation loving me. I understand that I am necessary to life and that life is necessary to me. I love life, and life loves me. I am grateful that all is well.

Affirmations

- I am always loved, honored and valued!
- Love is the core of my power. I honor God's love in me.
- My thoughts, words, and deeds touch the Spirit of God in everyone. I offer love and compassion to all and I receive love and compassion from all.

Mirror Work

The following process, called mirror work, is a powerful practice that can enhance self-love and transformation. You can use a mirror that allows you to see a reflection of your face. However, the better option is a full-length mirror that easily captures the reflection of your whole naked body. This way you can see each body part while addressing it. One may wear minimal or no clothing, (if this does not cause major discomfort). If there is just a little discomfort, this might be the time to stretch and perhaps become fully undressed and look deep into your eyes beyond any mask, then see your innocence.

Get into a private spot at a time when you will not be disturbed. Look at the reflection of your face or body and scan it completely and without judgment or any idea of what part should be fixed, nixed, filled, or obliterated etc. Smile as you look at each body part and say tenderly, "I love you dearly; you are so precious" or "I love you unconditionally; you are worthy of all that is good" or "I love you; your inner beauty shines brightly." You can say whatever is more personal to you. Be creative and say nothing negative. For example, you may be inspired to thank your beautiful eyes for helping you experience the beauty of the world. However, after working long hours, your eyes may be tired and red. You are aware of this, so you don't have to repeat that. What is important is that you thank your beautiful eyes for affording you such spectacular beauty in seeing all of creation or looking at the reflection of perfection, i.e. You!

Continue this process and for each body part; mention what that body part does. For example, thank your feet for supporting you as you exercise or walk around your office. Thank your body for being a vessel of service to God, to you and others, and also for allowing you to feel various sensations. Thank your body for being a temple of the Spirit of God and a vessel for procreation. **In conclusion, you may make one or more of the following statements of Affirmation.**

- I am so grateful that I am beautifully and wonderfully made.
- I thank you my beautiful body, for being a vessel through which I experience God.
- I am the person I love to be, and I am grateful.
- I love and respect myself for being kind and compassionate to others.
- I feel joy and gratitude for being such a caring spouse/parent/child/friend.
- I honor myself for being a willing co-creator with God.

The following exercise serves to open your awareness to the parts of you that have been neglected as well as the cause(s) for the neglect.

Meeting Your Inner Child

Sit quietly with your eyes closed and with your back straight or in the way that is most comfortable for you. Place your feet in the most comfortable position. Place your hands in your lap. Take a few deep breaths and allow your body to relax. Focus on your breathing and feel the air as it enters and leaves your nostrils. When thoughts come to your mind's surface, gently release them and continue focusing on the sensation of the air entering and leaving your nostrils. Allow your body to relax completely. Feel any tension drop away from your head, forehead, eyes, face, ears, and shoulders, back and wherever else the tension may be felt.

Keep breathing until you feel stillness. Know in your heart that you are at complete peace. In your visualization, see yourself walking in a beautiful garden with a large area for children to play. You notice a child of about five years old and the same sex as you are dressed in white—a white dress for a girl or white shirt and pants for a boy. This child is playing happily, and you can't help but acknowledge that this child is pure and innocent. You feel drawn to this child.

You begin to walk toward the child, who instinctively begins to run to you with a big smile on his or her face. You begin to smile too. You meet each other, and immediately you bend down to this child's height, and you hug each other; you sense this child's innocence. Instantly you both realize that you are a part of each other. You romp and play, and memories of when you did not allow the little ego to dictate your life come swirling back into your memory. You kick off your shoes and feel the soft grass under your feet. The flowers smell lovely, and their colors are vibrant.

A sense of freedom comes over you, and as you play with this child, he or she asks you where you have been for so long and why you haven't visited. You reply that you are busy working, or caring for a family, and taking care of your life etc. The child says that he or she missed you and invites you to come often. Instantly you realize that this child is the part of you that you have neglected and ignored. You had replaced joy with worries, shame, blame, neglect, and whatever else is a shadow for you. You also realize how and why you have done that.

With this new awareness, you quickly resolve to love yourself unconditionally. You feel worthy of the good life has to offer. You realize an unbounded joy in that moment and realize your life is meant to be wonderful. You continue playing, romping, laughing with this child. As you end this play time, you promise this child you will be back soon. You follow through.

Note, this exercise can be followed by a resolve to take time out for self-care, relaxation, and recreation at set times. Follow the information received from your inner guide. Please put these practices into place quickly. Neglecting to do so leaves room for the more familiar self-defeating habits to set up resistance and flourish. It takes physical and mental practice to put new behaviors in place. Be willing to take responsibility for any negative state you have helped to create in your life and consciously cooperate with God to end it. Honor yourself for taking this bold step!

The Sacred Journey

There was love in the beginning. Love is the source of all creation. As we practice love and let it guide us, we are indeed on a sacred journey that is oh, so far removed from the boring or the humdrum. As we love and nurture ourselves as a standard way of being, we become open to accepting love and forgiveness from ourselves and others. When we love ourselves, we *know* ourselves as people who are loved. Our spiritual self-esteem then impels us to love others, especially since it is accountable for its own progress. The negative little ego becomes uncomfortable. It can no longer claim to be a victim. It loses the negative attention it craves and desires in order to self-sabotage. It can soon look for new ways to recreate the victim's role so be vigilant! Self-doubt can begin to creep in. The key is to recognize the little ego at these times of doubt and to think or quietly say to it, **"Thank you for letting me know**

that you're here, but I can take care of myself now that I am no longer a victim seeking pity. I love the new, empowered me!"

The following affirmations can help the Spiritual ego to flourish. These can be said during mirror work as you look at your face or body, as well as at other times of wholesome contemplation. The key is to involve your feeling nature, or emotions. **Feel** whatever you say. Remember, you want to bathe your entire being in the positive healing energy of these words. **Emotions seal your work; it becomes your own work.**

Affirmations

- This is a day the Lord has made; I rejoice and am glad in it!
- Almighty Father, today I am available for you to use. Love through me, think through me, talk through me, and act through me; I am willing.
- I am created for a holy purpose. I am a unique masterpiece; there was no one like me and there will never be anyone exactly like me. I do the specific work that God has called me to do. I am about my Father's business.
- I am too blessed to be stressed.
- I love, I am loved and this feels good.
- I am kind and compassionate.
- I love all people, and all people love me
- In my place of work/service, I am loved, valued, needed, and important; I love and value my peers and those I serve.
- I am a wonderful spouse (husband/wife). I honor my spouse with unconditional love and respect.
- I am a wonderful parent. I have unconditional love and respect for my children. I honor them as my precious gifts from Jehovah God. I offer them unconditional love, forgiveness and support.

- I am a wonderful child. I hold my parents in my heart with love and admiration. I am grateful for them and the lessons we taught each other. I offer them unconditional love, forgiveness and support.
- I am healthy, wealthy, wise, and happy. I am prosperous.
- I am generous with my time and money. I allow the Spirit of God within me to inspire my use of my time and wealth.
- I attract, cherish, and maintain divine friendships. All who do not mean me well peacefully leave; they stay away from me and prosper elsewhere.
- I am God's love manifested to myself and my fellow men.

Cultivating Love for Others

When our prayer lives seem stagnant or unfruitful, it is wise to take a look at how we are expressing love to others. We all have an innate desire for connection to others. We have a need for relationships, whether they are based on brotherly love or romantic love. The gift of love that is a part of us is a magnet that rewards love with love. We cannot genuinely love others without loving ourselves. We have a shared oneness with each other that is spiritually profound. Practicing love is a Spiritual practice!

With wisdom, we can realize that we all have been blessed with the gift of choice. However, desiring the good that has been created for us leaves us with the choice of whether or not we want to obey the commandment to love one another. We understand that love is the way to manifest our desires through prayer. We must be love in thought, word, and deed. All spiritual laws, as stated before, are immutable, which means we cannot bend them to suit any particular person or desire. The law of love manifests as brotherly love. This is the quality of the love we must embrace. This is not to say that romantic love is not important; it is indeed blessed and forms a vital part of the intimate and marriage relationship.

However, it is an effect of brotherly love. When brotherly love is present romantic love flourishes.

Loving others as a Spiritual practice

We must prayerfully ask just how we must love. There is always a specific way that we must love in the "now"

Despite the negative ego's tantrums, which may show up as the thought that every man fends for himself, we owe it to our Heavenly Father and our own divine selves to be love to ourselves and others. The sacred journey to transformation dictates that love expands from us to all creation. We must be in service to Almighty God and each other. I believe love transforms this world one loving act at a time. **Love works as we work it! We are in turn served by the love we express; this is a Spiritual a law.**

Practice thinking kindly of others. **Observe your private thoughts** about others when you see or think of them. Ask yourself, "Do I think kindly, lovingly, or respectfully of others, regardless of their race, religion, class, skin color, body size, or any other aspect?" Let's face it; sometimes our past experiences, our parents, societal norms, or norms in general dictate who we do or do not like. People can love or hate because they were treated well or because they were mistreated, respectively. Race relations have been birthed out of this premise.

The following are some useful practices that help in cultivating love for others:

Upon seeing someone, say silently or think, "I salute the Christ in you."

- Watching a total stranger go by, say silently or think, "The peace of God goes with you" or "May you have joy."

- Say a happy hello or greeting to someone, whether he or she is a stranger or acquaintance. It truly makes no difference whether you know this person or not, or what their race or ethnicity is.
- Affirm the following often: "I love with the love that uplifts and blesses my fellow men. I allow this love to guide my thoughts and actions."
- Provide childcare for an evening so someone can have the time for recreation. Do this on a volunteer basis.
- Via phone, Skype or other means, call and support a friend who may be experiencing some difficulty.
- Return money or merchandise given to you in error.
- Hold the door open for someone and be okay if they say thank you or not.
- Practice speaking kindly to others, even in times when you would have otherwise not done so. Refrain from mean gossip and judging others.
- Volunteer by mentoring a child, taking groceries to a food pantry, helping the elderly, or working at an animal shelter. Share your skills, wisdom and knowledge.
- Pray for the poor and others worldwide.
- Smile at a complete stranger. Commit random acts of kindness.
- Pray for prisoners as though you are imprisoned with them. Pray for the sick, and people in war-torn areas. Pray for orphans, widows and widowers.
- Pray for the world's political leaders, asking that love and wisdom guide and support them for the benefit of all people. Pray also for their protection. Pray for their families. (See chapter 13)
- Take care of the environment. This shows love and respect for our creator, our world, and each other.
- Plant trees, flowers, and vegetables. This has the same effect as taking care of the environment. Plants reward us with life sustaining oxygen.

- Allow others to be themselves; this allows you to freely be yourself as well.
- Share your time and other resources in service to others always with the goal of improving the human condition.
- When you wrap a gift for someone or make a package of something to share, say a silent prayer that it blesses the receiver in the way that is most appropriate for them.
- Be bold enough to discourage anyone who intends to harm or hurt others.
- Be kind to lower class animals, including your pets.

"To receive love, we must first become the love we seek."

When we speak of loving others, we must be able to cut through the obvious chatter and connect with that Christ's essence in the one who is in our presence. Dr. Wayne Dyer once demonstrated this to me. On a tour, I met him and his family. I greeted them and after our greetings, proceeded to tell him how he mentored me through his books and how I use his children's books as a teaching tool for children etc. He patiently, quietly, and calmly looked at me with a smile on his face. His first words were "Where is my hug?" He connected with the Christ's presence in me first. Although what I did with his books is very necessary for transformation, he showed me that **being who I am takes precedence over what I do**. I am grateful to him. This reminded me that we first must have reverence for the essence in each other as a first priority; "people before things; being before doing!"

Our Health

As we show love to ourselves by practicing self-care, we must also come to the awareness that we have a divine privilege of hosting the Spirit of God in our being. God needs our minds and bodies through which to work! Everything has its place in this beautiful world. In order for the spiritual evolution of the world to continue, there must be physical bodies through which the Spirit of Jehovah can manifest its work!

We don't see an elephant standing in front of a classroom, in front of a crowd or in our homes, teaching us about affirmations, prayers, or some new technology. You don't see human beings flying from flower to flower, extracting nectar with their beaks or laying their eggs in nests. Everyone and everything has a divine purpose which is aligned with their innate nature, and we need to be available physically, mentally and emotionally to fulfill it. Some might ask, "Since everyone has a purpose, how can people who are mentally challenged or profoundly physically disabled serve their divine purpose?" The answer is that they can serve when they provide the opportunity for someone to practice mercy and compassion toward them. They also serve when they provide the vehicle (their body) on which someone can use his or her talents and skills while serving them. In turn, these people when and if they are able can show gratitude, and we all can glorify God for this arrangement. Every physical body has a divine purpose!

The health of our bodies is such a priority that Jesus' miracles focused largely on the healing of our bodies. Through his miracles of feeding the hungry multitude, he demonstrated the importance of feeding the body to maintain it. He even turned water into wine. This shows that he cares about our nutrition and our moods. Be aware that this truth is not intended to endorse drunkenness; neither does it support underage drinking.

In this discussion of self-love there, is included different ways to care for ourselves. Again, I am also recommending best-selling author Louise Hay's book *Heal Your Body*. Please read it carefully and with an open mind. It explains the causes for many illnesses. Please keep in mind that we have different life experiences that affect different people in different ways. What is true for one person may not be true for the other. This book provides a general view of the mental causes of many illnesses and the Metaphysical ways to overcome them. It is not meant to replace the recommendation and treatment of any health-care provider.

This affirmative life-giving way of praying provides guidance and support as we prayerfully care for our bodies. Metaphysical writer Ralph Waldo Emerson said that the soul needs an organ. By this Emerson meant, that the deeper soul level needs the physical body through which it must express; we are living souls. Knowing this, we ought to make a conscious effort to care for our bodies, willingly maintaining this vessel through which God must work and manifest.

The following healing exercise is one that came to me while I was in silence. Please read it in its entirety before you do it, so that with some familiarity the process can flow smoother.

Healing Exercise

Sit comfortably in a comfortable space. Temporarily turn off any device you think might disturb you. Set an intention in your mind to go deeply into this process and to receive guidance and healing. **You may use soft music that features the sounds of nature, as this can soothe your senses while providing mental imagery.** You may choose complete silence and imagery.

Close your eyes and take three deep, slow breaths. Begin to focus on the center of your body around your abdomen. In your mind's eye, see your abdomen as hollow. See a warm light the size of a hen's egg warmly glowing and emitting bursts of bright light. Each burst of bright light emits micro droplets of light forming a mist. This mist of light has the healing love and intelligence of God in its nature. This light begins to travel through your body. Turn your attention inside your head. see this healing mist moving through all cells and tissues through the brain and blood vessels. This mist settles, and no cell escapes its healing touch. It moves through bones and cartilage, settling on the skull and hair follicles. It then moves through the pores to the entire facial area. Its only action is to heal, and it must heal everything it touches.

If any stray thought comes in at this time, gently let it go and refocus. See the mist moving, settling, and healing in the throat. See it settling on every cell that makes up the glands in the throat and then move through the skin. It radiates and settles on the shoulders, down the forearms, wrists, and hands and to the palms and tips of the fingers. It moves through the pores and settles on the skin. In your thoughts, think the words, *I am grateful that this healing is taking place in my body now.* See the healing mist in your chest, settling on then in every organ, including the heart, breasts, ribs, muscles, armpits, and lungs. The mist moves through the pores of your chest and back, healing gently as it moves along. It moves through the abdomen and reproductive organs, spine, intestines, liver, spleen, pancreas, and stomach. Every cell and system in this area is touched and healed.

See the mist settling and flowing in the hip area, sacral area, and buttocks. See the healing mist flowing in and through every bone, muscle, fiber, tissue, and cell. It moves through the ureter and the urethra, colon, sex organs, and all glands, muscles, systems and tissue. It moves through all the cells and out to the skin that covers these regions. See the mist moving down the thighs to the knees, legs, ankles, and feet, including the heels, toes and soles of the feet. No cell has been left untouched. Be grateful in your mind that healing is now complete. Send love to your body by lovingly thinking, *"I love my healthy body!"*

So often we give attention to sickness and may talk about it constantly. It is truly most beneficial to praise our bodies in times of health. We must remember that what we praise we raise or increase. Take three deep breaths and feel the warmth of gratitude well up inside of you, then offer praise by saying any or all of the following healing affirmations.

Affirmation

- I am healed, made whole and perfect now.
- Divine love draws health to me; I am strong and able
- There is one life that is perfect and whole; that life is my life now.
- I love health and health loves me; I am grateful!
- I praise Our Heavenly Father for my perfect health.

Treatments

Divine life in my body denies anything unlike itself. Whatever is not wholesome is eradicated. I experience perfect circulation, perfect assimilation, and perfect elimination. I surrender any limiting thoughts about my body and its functions. I cultivate thoughts and actions that maintain my perfect health. There is one perfect life; the life of God. I claim and accept this God- life now. I give thanks for my perfect life.

God's gift of health is perfect and complete in me. There is nothing in my subconscious mind to cause or maintain illness. I cooperate with ideas that support health. I am receptive to health, I embrace health, and with faith I give thanks for my perfect health.

As we pray affirmatively about matters concerning our health, there must be a spiritual recognition that God is life, Love, Perfect health and wholeness. This conscious recognition informs the subconscious mind which produces the corresponding condition.

Affirmative Prayer

Our Father God of wisdom, you are perfect health. I believe that you wonderfully created me in your image and likeness. and that your breath continues to give me life. There is only one life and that life is your wonderful life which courses through my body.

Abba Father, you are so loving and wise; every cell in my body is a center of divine intelligence! Therefore any function that is not healthy is now corrected through grace.

I ask for and open myself to receive the guidance that supports and informs me, as I select and consume wholesome foods in the right portions. I practice self-care as an honor and appreciation for my body which is your temple, and a vehicle through which I must serve. Dear Father, I realize that you must work through my body and I am very grateful for this privilege. My desire is to maintain my God given body in the way that aligns with my love for you and my gratitude to you. I love health, I embrace and accept health. Dear Father, I thank you for my perfect health and my many blessings. In the name of Jesus Christ I pray.

Chapter 8

Forgiveness

"And whenever you stand praying, if you have anything against anyone, forgive him that your Father in heaven may also forgive you your trespasses." (Mark 11:25).

Webster's New World Dictionary and Thesaurus defines the word *forgive* as to pardon; to remit as a debt, fine or penalty; to grant free or pardon to cease to blame; to overlook an offense and treat the offender as not guilty.

In the hour of great distress came the Christ's plea: "Father forgive them for they know not what they do" (Luke 23:34). The mandate was echoed; for our prayer practices to be fruitful, we must cultivate in ourselves this consciousness that embraces forgiveness. The entire purpose for learning about the transforming power of affirmative prayer will not be realized if the spiritual law of forgiveness is not embraced. Not forgiving, which is one of the weapons of the little ego, is often one of the most challenging strongholds to break through. Nevertheless, this can be achieved with God's help.

Examining the Lord's Prayer, which the Christ taught, we read, *"Forgive us our debts, as we forgive our debtors."* This implies that the degree to which we forgive is the degree to which we will be forgiven. There is a dynamic spiritual, scientific, and physical process embodied in the act of forgiveness. Through grace, which is unearned favor from God, we find the strength to forgive. We cannot fathom how this happens because it is a mystical event. When we harbor grudges, the body becomes stressed, leading to many illnesses. As we harbor the negative energy of unforgivingness, there is no place for grace, health, peace, etc. We are told to make amends with our adversaries quickly! As we begin to surrender to forgiveness, we allow the goodness of grace to come into our experiences. For this reason, we also experience forgiveness as we forgive. With whatever measure we meet, so it will be met to us.

Through experiments, scientists have concluded that humans have a mind-body connection. Mental health professionals are proving that our thoughts, whether conscious or unconscious, affect our emotional, mental, and physical selves. It is said that most people who are in therapy have at least one thing that they can forgive. Of course, none of this is new, for this has been the truth throughout history. St. Paul stressed the renewing of our minds for our transformation. The mind-body connection shows up clearer in situations where there is an emotional component like love, hate, fear, anger, calm, etc. Therefore, when I fearfully and mistakenly thought in my mind that I had been stuck with the needle, pain was created in my body. Forgiveness and unforgivingness ultimately affect us mentally and physically, positively or negatively.

Forgiveness is the spiritual law that was painstakingly demonstrated at the crucifixion of Christ. Imagine the culmination of such a savage, humiliating, and sorrowful event punctuated by Christ's plea for forgiveness for those who mocked him, beat him, and shed his blood. This was a profound lesson at the ultimate price! Christ taught forgiveness and showed us how to forgive. Jesus knew that unforgivingness toward self or others forms a hindrance to prayer. Prayer is the key to healing our minds, bodies, and affairs, and it is how we come into conscious union with God. If our prayers' effectiveness is blocked by thoughts and acts of unforgivingness, the healing of our minds, bodies, or affairs will be hindered, and we certainly will not be able to enter into union with God.

Jesus understood that a mind cluttered with unforgivingness, even against oneself, would have an unhealthy effect on the body. He demonstrated this when he healed the man who had an appearance of paralysis. This man's friends had faith that Jesus could heal him. They were determined enough that they let him down through the roof, in the Christ's presence. "When Jesus saw their faith, he said to him, Man, your sins are forgiven you" (Luke 5:20). Because of Christ's declaration, the negative energy of unforgivingness that blocked the healing process was transmuted into healing energy through Christ's forgiving power. There was no petitioning. Christ affirmatively declared that the healing was complete, and it was completed.

St. Paul wrote the following to the Ephesians: "And be kind to one another, tenderhearted, forgiving one another, even as God in Christ forgave you" (Eph. 4:32) Immediately after the master teacher taught the model for prayer known as the Lord's Prayer, he said, "For if you forgive men their trespasses, your heavenly father will also forgive you" (Matt. 6:14). Of all the statements in this model, Christ chose to repeat the one that expounds forgiveness.

When Peter, a disciple of Jesus, asked Jesus if he should forgive someone who had offended him as many as seven times, he probably thought he was impressing Jesus with his great generosity. The Jewish law in those days allowed a person to be forgiven three times. Jesus answered him, saying, "I do not say to you up to seven times, but up to seventy times seven" (Matt. 9:22). This simply means that we must forgive each time it becomes necessary. We must keep in mind the truth, that when Jesus performed healings, if forgiveness was necessary it was done first. Unforgivingness, with its negative energy, can block the manifestations we seek. Dr. Martin Luther King Jr. promoted nonviolence and forgiveness in his promotion of justice and unity. He said that we must develop and maintain the capacity to forgive and that the person, who is devoid of the power to forgive, is devoid of the power to love. He believed that there is some good in the worst of us and some evil in the best of us; believing in the sacredness of the human personality, he reminded us not to reduce people to their mistakes. Mahatma Gandhi said that the weak can never forgive and that forgiveness is an attribute of the strong. Archbishop Desmond Tutu of South Africa wrote extensively in his book, *God Has A Dream*: A Vision of Hope for Our Time, about the cruelty and injustices of apartheid in South Africa. His ultimate lesson was that we should all embrace the power of forgiveness. (2004)

Although forgiveness has profound benefits, many people choose not to forgive. Many misconceptions about forgiveness play a major part in making it difficult to accomplish.

Some of the most frequent explanations that form misconceptions are

- Forgiving an offense means that the person who is forgiving condones it.
- Forgiving means that the offence is negligible, and soon the offender will see things that way too, as negligible.
- The offended has to make up or become friends again with the offender.
- Any legal process of justice necessary will be hampered.
- Remembering the offence means you cannot or did not forgive it.
- Forgiveness means that the offended has to mask his or her anger.
- One must forget the incident in order to truly forgive it.

The Truth about Forgiveness

We all have the capacity to forgive; otherwise, Christ would not have mandated it. It is a remarkable way to finding or rediscovering peace and freedom within us. Still, some people become stuck in the self-righteous stance and refuse to forgive. When we cannot forgive, it often causes physical symptoms such as muscle tension, hypertension, heart disease, back and neck pains, etc. It also manifests emotionally as frustration, anxiety, depression, hopelessness, low self-esteem, poor relationships, guilt, and shame, to name a few. When we hold grudges in our thoughts, it affects us mentally, and we become stuck in the victim's role, focusing on the cause of the hurt. Our bodies' flight-or-fight mechanisms become engaged, sending stress signals throughout our bodies. Let's admit that there are times when it is very difficult to forgive; it may even seem impossible. The wounds and hurts may be so deep that we are mesmerized by a constant mental replay of the experiences. We may even come to describe ourselves as the situation itself. When we realize the magnitude of the effect that holding grudges has on our well-being, we can understand that forgiveness chiefly benefits the one who needs to forgive.

Forgiveness heals our life's circumstances in every way! This act shows that we are wise enough to recognize an offense and big enough in character to forgive it. Forgiveness can also create a positive change in the one being forgiven; when forgiven, he or she will have received a lesson on forgiveness and grace. This does not mean that one has to reconcile with the offender, although it is a noble act worth considering if appropriate. Some people reconcile sooner, later, or never. It is always a personal choice to become friends again. Feeling forced by ourselves or others to resume a friendship is not healing and may trigger resentment towards the offender. Forgiving does not mean that the offender pays no consequences. Consequences teach lessons that can help correct behaviors; at the same time, the one harmed feels justified and learns to have faith in justice. Ultimately, we ourselves cannot make forgiving possible; this mystical experience can only be achieved through God's grace. Grace gives the power to forgive.

Some people feel that if they are not forgetting an incident, it cannot be forgiven. The truth is that as human beings with minds, we are also thinking beings with memories. Occasionally a traumatic memory may be repressed, but it never leaves the mind. To completely forget a harm we have experienced is unnatural. For example, let's say someone was robbed as he or she walked in a lonely alleyway. The perpetrator was caught, legally dealt with, and forgiven by the victim. Would it be wise for the person who was robbed to forget the incident or the lesson learned and then go walking in the lonely alleyway again? Of course not; one should remember the experience and the lesson it brought. In this way, safety can be practiced in the future. We also are not obligated to associate with people who hurt, mistreat, abuse, or violate us in any way, even after we forgive them. Once forgiveness occurs, the memory of the incident does not usually carry the power to evoke strong negatives emotions. Remembering the forgiven incident could be a reminder of the mystical gift of grace that supports forgiveness and heals all wounds!

Inner and outer work are required as part of the forgiveness process. Results may or may not be arrived at quickly. Sadly, some people die without allowing themselves to forgive or be forgiven. Forgiving oneself seems more difficult. We must allow ourselves to remember that forgiveness also frees the one who forgives; **forgiveness is a path to peace and freedom**. Although we cannot change what happened in the past, we can certainly change our thoughts and feelings in the present about any situation. The time to forgive is always *now*.

Some people reason that they will forgive when they are not too angry to do so. Not forgiving actually sets the stage to maintain both the anger and the victim mentality. **Forgiveness supports** the release of the suffering, which the little ego uses as a tool to maintain anger. In forgiving, our goal must also be to free from our beings the negative energies of resentment, anger, hate, sadness, malice, etc. We release the dull, heavy, slow energy of resentment and embrace the quick, healing, loving, light energy of forgiveness. This propels us to move forward joyfully and to experience the transforming power of Affirmative prayers in our lives. All we need is willingness to begin; are you willing? The universe beckons!

Forgiveness—Practice

We understand that affirmative prayer works wonderfully when our consciousness is conducive to forgiveness. Prayer always works in and through us. Limiting ideas or negative emotions create an atmosphere that blocks the internal landscape where prayer first begins its work. Forgiveness cleanses and frees the mind to receive answered prayers. There are practical ways that support the forgiving process. Listed in the following sections are some processes that can be embraced and used in forgiving.

One of the body's natural ways of coping with hurts and trauma is to repress feelings and memories. Then, as we experience this repression, we say we are "numb" or that we "forgot." At times, hypnosis is used to aid in unearthing memories. Working toward forgiveness, it is necessary to unearth these memories and feelings. In addition to allowing our prayer lives to prosper, complete healing begins as we forgive.

An incident that wounded us really has no power. However, we give power to the beliefs and feelings we have about it. The term *wounded* is used because of the deep emotional hurts that have far-reaching adverse effects. For example, there may be direct effects such as loss of libido or sexual dysfunction because of a sexual violation.

Proceed with some caution, as the unearthing of feelings can cause us to relive them. However, this gives us an opportunity to move through these feelings with a more empowered consciousness. As we face the feelings peacefully and with authority, we address them and reduce and eventually eradicate their stings. Persons who are undergoing counseling or who have emotional or anger management challenges should consult with their mental health-care providers before doing the following exercises for forgiveness. It is also wise to consult one's religious or spiritual advisor for guidance because reliving the feelings can cause emotional pain, anger, frustration, etc., and these professionals can lend support according to their disciplines.

Forgiveness—Prayers

Prayer is the act that truly brings us in union with God. It works from the inside out and changes our mentality to one that is receptive to the love and guidance of our Most High God. Before we engage in any spiritual practice, it is wise to open our consciousness to guidance and clarity. We can accomplish this through prayer and meditation. Before beginning the spiritual work of forgiveness, offer a prayer of submission and become receptive to the guidance received. Prayer is not only about submission and asking; it is also about decreeing or affirming the truth about the situation. Prayer is done through the mind; therefore, one can meditate which simply means to focus on the prayer and God. One can pray without moving his or her lips, or they can pray audibly. Regardless of the method, the consciousness will be equally involved.

Prayers for Guidance and Support in Self-Forgiveness

Dear Heavenly Father, I am ready to honor your Spirit in me, and I seek guidance. Feelings of guilt remind me constantly of [insert the offense here]. I admit that I do not feel worthy of forgiveness. Please help me accept that I made a mistake and that I will learn from it through my willingness to surrender my will to you. Help me understand that my successes and failures are my lessons along life's journey. Help me forgive myself, no matter the offense. I allow your word to be a lamp unto my feet and a light unto my path; in this light I walk. For your grace, I am eternally grateful.

[After praying, silently listen. Obey the guidance received. You can also complete the writing process described later in this chapter.]

Prayers for Guidance and Support in Forgiving Others

Wonderful Counselor, Creator of harmony, it is my desire to always be in your will. It is your will that we forgive ourselves and each other. I ask that you help me to be open to the grace that empowers us to forgive. I admit that with you all things are possible, and that I can do all things through Christ, who strengthens me. I desire strength to forgive, so I now let Christ strengthen me. [Breathe.]

I forgive whenever the need arises, as I see everyone through the eyes of Christ. I let go of the hurt, shame, anger, grudges, and condemnation. I allow the emotions they stir to gradually lose their sting. I free myself from their bondage, and I ask you, God, to protect my wounded self as I heal. [Breathe.] I accept and embrace the peace and freedom that forgiveness offers now. For this peace and freedom through grace, I rejoice and am grateful.

Group Prayer for Forgiveness

Dear Almighty God of love, we ask that you help us to become fully aware that through Christ's death and resurrection, you have already provided forgiveness for all. We recognize that we cannot only ask for it, but we must also do the inner and outer works of love that seal our forgiveness. Help us to let go of judgments, resentment, hate, and the condemnation that limits the flow of good in our lives. Help us to remember that no harm is ever worthy of causing us to destroy our lives. We surrender ourselves to you and ask that you keep us steadfast as we forgive and accept forgiveness. [Breathe.]

Lord, it is through your strength that we allow the healing power of love to wash our minds, cleansing them of nonforgiveness. We see everyone as children of God created in your image and likeness and in whom your spirit dwells. We see everyone as worthy of only good. We release and forgive those who wounded us. We forgive ourselves for wounding others. We accept forgiveness through our Christ minds. We let it be so, and so it is, now and forevermore.

Scanning Process (scan before forgiving self or others)

It is productive to scan one's memory to check for and unearth any memory that caused hurt. It is better to be thorough; the freedom gained in this process is priceless. Get into a safe, quiet place where you are least likely to be disturbed. Become still and comfortable. Take three deep cleansing breaths. Close your eyes and stir up the feeling of love and compassion toward yourself. In your imagination, see yourself at the youngest age you remember being. You may or may not remember where you were. Pay attention to smells, voices, music, and words. Were they harsh or soft? Pay attention also to colors and lighting. Check your memory to find out if you were at home, daycare, school, or any other place like work, a relative's home, etc.

Continue to breathe slowly and deeply. Observe your feelings. Does any sight, sound, or smell (in your mind's eye) stir up any emotions? If this happens, stay with the emotion. Observe what brought it up because this is the situation that encompasses the reason to forgive. As you feel the emotion, breathe. You can whisper,

"Peace, be still," to the emotion. Try not to let the emotion go away without addressing it. This way, when you remember the incident again, the cellular memory of it will produce peace instead of hurt. You may shed tears; just see the tears as the body's way of washing away the hurts. Remember not to push the emotion away; it is better to release it. When you push something away, an antagonistic force of resistance is created. What we resist, persist. Pay attention to people involved; they may include the person/ persons you must forgive.

Some people choose to scan their memories up to a certain age and then complete the forgiveness process. They may later in another session, start scanning from the developmental stage where they left off. Other people choose to scan until their current age and then complete one process. The person engaging in this process knows him or herself best. This is why it is good to pray for divine guidance before beginning this process.

While scanning one's memory, it is important to also recall any involvement with social circles such as groups and religious or spiritual organizations. Pay attention to times of illness, sadness, or joy. Focus on relationships. Were you abused by a boyfriend, girlfriend, husband, wife, children, or others?

You may be surprised at the unexpected negative emotions you might have unearthed. Fortunately, as you speak peace to them, you are disarming them. This might take time to accomplish. The controlling factor is our consciousness. While forgiving is noble, when we choose not to forgive, we are in truth blocking the flow of our physical, mental, emotional, and spiritual wholeness. Forgiveness is a process of love, and it begins in our inner beings. The outer exercises are just the outer works. We must bring our whole beings into the forgiving process. **Jesus Christ did not just think about forgiveness; he spoke the words. These exercises allow us to also speak and write our words of forgiveness.** In the following section are some exercises that support the forgiving process.

The following exercises serve as outer acts of faith. They also support the inner forgiving process. These exercises can be completed or omitted as one is led to do. They serve as visual representations of the work done in the invisible. There is nothing sinister about these exercises, and no more should be read into them. Jesus, the way-shower and master teacher, used a mix of saliva and clay to heal a blind man's eyes. It was a physical demonstration of what had already occurred in the invisible. The onlookers witnessed the healing that had begun in the healing mind of Christ. **(John 9:6-7)** The writing exercises in the following section also help us muster up the painful feelings as we face the experiences we are moving forward to heal.

Writing Exercises for Forgiveness

We know there is power in our words, whether they are written, spoken, or they form our thoughts. In this exercise, we will think and then write them. We will write statements about forgiveness for the harm and their effects on us.

Materials needed for this exercise include paper (preferably magic paper, which burns swiftly and cleanly), matches or a lighter to ignite the paper, a pen or pencil, an envelope (optional), and tissues with which to wipe away cleansing tears. The steps for these writing exercises are as follows: Always pray before beginning the Spiritual work of forgiveness.

1. Write the statements of forgiveness.

2. Take occasional deep cleansing breaths during the exercise; they are calming and help with memory. They also keep us centered in the present.

3. Check your emotions; be gentle with yourself. Write at a comfortable pace. Remember to take deep cleansing breaths.

4. At the conclusion of each exercise, you can destroy the paper by shredding or burning it. If you prefer burning,

please be sure plenty of water is on hand to wet the burning paper as soon as you burn it. This should not be done near flammable things, nor where embers can fly to trees, shrubs, or other structures. Using magic paper is safest because it disintegrates immediately, leaving no flying embers. Take all necessary precautions to prevent a fire! You can also safely throw the paper into a body of water such as a pond or lake.

These actions are metaphors for the healing process. For example, fire burns away the hurt while the smoke rises in surrender, thanksgiving and as a peace offering to all creation. Water, in this process, signifies the hurt being washed away and the cleansing of one's consciousness.

Self-Forgiveness Writing Exercise Examples

- I forgive myself for allowing others to mistreat me.
- I forgive myself for not speaking up for myself.
- I forgive myself for procrastination.
- I forgive myself for making unwise financial decisions.
- I forgive myself for inappropriately expressing my anger.
- I forgive myself for judging others.
- I forgive myself for being impatient with the cashier.
- I forgive myself for forgetting that I am God's beloved child.

You can add your own forgiveness statements. Remember every act of omission or commission that causes you guilt, shame, anger, or resentment. This is a private exercise. Even in workshops it is kept private. You are the only person who sees what you write.

Forgiving Parents Writing Exercise Examples

- I forgive my parent(s) for telling me I would amount to nothing.

- I forgive my parent(s) for treating our pets better than they treated me.
- I forgive my parent(s) for not giving me adequate healthy food.
- I forgive my parent(s) for abusing me by [state how] and making me feel bad about myself.
- I forgive my parent(s) for not meeting their financial obligation to me.
- I forgive my parent(s) for all mistakes. I realize they did the best they could, as a result of their experiences, need for safety, expectations, and consciousness. They are God's beloved children and deserve only what is good for them.

Forgiving Others Writing Exercise Examples

- I forgive Jenny for always hitting me and making me feel sadness, pain, and shame.
- I forgive my classmates for bullying me and making me feel not good enough.
- I forgive my sister(s)/brother(s) for speaking untruths about me and causing me to be unfairly punished.
- I forgive my kindergarten classmates for not playing with me.
- I forgive my employer(s)/employee(s) for not being fair and causing hurt emotions, disappointment, loss in profits etc.
- I forgive Suzie for being selfish and not dependable.

Additional Exercises

The Empty Chair Process can be used when the person is being forgiven is absent. This can also be used to forgive someone who is no longer alive.

Materials needed for this exercise include two chairs of the same height. It is important to have chairs of the same height so that the mental image of the one forgiving and the one being forgiven is balanced. If available the picture of the person may be placed upright so that it is clearly visible in the chair.

After saying the prayers for guidance, sit in one of the chairs and face the empty chair or the chair with the picture. Close your eyes and take a slow deep breath. Imagine that the person you are forgiving is sitting in the chair. In your mind's eye, see yourself looking at him or her with compassion. See yourself making eye contact as you tell the person that you are grateful he or she is there with you. Explain how you feel and why (whatever the offense was). Tell him or her that you are willing to set both of you free from the effects of the harm done and from the guilt and the burden of nonforgiveness. Offer this person your forgiveness and see and hear them peacefully acknowledge and thank you. You may be led to "see" a pleasant and extended conversation form, or perhaps a brief one. See this encounter ending on a peaceful tone.

Prayer

This prayer is an example of one that can be used after forgiving oneself or others. This may be adapted to suit your unique situation.

Heavenly Father, in this moment of grace, I honor the integrity of my actions, which I know are guided by your sweet spirit within me. I release to you all tendencies to think and act in ways that are not of love. I embrace the truth that I am one with you and my fellow man; there is only one Spirit. As I forgive, I am forgiven. I thank you, Lord that through the healing power of forgiveness, I now walk with ease in peace and freedom. Through Christ's lessons on forgiveness and my willingness to accept your grace, God, I am free. I am no longer bound by mistakes of the past, and all negative effects are negated. I accept that today, bright with hope and filled with promise your gift of grace comes to me. I accept this grace now. For all these blessings, I say thank you Father, in the name of Jesus Christ.

Remember, nature abhors a vacuum; after forgiving self or other, it is wise to immediately fill the consciousness with the positives. This prevents any counteracting thoughts formed by the little negative ego from creeping back in. A prayer, treatment, affirmation, or denial such as the following can suffice.

Denial

No unforgiving thought can trouble me. I forgive, and I know that am forgiven.

Affirmation

Through forgiveness I free myself from the past. Anyone needing my forgiveness, I forgive. I release all wounds and bitterness to God. I now fully experience the peace that life offers.

Treatment

I forgive things past and present. All acts of commission or omission needing forgiveness, I forgive. I surrender the need to be a victim. I am willing to release anger and I do so now. I surrender to Jehovah any negative attachment to anyone or anything. I forgive myself and others, and all matters are resolved now and forevermore. I forgive, I forgive, and I forgive. Thank you, loving Jehovah, for this grace and wisdom to forgive.

Forgiving Our Parents

The fifth commandment requires us to honor our fathers and mothers. So many of us have had difficulties doing this, even if only initially. Most of us have had at least one, to say the least, disagreement or unfavorable interaction with them. I also include guardians who played the role of parents in this category as well.

In honoring our parents, forgiveness must often be a part of the process. This can be a very difficult feat because of the fact that the wound came from someone related to us. Childhood wounds go deep and can be the catalysts of what we believe about ourselves. Through our young childhood and adolescent years, there is an innate vulnerability in us that creates an openness and susceptibility. We mentally accept positive as well as negative messages. As mentioned in the beginning of this chapter, the resulting anger, resentment, and ill health that occurs because of not forgiving is not worth harboring.

Forgiving of our parents can be done as mentioned in the previous process. However, I believe an adult child should be on equal footing (mentally) with his or her parents. Some adults, who may also be parents, interact with their parents the way they did as children. It can be empowering to confront the parent in person, peacefully and confidently. The child whether an adult or not should let the parent know how he or she feels and why he or she feels that way (state the offense). A lot of patience will be required here; be prepared to wait for an answer if necessary. If no apology comes, you can ask for one. If both parents are to be forgiven, you can do this process with both of them or one at a time. Of course, do these processes separately if the offense and offender are separate (one parent). Each person is different, and this might result in a very big issue, or it might not. The ultimate goal is to let your parent(s) know that you are open for his, her, or their apology and to let your parent(s) know you have forgiven him, her, or them when you have done so.

This writing exercise can be completed whether you receive an apology from your parent(s) or not. Christ, our master teacher, forgave those who wounded him; he did not ask or wait for a reply. His mission was freedom for all, and so should be ours. We should not subject ourselves to further punishment by waiting for an apology before we decide to forgive.

In his book *The Ten Challenges*, Leonard Felder, PhD, (1997) advises the following process:

Get a picture of your parent; one from their childhood or young adulthood. Start a conversation with this young, vulnerable, curious, loving person. Ask what their fears and hopes are. Ask how it really was growing up with their parents and with the pressures and influences that made them into the adult you know them to be. If you don't know much about them, you may ask relatives or friends of theirs. During this exercise as you talk to the photo, sense warmth in your heart connecting to this person's innermost being.

This exercise can provide information and insight that can support the forgiving process. Many of our parents also carry the need to forgive their own parents or guardians for acts similar to the ones we need to forgive them for. Some parents were also abused as adolescents and some, even as adults. You may find that if you are a parent you may have wounded your child/children, either through acts of commission, omission or both.

The empty chair exercise can also be done as a process for forgiving parents. Also remember to adapt and say one of the aforementioned denials, prayers, or treatments. Honor yourself for this bold and loving step.

Asking for Forgiveness

The toll of waiting to be forgiven can be severe; guilt can trigger illness in our bodies and negativity in our lives. Shame often accompanies guilt, which compounds this negativity. The little personal ego can make asking for forgiveness a very difficult feat; in fact, it might reason, "I'm always right, I don't need to be forgiven." Beloveds, as we move forward in our transformation, we must embrace the Christ consciousness that empowers us to forgive ourselves, until we know no joy in erring. It is always better to ask for forgiveness sooner than later; the offender eases his or her guilt quicker, while the offended can begin to heal quicker. This is a win-win situation.

Process

As in any forgiveness process, you must begin with prayer. This holy activity should be spiritually guided. You must scan your memory to clearly remember and understand your actions and what transpired. This can also prevent inaccuracies and further hurt. Of very high importance is that one must be clear of the safest, most lawful, and most honorable way to make contact with the one(s) offended. Situations are different; you might be asking forgiveness of someone who lives in the same home or halfway around the world. You can make contact in person or through some other means (e.g., letter, phone, Skype, etc.).

Upon making contact with the person(s) who was offended, you should state the reason for this contact (to ask forgiveness). Next say why by clearly stating the offense. It would not be very healing to say, "I apologize for hurting you." That is too vague. It would be more healing to say, "I apologize for hitting and insulting you in public, causing you to feel pain and shame." This way, the person(s) who was offended hears and feels that you (the offender) have really thought about your actions and the wound you caused. You can add how you feel; for example, "I feel sad, angry, and ashamed that I allowed myself to be in that state of fear and hate."

If this is an in-person meeting with genuine facial expressions, you can now ask, "How are you doing or feeling?" When there is a response, listen intentionally, make eye contact, and refrain from defensiveness. **Remember, the little personal ego might have begun to scream, so focus on the goal of asking for forgiveness**. There may or may not be a conversation. If there is one, you can ask for forgiveness and even suggest reasonable ways to make restitution or at least support the healing process. If this is accepted, you must fulfill all promises in true repentance. If there is no indication of forgiveness, you can express gratitude to the other person for listening, for being there, or for whatever way he or she participated. You should not lose hope, because this encounter may be the start of the forgiving and healing process. Whether you feel, believe, or know you were forgiven or not, you must forgive yourself and allow a feeling of loving kindness to wash over you. True forgiveness can only be accomplished when our consciousness is one of true repentance. In this case, you can honor yourself for taking this bold and loving step.

Forgiveness—Help Along the Way

When we forgive in a spirit of willingness, the universe always conspires to help us, sometimes in ways that would cause us to rebel. We might be willing; however, we may continue to hold on to some remnants of the grudge. We are usually gently tapped on the shoulder and made aware in ways that align with our own consciousness. For clarity, I have chosen to share how it once worked for me.

Someone (I'll call her Jane) once caused me to feel terribly hurt; to crown it all, her apology was, "That was messed up." No part of that comment indicated that she had committed the act that caused me pain. I forgave her but still felt a twinge of resentment. She seemed to show up more often, always "bugged" me, (as I saw it) asked for favors, and was excited to see me since I would grant the favors. I would often think, "*She has some nerve being glad to see me and to hug me."* I felt like the prodigal brother, but I was the prodigal father, throwing the feast for her.

When I began to embrace forgiveness as a spiritual practice, I became aware that I had not fully forgiven her. Whenever I saw her or heard her voice, I experienced a subtle jolt in my stomach area, or my heart rate would change. Flight-or-fight responses were triggered as my body sensed danger. Whenever I had truly forgiven someone, the opposite response was evident; I felt no emotional charge. When I encountered a person I forgave, memories of the incident were brief or would not surface at all. There was no alarming bodily response, and I was happy to see that person. I would feel peace. In the scheme of things, this is a tremendous difference!

In this instance, when it was most difficult to forgive (Jane), she showed up in my life the most often. I believe that was the universe's way of making me aware of my commitment to forgive. Once I forgave her, she showed up less and I felt ease when I would see her. Beloveds, just allow the Spirit of forgiveness to lead you. This is one of the most sacred and exonerating things we do for ourselves and this planet. Always rely on Almighty God's help to bring this mystical event to pass.

The Ego's Challenge

We must watch for the little ego. It likes to maintain drama. This ego directs that you must talk about the hurts over and over again. Blaming and shaming are its modes of operation. Remember that forgiveness is a direct threat to the little ego because it means this ego will have to stop projecting and wearing the victim's hat for protection. Never give the little ego any place in the forgiving process, or the process will not be authentic. True forgiveness should originate from the place of unconditional love within you. Know that God loves you

and the person who wronged you just the same. Honor yourself for your willingness to surrender harm for freedom, peace, and joy. Stop retelling the story in the same way. Tell it in a way that demonstrates how forgiveness through grace offers freedom and upholds the divinity of mankind. Forgiveness is your key to freedom. Use it now!

Racial Healing

We live in a world in which we see far too many instances of "otherness." Although humans continue to evolve spiritually, much work needs to be done in support of creating racial and ethnic unity. Jesus Christ's Sermon on the Mount and St. Paul's teachings embraced brotherly love. Dr. Martin Luther King Jr., Mahatma Gandhi, Archbishop Desmond Tutu, President Nelson Mandella as well as more recent teachers focused on peace through forgiveness.

The legacy of atrocities across the world requires much to be forgiven. The catalyst for these atrocities is often formed by what we believe about the differences of other people. We often rely on someone's outer appearance, religious or spiritual affiliation, race, ethnicity, etc., to determine if he or she is good enough or worthy enough for anything good or if he or she deserves our respect and friendship. The atrocities of slavery, the Holocaust, the mistreatment of the Native Americans, wars, and ethnic cleansings and so many other atrocities worldwide have caused deep emotional wounds to generations of people. Today, many of us stand with the need to forgive and be forgiven.

The fact that slavery and its scourges were allowed to happen worldwide for centuries left a raw wound in the psyche of so many. The visible wounds on many slave's backs paled in comparison to the scars in their psyches. The visible shackles were removed, but for many people the mental and emotional shackles remain.

Physical healing was possible at times; however, psychic wounds require radical love, spiritual work and care. Regardless of our race, ethnicity, or class, we can all be healed from the effect of these ills; **when one person is wounded, the whole human race is wounded**. The fact that I got teary writing this paragraph today, lets me know that I, like others, carry some cellular memories. **There is only One Spirit that dwells in us all.**

A Voice in the Silence

While in the silence, the following exercise was revealed to me as a tool for healing. I caution you that this exercise is profound. If you, my beloveds, do not feel that you are emotionally stable enough or if you have anger issues, please skip this exercise. Please also note that each exercise in this book is not appropriate for everyone. The following exercise is suitable for people whose ancestors lived in places that currently have or once had cotton and sugar plantations or other place requiring slave labor. Feel free to recreate the place where your loved ones were harmed.

Process (Scene I)

[Take three deep cleansing breaths. Close your eyes and become still and relaxed. Imagine being on a cotton plantation.] You are an observer and not involved with the slave trade. You observe a pregnant slave who appears to be in her third trimester of pregnancy. She seems ill or tired but is working slowly and steadily. A man with a whip comes up to her and reprimands her for working slowly. She looks up at him sadly and seems unable to work faster. He makes her walk about forty yards to a spot with a large rut or indentation. While walking toward it, he follows close behind, yelling for her to walk faster; she does not. Once they arrive at the rut, he makes her lie face down with her large abdomen in the rut, which is large enough to fit it. This man, who supervises workers in this area, then lashes her with the whip across her back. He seems to muster up all his strength, yelling at her after each lash. She screams weakly. He leaves.

[Breathe. Keep your eyes closed.] Whether you feel anger or sadness, bend over and offer to help her. She very slowly mutters, "There is a God" and then softly says, "Yes, please." She is crying and trembling and seems weak as you helped her up. You tell her that you saw what happened and that you feel very sad because she was treated so cruelly and disrespectfully. You hold her by the arm and begin to walk with her to her cabin, which takes about ten minutes. She leans on you, so you hook your arm under her arm to offer more physical support. She thanks you. (Breathe in and out, whisper, "Peace be still," to your emotions. Stay with your emotions for several minutes and keep the image in your mind.) Continue to say "peace be still" to your emotions.

Once you both get to the cabin, you help her by cleaning, applying salve to, and bandaging her terribly bruised and bleeding back. You wonder about the baby she is carrying. You pray with her and ask her to forgive while offering words of love and comfort. You bid her farewell as it is unlawful for you to stay.

(Breathe in and out "Peace, be still" through your emotions.)

Process (Scene II)

As you walk across the cotton plantation to leave, you notice a commotion and a crowd of about sixty people. Once again, you are a silent observer. Upon investigation you notice a slave auction occurring. A slave couple with their son, who is about eight, and their daughter, who is about age six, are being auctioned off. They all seemed in shock, staring with wide eyes at everyone and every move the people around them make. You see tears in the eyes of the mother and the children. They all seem nervous. This father trembles, perhaps with fear, anger or both, as slave traders examine his nearly naked body. There are no tears in the father's eyes, and you wonder if he has detached emotionally just to ease the pain of eventual separation. You feel angry, helpless, and sad all at once.

(Breathe in the thought," Peace be still" for several minutes. Stay with your emotion and keep the image in your mind.) You look at them individually as you hold in your mind a prayer for their protection.

Each family member was bought by a different trader. Each goes to a different state, with tears of sadness. The father begins to cry. (Breathe. "Peace, be still to your emotions" through several breaths.) You wonder if they will ever see, hear, smell, touch, or embrace each other again. You wonder whether any of them can survive physically or emotionally. (Breathe. Peace, be still through your emotions.)

The previous exercise exposes one to anger provoking thoughts while using healing statements. This helps to nullify the sting of the emotional wound and to reduce the need for anger, revenge, or holding grudges. It promotes healing and forgiveness as well; future thoughts of this travesty will eventually lose their emotional charge. The emotional charge is what triggers more anger, hormone fluctuation and subsequently illnesses.

Healing for People of various Ethnicities

I chose to use a slave plantation scene in the exercise above because when looking at the ill effects of past atrocities, the effects of the travesty of slavery in my view are more pronounced. These patterns can be adapted to suit other ills that have occurred.

There are people of various ethnicities and nationalities that stand in the need of healing from the effects of generational wounds as well.

When doing their forgiveness rituals, Native Americans could change the scenes to depict being chased off their land, being brutally attacked, losing their land, food, and livestock, or having their children taken and made to live outside their native culture. Jewish persons could reflect the atrocities of the Holocaust, family members being killed or taken away, the blatant starvation, and the degrading camps. They could reflect on the gas chambers and fears of not knowing their fate.

Other groups of people can reflect on ethnic cleansing, such as the atrocities seen in Rwanda and other places in our world. Some people can reflect on the devastation of terrorism and the fear it engenders. Most of us can reflect on some degree of direct or indirect experience with racism, sexism, or discrimination on the basis of skin color, religion, faith, hair texture, ethnicity, or any other perceived difference.

Exercise—Forgiveness for Slavery

Write a letter to your ancestors who were enslaved. This letter serves to acknowledge their love, power, strength, and sacrifice. It also serves to help you focus on the blessings and gifts their sacrifices brought to this world, as well as the ways you can use their experiences to support your well-being and spiritual evolution. Different families have different stories; you may incorporate your own familial stories into your letter. The following is an example:

> My beloved ancestors,
>
> I salute the divinity in you. I greet you in the name of the love that you are. There is so much I have to say to you. My earnest desire is that you hear these words; I believe that in spirit you hear, as we have a part of each other in our beings!
>
> I acknowledge that you were forcefully torn away from your native land of Africa, and your families were disrupted in an instant. You were transported to different parts of the world in the most inhumane way. During the slow and brutal transatlantic journey, you were denied a decent way to find

physical ease and elimination of your body's waste when nature demanded it. Instead, you lay stacked in hatches like sardines amid the cold, heat, and stench. Sadly, some of you thought it best to throw yourselves or your children overboard to the hungry seas. You must have been terrified, sad, lonely, sick, hungry, thirsty, weak, and afraid. The universe saw. Let's forgive now.

When you landed on new shores, you landed with love and sadness in your heart. This love you eventually learned to share in humble services; you were not always willing. You may have rebelled, but what a sacrifice you made. Shackled, oiled, and waiting to be bought, you stood like lambs going to the slaughter. The universe saw. Let's forgive now!

Once you were bought, you were stripped of your names and what seemed like your dignity. You were forbidden to practice spiritually, read, write, and congregate with others. You were separated from those who spoke the same languages as you. Oh, how lonely you must have been! Some of you had your lives taken from you through injustices. The universe saw. Let's forgive now!

Strangely, your strength and gentle ways caused you to be seen as beastlike, less than human. Amid your difficulties, you learned to sing, dance, pray, and dream of freedom. What strength! Some of you secretly learned to read and write; you were so determined! The universe responded to you, let's forgive now!

My beloved ancestors, I now join with you through the one Spirit of God that is omnipresent and dwells within us. I join you in this freeing act of forgiveness:

> All who captured you, I forgive.

> All who sold you, I forgive.

All who bought you, I forgive.

All who bruised your bodies, I forgive.

All who took your children, I forgive.

All who stripped you of your names, I forgive.

All who raped you, I forgive.

All who killed you, I forgive.

All who gave you unhealthy scraps of meat to eat, I forgive.

All who couldn't acknowledge your humanity, I forgive.

All who couldn't see your beauty and divinity, I forgive.

All who could not find a place inside themselves to love you, I forgive.

I forgive all hurts and surrender all anger, resentment, and thoughts of retribution or malice. I am free from the baggage of nonforgiveness. I realize that all who participated in enslaving and mistreating you were not acting from a consciousness of love and oneness. They were acting from a consciousness of fear and separateness, believing that it was the best way to survive. I forgive them now.

Exercise—A Letter to My Brothers and Sisters

My intention in including this sample of a letter is another way to inspire an awareness of the issues that must be healed. Guilt can be a burden that takes a toll on the human psyche. In order to maintain slavery and not feel guilt, the general trend of slave traders or owners was to dehumanize the slaves. They saw them as less than humans and this made it easier to oppress and mistreat them. Centuries of oppression caused the slaves and their descendants to see themselves as victims who are lesser than their masters and those who had similar features. Slaves were often sold without warning and often sent away, leaving their family members behind. I believed that some male slaves learnt not to become emotionally attached to their families; unexpected separation would be too difficult to endure and their response may have had tragic consequences. Information gathered through research, revealed that a male slave reportedly said that he would never marry, because if the master puts his hands on his (the slave's) wife the result would be terrible. I believe that these beliefs and actions of non- commitment by some male slaves became their defense mechanisms, which subsequently and over time, manifested as generational patterns that must be healed.

My beloved brothers and sisters,

You are the descendants of people who in their determination made sacrifices so that freedom would flow fully for all people. **We are now free to...**

- Get out of the box of victimhood.
- Surrender anger, hatred, blaming and shaming.
- Shake off the shackles of learned helplessness, live in opulence and live and die with dignity.
- See past the outer appearance of ourselves and others, knowing that only what is not visible is eternal.
- Put on the armor of brotherly love through service to all people.
- Exercise our rights to equal education and become wise as serpents and harmless as doves.
- Hold the highest political office that any human being can.
- Exercise our right and freedom to a spiritual practice that is the path to our transformation.
- Stand firm and allow God's will to be done through us, for us, and by us.
- Support and keep our families intact.
- Always be in a state of love and gratitude...and expect and accept our good.

My brothers, you are free to emotionally embrace your children. The threat of you suddenly being removed from them is gone. Surrender this unconscious defense, this learned dysfunctional pattern that shows up as you abandoning your offspring. Ask for forgiveness, forgive yourself, and make amends. If this has not been your pattern, pray for those you know have done so. Forgive them now.

My beloved sisters, please realize now, that as a magnificent creation of God, you are never more or less valuable based on how many children you bore or not; whether you are married or single, rich or poor, feel broken or not. You are always more and never less! Be gentle in your natural beauty, strength, wisdom and power; use them for the betterment of yourself and all others.

My brothers and sisters, you must love yourselves so that you can willingly love others. Love is the door to everything that is good. Listen to your thoughts; attend to your deepest needs. **Often affirm, "I am love, I love, and I am loved. I am forgiving and forgiven. I am respectful and respected. I am joy, I spread joy and I am joyful."** Doing this in front of a mirror is empowering and fun. Be worthy of all that is good; you came from blood lines of Kings and Queens! Dare to show up in this world with love, wisdom, compassion, power, courage, and authority! Always be in a state of gratitude. The Universe beckons! Are you willing?

Exercise—Asking Forgiveness for Our Ancestors

Having had the privileges of both participating in workshops and carrying workshops, I have witnessed various noble actions in the process. There is one process that, if undertaken, must be done with wisdom so that someone does not internalize unnecessary ownership of someone else's misdeeds.

Anyone who knows or believes that their ancestors took part in any of the above atrocities or even more recent discriminatory practices has no reason to take on personal or conscious guilt, because they had no direct part to play. However, when one truly regrets that these atrocities occurred and feels remorse, he or she can do the following:

1. Begin with a prayer for guidance.

2. Pray for the ancestor's forgiveness.

3. Write a letter expressing love to them. (If they are alive and it is possible for them to understand and participate you can complete this process in person.) Let them know that you are forgiving them. State your regrets that they made those errors. Forgive them for acting with a consciousness of fear and hate. Tell them that you can only imagine how heavy their loads of guilt and shame were. Tell them you are sorry if they had no feelings of love and that it was a sign of a very unhealthy personal ego. Assure them of your love and say that you now offer them forgiveness. Ask them to please accept your forgiveness. Imagine that they accepted your forgiveness. Ask them to please forgive themselves. Imagine that they have. Thank them for undertaking a freeing and loving act of accepting forgiveness and forgiving themselves. Promise them that you will, as a mark of your gratitude to them, be a kinder, gentler, and more loving person.

4. Keep your consciousness raised high. Abstain from thoughts, words, or actions that do not demonstrate love, kindness, or compassion.

5. Remember that forgiveness builds character. Take a stand for love and justice and never falter. You can put an end to any generational shadow effect such as hatred, guilt, shame etc.

6. Beloveds, feel free to create forgiveness exercises from family stories, history books, etc. I can still remember when I was an adolescent in history class, reading about the transatlantic passage of the slave trade. I was appalled when I learned that those captured and shackled had no bathroom breaks for weeks. They lay stacked in hatches amid the stench of human waste. I also read Lois Lowry's book *Number the Stars* which told of the difficulties the Jews suffered at the hands of the Nazis. I cried as I read how the mother in the story was slapped across the face. Books on the plight of the Native Americans brought me sadness as well, as did stories of wars, ethnic cleansing, and other crises. These books are great to read because they can set the tone for deep forgiveness work.

We must go deep if we want to experience significant healing. It may appear that we are only forgiving our ancestors; however, we are relieving ourselves of the ancestral baggage that is etched deep into our spiritual DNA. This baggage shows up through generations as negative family patterns. We who now have this technique can work on behalf of our loved ones. There are no mistakes in God or with God. If you are reading this, get quiet and assess what work you must do! **We must also be careful not to dwell on old issues once we have unearthed and forgiven them.**

If you are tempted to feel damaged, remember that you are a perfect spiritual being. We heal the effects these issues have on us through prayer, counseling, journaling, forgiveness; going to school, serving others according to God's will and building up our lives. We do whatever it takes to lift us above mediocrity, learned helplessness, lack of self-worth, anger or whatever the negative state may be. We then move forward as wiser and more compassionate beings. When we retell the stories, we must now tell them differently. Tell them in the way that demonstrates how the constant grace of God works through forgiveness. When we instill in ourselves and in our children the ideas that these atrocities must never occur again, we align ourselves with agape love. The universe rejoices!

The following treatment can be used for support as one does the loving work of surrendering old issues.

Treatment

I allow the shining sun of Truth to shine in my consciousness revealing to me God's idea of who I am. I choose to surrender any false ideas that hold me bound. I know that I am born of the spirit. I show up in this world as a free being, daily demonstrating dominion in my affairs. I refuse to function at the level of problems and instead function with wisdom and love at the level of perfect answers. I am a vital participant of life and I participate with love, wisdom, power and authority. I identify myself as the perfect and worthy child of Jehovah Jireh and I stand tall in my Divinity. This is so and it cannot be otherwise.

Treatment

I am grateful! Today I realize my perfection. I know that God's kingdom is within me. I speak my words from this truth, knowing that Divine wisdom flows through me. I use my words of wisdom, with power and authority. I command every false idea to depart from my consciousness and I stand firmly in my greatness. Every cell, organ and function of my body vibrates with the Divine life of God. My mood is colored with joy. Divine Love fills me, loves me and moves through me to all creation. All is well; I gratefully allow this to be so and so it is.

Do all in your power of decision to heal your consciousness of past harm, old hurts and worn stories. You can marginalize or expand your wellbeing by what you accept about yourself. Make room for the gentle healing breeze of freshness, elegance and wholeness in your life. Dare to be blessed in every way!

Chapter 9

Faith

"For assuredly, I say to you, if you have faith as a mustard seed, you will say to this mountain 'Move from here to there,' and it will move; and nothing will be impossible for you (Matt. 17:20).

"And he said to her, Daughter, be of good cheer; your faith has made you well. Go in peace" (Luke 8:48).

Our faith is a life-giving force to our prayer practice. A lack of faith blocks our prayers from being answered. On this dawning of our universal shift in consciousness, the worn-out mindset of fear and doubt must also be transformed. In order for us to experience the working of spiritual laws in our lives, our minds must rest on a foundation of faith. Spiritual laws such as the laws of attraction, cause and effect, love, faith, forgiveness, and thanksgiving, etc., are the connecting spokes to the hub on the wheel of Affirmative prayer. Affirmative prayer is also called effectual prayer as well as Spiritual Mind treatment. Faith balances the act of prayer as we make demands on universal substance; whatever is unbalanced cannot stand firm.

According to the law of Mind Action, things in our experience become real to us according to our recognition and acceptance of them. This recognition and acceptance is an active faith, a declaration of the evidence of things not yet seen. As we pray, making our requests known to our creator, we are admonished to have faith; faith has creative energy that brings the formless into form. When faith is developed, it too can be a great harmonizer. Faith supports our confidence in the "big picture," which stimulates I-can-do-it thinking. This is then transformed by asking, "How can I get this done? What do I have that can help me achieve this? Who do I need to call for support?" That person then reaches out and in the process opens up the self to receive while at the same time stimulating someone or something to open up and give. The person, who becomes aware of the effects of faith, is more likely to understand that every person is equally capable of manifesting his or her desires. Another realization is that there is no need to struggle or compete. This awareness creates harmony among people.

Brother Mandus, in his book *The Grain of Mustard Seed* (1959), reports,

> *In January 1959, a British Sunday newspaper published the results of a controlled experiment conducted by American scientists. The scientists sowed lima beans in two pans under the exact conditions. They prayed for only one set of beans. Conditions were same soil, same care given to all the seeds, and they had the same time to grow. The beans that were prayed for grew 15 inches. The beans which were not prayed for did not break through the soil.*

Their prayers were done with the belief that there would be a difference between the beans that were prayed for and the beans that were not prayed for. These scientists proved the law of faith, which has existed since creation.

Researchers have also discovered that there is a greater correlation between expectation and performance than between IQ and achievement. The key determining factor is the belief or faith. Educational research supports the findings of the correlation between teacher expectation and student performance. Belief is the precursor to performance. This supports the understanding that when we desire the transformation of any situation or circumstance, the work based in faith must begin in the mind. Our believing minds must be on the same frequency as our giving God. This can only be accomplished through faith in the goodness of God, who seeks only to bring us good.

Spiritual doctrine and science do not deviate from the principle that was taught in the gospel: **"Whatsoever things ye desire when ye pray, believe that ye receive them, and ye shall have them"** (Mark 11:24). Christ, the master teacher, taught that when we ask, we are to believe we have already received the fulfillment of our desires. He taught that faith the size of a mustard seed can move mountains. Of course, this means that it requires a small amount of faith to remove a great deal of adversity, difficulty, or challenge. Some people have interpreted the word *mountain* in its literal sense. As a result, they have difficulty believing the validity of things of a spiritual nature.

Christ's Ministry of Faith

The examination of the ministry of Christ reveals that faith was required before he performed miracles. When healing was sought, he would often ask the one seeking healing or an intercessor for someone else, "Do you believe?" When the answer was the affirmative, healing occurred.

We can use the power of faith to create whatever is ours by divine right. Christ understood this; before he healed the man with the withered hand, he told him to stretch out his hand. In an act of faith, this man stretched out his hand and was healed. In a biblical account, Jesus Christ's friend Lazarus died. Jesus was also a friend to Lazarus's sisters, Mary and Martha; he loved all three. Four days after Lazarus died, Jesus learned of the death, and he became sorrowful. Mary expressed her faith by telling Jesus that if he had been there, Lazarus would not have died. Jesus, the man of faith, went about his Heavenly Father's business of resurrecting Lazarus. In yet another profound use of spiritual laws that served to teach mankind, Jesus commanded that the stone covering the entrance of Lazarus's tomb be taken away. He then lifted his eyes (and his consciousness above the level of the sorrow) and said, "Father, I thank you that you have heard me. And I know that you always hear me." He then used the power in his faith-filled words and loudly cried, "Lazarus, come forth!" Lazarus regained life in his body. Then Jesus directed that they remove the grave clothes and set him free.

With faith, we can also call on Christ's resurrecting power to resurrect us from vicissitudes, whether they are issues with relationships, work, parenting, health or other challenges. We can command the stone of fear and doubt to be moved out of our experience so that our courageous self can come forward. The faith that Christ taught is a radical and practical faith. As mentioned earlier, Jesus once mixed clay with spittle (saliva) and placed it on a blind man's eyes. As a result, the man began to see. Regardless of the situation, Christ demonstrated faith. More recent spiritual teachers emphasize faith based spirituality as well. New thought teacher and Science of Mind founder Ernest Holmes wrote in his book, *This Thing Called You*, that one of the greatest adventures in life is our conscious use of the power of faith (1948). Of course, it can be an adventure as we enter the caves of our minds and unearth the treasures that were always there! Practical faith is attainable by anyone who persistently seeks to develop it. We know God meets us at whatever level of consciousness we are on. However, this is not to say that we should stagnate at a shallow level of faith. **We must always reach for a higher level of faith and refuse to exist by default**. Through faith, we can surrender any limitations, guilt, feelings of being not good enough and even feelings of being better than.

Developing Faith

The **first step** in developing our faith is to remember that we are all created in the spiritual image and likeness of God. The **second step** is to accept that God loves us unconditionally and is always seeking to bring good into our lives. The **third step** is to accept that as creations of God, it is our divine right to inherit the goodness of God. This goodness is a gift to all humanity; God does not play favorites! Realizing our worthiness motivates us to take positive action on our own behalf as we begin and continue the work of faith.

The act of daily prayer and meditation also supports the increase and strengthening of our faith. Adverse situations in life are more difficult to overcome when we have not sufficiently increased our faith through prayer. Faith inspires us to call on other spiritual principles, such as freedom, wisdom, strength, will, enthusiasm, joy, courage, and authority. Oh, how the Spirit awaits or demands! Using the above mentioned principles, adds wings to our prayer practice.

When Paul addressed the Romans, he said, **"Faith comes by hearing, and hearing by the word of God" (Rom 10:17). For example, while reading the scripture; one encounters many promises of goodness meant to persistently improve the human condition. It is fruitful to audibly and confidently read and repeat promises such as, "I can do all things through Christ... " Or "With God all things are possible." One can repeat with faith the words the Psalmist David affirmed: "The Lord is my shepherd, I shall not want" (Ps. 23:1) and "I will lift up my eyes to the hills from whence comes my help" (Ps. 121:1). Those are also affirmative statements!** There are many books of wisdom by authors who powerfully support the evolution of faith in humanity. Attending workshops, seminars, and classes and listening to ministers, spiritual practitioners, and other teachers can also offer a vital boost to our faith. **Remember, the universe is always responding to us. When the student is ready the**

teacher will appear; when the teacher is ready the student will also appear!

Since God can only work for us, through us, we must allow ourselves to be suitable channels through a willingness to believe that with God all things are possible. As a signature of our faith, we must deliberately and confidently say our prayers, denials, affirmations, and treatments, etc. This will further strengthen our faith. We must also have a firm knowing or acceptance that it is done to us as we believe. This knowing, when it is the authentic state of our consciousness, seals our renewed faith.

Acts of Faith

We read in the Scripture that **"faith without works is dead"** (James 2:20, 26.) To fully embrace faith, work is required in the invisible realm within our minds as well as in the visible physical realm. Faith without works is dead, as written in the Scripture. Christ demonstrated this holistic way of manifestation. Our outward acts must be in alignment with our inner lives and intentions. For example, a person seeking a spouse or a mate may pray, used denials and maintain a firm, quiet knowing that their desire is already fulfilled even though he or she may not have yet met this person. This would be his or her inner work. The outer work might be asking friends to introduce them to someone, grooming, or visiting places where a particular person with particular qualities might frequent. More recently, people are joining Internet dating sites. In terms of quantity, this is similar to "casting the net on the right side!" Someone who prayed and affirmed for a job may follow up by preparing for an interview, preparing for required tests, learning about the particular field, and getting appropriate clothing for the interview. A person who prayed for health and said a treatment may follow up by caring for his or her body, eating healthily, exercising, and meditating. These actions give a true balance to our faith because as a declaration of our intentions and faith, and apart from believing, **our outer actions must support what we believe and must align with the creation and manifestation of the desire.**

Challenges to Our Faith

As humans, we are thinking beings. **Our thoughts, which are living things, affect every aspect of our lives. We think the thoughts, which then become programmed into our subconscious minds. Our subconscious mind dictate our state of affairs because it stores the thoughts we feed it. It then impels us to act according to the thoughts we feed it, whether these thoughts are positive or negative.** Our subconscious mind does not discriminate. We each must think for ourselves. Throughout the day, we are bombarded with many negative and some positive discussions in the media, such as television, computers, phones, radio, newspapers, magazines, etc. Negative chatter can wreak havoc in our minds if we allow it. This causes us to habitually act from a base of fear instead of faith.

The personal ego tells us that all is not well, and more often than not, we believe the lies. This personal ego is that mindset or inner voice that works tirelessly to convince us that we are not good enough and that there is not enough for us and asks, "What if you fail?" This ego, which thrives on fear, becomes excited with negativity and drama and habitually spreads it to others. It likes to remind us of e.g. past failures and the put-downs we received from parents, siblings, relatives, peers, or other significant people in our lives, and we often listen. We let the little ego dictate our destinies and beat our voices down to whispers. We may have experienced and listened to negativity since our childhood so often that it has developed a stronghold in our consciousness.

On any given day, if our faith is not firm, negative beliefs can dominate our thoughts. This causes our experiences to reflect this negativity. It is said that our routine thoughts and actions are controlled by a miniscule 5 percent of our conscious minds and by a whopping 95 percent of our subconscious mind. The subconscious mind forms the seat of our conditioning. When it seems we cannot develop faith or our faith wanes or is weak, it can be the result of our unconscious resistance to the positive. This resistance is formed in the subconscious level of our minds and, again, by the information we think into it.

The fact that you are reading this book is an indication that you desire and deserve to live according to the glorious way you were created to live—with authority and dominion over your circumstances. You are asked to have faith in this authority, which is your divine birthright. You must believe that the law of faith acts upon your words when you speak them with conviction. In the Scripture we read, *"So shall my word be that goeth forth from my mouth; It shall not return to me void, but it shall accomplish what I please, and it shall prosper in the thing for which I send it" (Isa. 55:11).* Beloved, this is for everyone! This truth is for anyone who has the consciousness and does the outer works of faith, supporting their belief and words.

The following prayer and exercises can be used as practices for strengthening one's faith. When we desire something tangible, we do the inner and outer works. When we desire understanding or faith (i.e., that which is not tangible), we must do the same. Prayer, meditation, visualizing and keeping our thoughts in a wholesome state can be the inner works, while affirming, denials, reading, seeking a job etc. can be the outer works. **We begin the process of increasing faith with a prayer of surrender. At this time, we ask God to help our unbelief or strengthen our belief**. We then cooperate with God's Spirit within us by allowing ourselves to be fully tuned in and receptive as we listen. As a result, we are reawakened to grace, which inspires us to believe. **Grace is always unfolding in our lives; however, a lack of faith is the very thing that obscures it from us.**

As demonstrated by the following prayer, it can be empowering when we approach God as our loving Father, open up to him verbally and tell him of all our cares; also when we thank him for what we already have and for even more, which must become tangible at the divinely appointed time.

A Prayer to Support the Development of Faith

Almighty Father, your Spirit dwells within me; yet here am I, seeking to increase my faith. I am aware that my well-being is limited according to my belief. I ask that you help me to fully embrace the truth so that through faith I can overcome all ills. Let me feel the presence of faith rising in me. With this faith, I shake off the burden of doubt and embrace my freedom now. I ask this in the name of Jesus Christ, who showed us how faith works. Dear God, I thank you for this blessing of faith. I joyfully let it be so, and so it is now and forevermore.

Affirmations and Other Practices for Developing and Strengthening Faith

Affirming is a very powerful practice for strengthening faith because it is in alignment with the process of creation; God spoke affirmative words that created. We too must use our power-packed words of affirmation to create our circumstances. What infuses power into our words? We know it is certainly not force or the volume of our voices. It is simply our beliefs, our intentions, and the condition of our consciousness. When these three things are based in agape love, they set the law of attraction in motion to bring to us what is best for us. At creation, mankind was given naming power. Jehovah God gave Adam, the first man, the authority to name the animals, and he did so. Today, we can name and call forth the circumstances we desire through affirmation and affirmative prayer.

See the earlier section on affirmations, denials, and treatments in chapter 3 for a full understanding of how to create your own. The following are more examples of affirmations, denials, treatments, and other practices that support faith.

Affirmations

- Today, I surrender thoughts of doubt and fear. I open myself to divine wisdom and the blessings of grace.
- God is the source of my supply. All my needs are met on divine time and in divine order.
- As I write this exam, I allow the Spirit of God within me to think through me. Having prepared, I expect and accept success. I am calm, and all is well.
- Divine life flows through my body now. All the cells in my body vibrate with wholeness, and I am whole and well.
- I am always safe and protected in this world.
- My place of work is a haven of peace and joy. I see the Christ in everyone there.
- I face every experience with confidence, knowing that the Great I AM governs all levels of my being.

Denials

- There are no blocks to the work of the Spirit. I freely invite and allow my blessings.
- No, I do not accept this diagnosis. There is no sickness in my body. I am well and whole. I follow guidance from the Healing Christ's Spirit in me.
- I do not accept any evidence of strife. My life and affairs are enmeshed in peace.

Treatments

- I forgive myself for not having a strong faith until today. I will no longer allow my faith to waiver and be swayed by the winds of change. I fill my mind with the truth that God's grace is my sufficiency. I believe that my Heavenly Father loves me and is always with me. I allow myself to move forward with trust as I take the next most appropriate steps to create a life of love, service, dignity, and happiness. I am grateful for the courage to do so. All is well.

• I totally and willingly rely on God's wisdom to guide me. I now begin to see my world through clearer eyes—through the eyes of Spirit! I dismantle all mental obstacles and no longer give them power. With God, all things are possible. So with God, I overcome now. I give thanks that Almighty God is always closer to me than my own heartbeat. On his presence I rely. In joy and gratitude, I allow myself to accept the support of God's presence, now and always.

Visualization and Faith

The practice of "acting as if" we have accomplished what we have set out to do builds faith. It helps us focus on the desired result and set the law of attraction in motion on our behalf. We can also do this through visualization. When we "act as if" through visualization, we hold an image of the desired demonstration in our mind's eye. (See the section on visualization and the law of attraction for an understanding of how these principles work.)

We must keep, asking, seeking, and knocking: *"Ask and it will be given to you; seek and you will find; knock and it will be opened to you; for everyone who asks receives, and he who seeks finds, and to him who knocks it will be opened" (Matt 7:7–8).*

We are all invited to ask, seek, and knock; no one is excluded. We do this through our faith-filled prayers. We ought to put our doubting thoughts outside. When Christ, the master teacher, came to a certain ruler's house, the flute players and mourners were already at work mourning the ruler's dead daughter. Jesus told them to make room for the girl because she was only sleeping. After the onlookers ridiculed Jesus, he put them out and took the girl by her hand, and she arose. At times the scoffers and doubters are our own thoughts. Like the Christ did, we are to *put them out!* We must put them out of our minds, and like Christ we must place our hands on what we want. Whether it is love, peace, a job, a financial strategy, family/relationship issues, health, education, the end of an addiction, issues with our children, a parking spot or any other issue down to its minutest detail, we can place our hands of faith on it. In this way we can bring to life the manifestation of our desires.

When we embrace the truth that nothing good is withheld from us, we are more likely to act with faith. The whisper of God moves through our burning desires, loving us into compliance. When with faith we allow the dream to be birthed through us, we find and embrace an unquenchable joy!

Chapter 10

Thanksgiving

"Be anxious for nothing in everything in prayer and supplication, with thanksgiving, let your requests be made known to God" (Phil. 4:6).

"Then they took away the stone from the place where the dead man was lying, and Jesus lifted up his eyes and said, 'Father, I thank you that you have heard me. And I know that you always hear me ..." (John 11:41–42).

"Enter into his gates with thanksgiving, and into his courts with praise, be thankful to him and bless his name" (Ps. 100:4).

"In everything give thanks; for this is the will of God in Christ Jesus for you." (Thess. 5:18).

During Christ's ministry, he demonstrated that the prayer of thanksgiving is an infallible practice that paves the way for answered prayers. When he exclaimed at the graveside of Lazarus, *"Father, I thank You that You have heard Me. And I know that You always hear me," (John* 11: 41-42), he was indeed thanking and praising God for his unending and constant mercy. The saying that whatever we praise, we raise, holds true. Here, the word *raise* means to bring forth or to increase. We ought also to pray with thanksgiving and praise. In Affirmative prayers, we understand that once we have prayed about a situation, we must release it to God. We are also told to pray without ceasing. This may sound like a contradiction because we often hear "pray then leave it to God" however, we must continue to pray, but these prayers must hereafter become prayers of thanksgiving as a testimony of our faith.

Our Prayer of Thanksgiving Is Our Unceasing Prayer

Uttering words of thanks and praise alone is not sufficient. There must be an inner working, a firm "knowing" that our prayers are answered. This must also occur whether we see evidence of answered prayer or not or if the answer begins to show up differently than we expected. This "knowing" permeates our consciousness where we hold our deepest thoughts. It is the catalyst of manifestation that overcomes any delay. Since this "knowing" is the ultimate act of faith, it births the invisible into form.

Upon examination of Jesus's resurrection of Lazarus, we realize that Jesus thanked God before this miracle occurred. A sorrowful Jesus said, "Father, I thank thee that thou has heard me (John 41–42). Lazarus, who had already been dead for four days, was resurrected! What a historic demonstration of the power of gratitude. Jesus's prayer of thanksgiving proved his faith; **faith and thanksgiving represent a powerful dynamic duo.**

The biblical account in John 6:11 talked about Jesus feeding five thousand people with what at first seemed like not enough food, for there were only five barley loaves and two fish. *"And Jesus took the loaves and when he had given thanks he distributed them ... and likewise the fish, as much as they wanted" (John 6:11). Five thousand people were fed with twelve baskets of crumbs left over after they were filled.* **This miracle and many other miracles began with gratitude.**

Christ, our way-shower, never said an idle word. Every word was meant to teach us then and down through the ages, even today. In the biblical account of the gospel of Luke 17:11–19, ten lepers asked Jesus Christ to have mercy on them. They were asking to be healed. He told them to show themselves to the priest because in his mind he saw them clean. While going, they realized they were healed. One leper returned to say thanks. Jesus asked, "Were there not ten cleansed? But where are the nine?" **Jesus' deliberate questions demonstrated that gratitude is a Spiritual mandate that must be expected!** He proceeded to tell the grateful man that because of his gratitude, he had been made whole. When someone is made whole, his or her entire life circumstance is healed; this includes his or her health, finances, relationships, and social as well as spiritual lives. **Gratitude has deep spiritual implications as a requirement for wholeness and subsequently transformation.** A healing in one area, as all ten lepers received, does not guarantee healing in all areas, as was the case with the one man. We cannot afford to be complacent with our privilege to be grateful. Gratitude makes us whole!

Thanksgiving helps us focus on the present moment. God's grace is always current. Our daily bread is truly supplied on a daily basis. As we continue to give thanks, we recognize that there are new mercies every day and that God is the giver of good gifts; yet still we come to understand that the privilege of being grateful is a bigger gift. We must not pretend that there is no past or future; however, when we think of those times, we ought to be grateful that lessons of the past have blessed us with wisdom and that God is the same yesterday, today, tomorrow and forever.

Thanksgiving Today

People across many faiths observe the practice of thanksgiving. In some regions of the world it has become a national day to give thanks. In other parts of the world, it is celebrated on an individual basis on any day of the year, and the observance may last for days. The observances include birthdays, weddings, scholarship awards, home or car purchases, business openings, overcoming illness, success in ventures or on an exam, a new job, etc. Worldwide, the observances of thanksgiving can be held in religious, spiritual, or secular fashions.

Thanksgiving creates expectancy as we set out with zeal to accomplish. Expectancy infuses our consciousness with ideas of possibilities; this makes it a suitable medium for creativity and a medium through which the Law of Attraction works. **The vibration of the energy of ingratitude works to attract to us more situations for which to be ungrateful, while the vibration of the energy of gratitude brings us more situations for which to be grateful.** St. Paul encouraged us to practice thanksgiving, which is a high form of prayer: "In everything give thanks (1 Thess. 5:18). No situation is too large or small for which to give thanks.

We can cultivate gratitude despite the little ego's rebellion. We must accept that we of ourselves are not doing the works as this ego would have us believe; the Spirit of God works within and through us. Christ our redeemer reminded us that it is the Father God who worked in him. We ought to always be in a state of gratitude until we become the power of gratitude itself! Gratitude ensures that our loaves and fishes are always enough to share and spare, and like the one cleansed former leper who said thanks, we will be made harmoniously whole just as he was.

Our gratitude will be broadcasted from the depths of our beings. Its energy will radiate outward, attracting the forces of nature to assist us in whatever we desire. Receiving support through the feeling nature of our beings, we experience the joy of accomplishment, even before the manifestation becomes evident. Consequently, we become less constricted and more yielding and open to receiving even more good.

Cultivating Gratitude

The beauty of cultivating gratitude is that even as one begins the initial mental work of cultivating it, the benefits can become evident. **The following acts can support us in these practices:**

1. **B**egin the day with a prayer of thanksgiving. It can be brief or longer if necessary. A prayer practice should not be burdensome.

2. **D**uring the day, when inspired, think or say phrases or sentences of thanks like, "I am grateful that this meeting went well." "I am grateful for life." Customize the statements to suit each; say it purposefully and lovingly to yourself.

3. **S**ay "thank you" to others each time the opportunity arises, such as when someone holds open a door for you or gives you a compliment. **Do not be tempted to diminish a compliment**. For example, if someone says, "That dress looks good on you," your response should not be, "Oh, this dress is old" or "I got it on clearance." That would be irrelevant. A thank-you is simple but powerful. Some people receive gifts and think they are being kind when they say, "Oh, you didn't have to do that." A simple thank-you demonstrates politeness, gratitude and appreciation.

If you're experiencing difficulties with anyone or anything, go into the silence or in prayer, and ask God to show you the solution and the lesson it holds for you. Be grateful for the revelation and follow what your inner wisdom dictates. When you express gratitude in all things, you will be shown a way out of any difficulty.

Express gratitude to people who render you services even if you pay them. Tell them why (e.g., "You are so conscientious"). Start a gratitude journal. Each day, write a few things you are grateful for. It can be water, peace, health, life, your family, money, your talent, tea, rain, or snow. It is good to write in short sentences or even one sentence that includes all you're grateful for.

A few years ago, a student came sheepishly to my office door and said these exact words *"Do you know when people come near you they feel good?"* I responded positively to her. A part of my journal entry that day included gratitude that God lets me know, often through the mouths of babes, just how I affect others. A few days ago, after a big snow storm, I noticed as I drove to work how clean the streets were. One of my journal entries that day was *"Thank you, God, for snow plows."* There is so much in our lives for which we can be grateful. Deliberately look for opportunities to express gratitude. Focus on what you are grateful for today and why. **Through the Law of Attraction, gratitude creates more for which to be grateful.**

We can show gratitude to God by simply praising him exclusively. This means we are not making any requests. We are praising him for who he is, for his power, his love, his intelligence, his magnificence, etc. Below are practices of thanksgiving you can use at any time, including a treatment of praise, affirmations of gratitude, and a thanksgiving prayer.

Treatment of Praise

Wonderful God, I praise your most holy name. I praise your wisdom and your creativity. You are the rock upon which I stand; I praise your matchless strength! I bless you! You hold your people dear to your heart; therefore, there is no need to fear. You are the peace, love, and joy I seek. You are the light to my path. You will never leave or forsake me. To you, Heavenly Father, be the glory and honor, I praise you!

(Repeat several times if you feel led to do so)

Affirmations of Gratitude

- **I** am grateful that there is nothing lacking in me. I am an energetic match for successful living.
- **My** Heavenly Father has offered me the Kingdom; I receive it with joy and gratitude.
- **I** expect and accept harmonious health and wealth now. For this blessing I am eternally grateful.
- **W**hatever I must know, I shall know on divine time. Whatever I must do, I shall do in divine order. Whatever I must become, I already am. I am whole and complete in the mind of God. I am grateful that this is so and cannot be otherwise. I rejoice!
- **I** am grateful for women, men, and children everywhere. I am grateful for all plants and creatures. What a wonderful world in which we live! I thank you, Jehovah.

Denial

- **N**o one was created with a spirit of fear. All mankind was created with a spirit of courage, love, and a sound mind. I am so grateful. All is well!

Thanksgiving Prayer

Wonderful creator, I am so grateful for your constant presence everywhere. You are closer to me than my breath and yet you are everywhere even now; I am so grateful. I align myself with you as I humbly reach for greater spiritual wisdom and understanding. I surrender to the perfect action of your Spirit within me, and I allow myself to be inspired. With diligence, I move according to divine guidance knowing that your will is being done in and through me now. For my divine privilege of having your inspiring Spirit within me and for so much more, I am humbly grateful.

The Benefits of Gratitude

There are many benefits to gratitude; whether we look at it objectively or subjectively; I suggest we do both. What metaphysicians, holistic healers, and mental health workers observe in their practices and what neuroscientists, biologists, scientists, and medical professionals learn are the same principles. Whether they are working with living cells or the whole person, they realize a law that has always been in existence; the truth that the states of our thoughts and emotions are out pictured in our lives. Negative states of consciousness produce illness, fears, sadness, and hopelessness and contraction while positive states of consciousness produce good health, courage, joy, hope and expansion. Make no mistake; these laws have always been and will always be spiritual laws. They may be described as laws of physics and science, but they are first spiritual laws of the mind.

Of significance is the fact that we cannot deceive consciousness or the laws of the mind. We cannot hide from our thoughts; we always know our most secret thoughts. In this light, our expressions of gratitude must be genuine, coming from a deep place within our being. Simply saying thanks or acting as though we are grateful when we truly are not will bring the same results as ingratitude. It is a Spiritual law that as a man thinks in his mind, so is he.

The power of gratitude in us empowers us to co-create with God if we so wisely choose.

The person who is grateful is positive and sees the good in favorable and unfavorable situations. He or she is grateful for the lessons learned in adversity as well. This positive outlook greatly reduces stress. Subsequently, this person is generally healthier, more optimistic, and more joyful. Having no or reduced stress, his or her immune system can be more resilient.

Gratitude creates space for us to laugh at ourselves. It helps us to relax and realize that we are good enough for everything good, and that there is always enough for everyone. This state of mind positions us to prosper.

The grateful person loves life, and life loves the grateful person. Such person evokes good feelings in themself and others.

The grateful person surrenders fear and desperation and embraces courage and trust. Trust helps us to be peaceful and satisfied in the present moment. There is trust that unfavorable situations will culminate in what is best for all involved. To the favorable and unfavorable situations, the grateful person can say, "It's all good." How does he or she know that it's good? Simply, because the situation is what's happening and it is sure to bring a lesson.

The grateful person is flexible, yielding, compassionate, and attractive. Gratefulness also has a positive effect on the person witnessing it; it produces in him or her trust in humanity. The grateful person's compassion, through the law of attraction, attracts to themselves people who are compassionate.

The grateful person is usually more satisfied and as a result, is also generally happier.

Gratitude releases Spiritual energy through us. This creates influence, breaks down strongholds and positions us to prosper.

Whether or not we live in a state of gratitude, we cannot alter the pure goodness of God. However, we can block the receiving of our good through ingratitude. As worthy children of Almighty God, we ought to follow Christ's example and cultivate gratitude; then expect and receive our good. The truly grateful person is a satisfied soul who learns to turn within for guidance. This person feels the peace of God that surpasses all human understanding. He or she can exclaim in the face of adversity, "I am grateful for all things! This too shall pass!"

There is always something for which to be grateful. The least someone can say or think is, "I thank you Almighty God for the breath of life." Say the following prayer.

Our Heavenly Father, in you I live, move, and have my being. I thank you for providing all that I need to survive. The air, water, sun, moon and stars all function in harmony supporting our beautiful planet with vibrant life. I thank you for my wisdom, power, and authority to create my life of wholeness. I join in consciousness, prayer and action with the caretakers of this universe. I willingly do my part and allow myself to be your instrument. I claim and accept these blessings. I declare that this is the truth about my being through Christ our redeemer. Amen.

Chapter 11

Relationships

I was in the silence when it occurred to me that I must write about relationships. I remember thinking that it would take a big book to discuss relationships. I remained open and receptive, and then I got it! Writing about relationships in a book about affirmative prayer and transformation through Affirmative prayer, is necessary; it demonstrates the practical journey to transformation. It shows how we "work it" as we serve and interact with each other, since **our interactions form the basis for our spiritual work.**

At creation, our creator understood that Adam must have a companion. Considering the fact that Eve was created from a rib taken from Adam shows our oneness and interdependence. The gift to humanity, however, is that although we must embrace our oneness as a human race, we each must live individual lives as unique beings. We were blessed with the gift of choice to do this. We are not like little robots without self-determination. We have dominion over our circumstances.

Many people see relationships as a way of becoming complete. Seeking or establishing a relationship with this intention is very disempowering. The general belief many people hold is that their partners will make them happy or will become their knights in shining armor. Under normal circumstances, an infant is loved, cared for, and protected, and we internalize this from infancy.

As we grow and mature, we come to see ourselves as individuals. Along our childhood journeys, we experienced childhood wounds, just as our parents and their parents did. These wounds may seem insignificant, such as when our preschool friends excluded us from a group activity, yet these wounds become etched into our psyches and take on lives of their own, often causing various types of self-esteem issues. We also may be wounded at later stages, such as young adulthood and beyond.

Our quests for relationships might lead us to look for love in "all the wrong places." We may venture out in search of this person who will give us the love we never had or buy us things we never had. However, many of us are not aware that when we have a desire, it is really a yearning for the soul to begin to grow spiritually. There is a call for us to step up into our greatness and our wholeness where we experience God manifested within us. Our search for love is the need to connect with others at that profound level: the Spirit of God in me loving the Spirit of God in you. We know there is only One Spirit; therefore, we really yearn to love the Spirit of God in us and to love ourselves as well.

There is a great difference in our experiences when we allow the laws of God to guide our choices as opposed to allowing the ego to **E**ase **G**od **O**ut and not seeking first the Kingdom of God!

Forming Relationships

Many relationships begin with a common exclamation. We may hear someone say something like, "I have found my soul mate" or "I cannot believe how similar we are" or "We love the same music" or "We love the same foods, and guess what! our parents have many of the same attitudes." or "Oh my, this is really a match made in heaven." The truth is that most often we don't realize the depth of this truth. This is indeed a match made in heaven, designed to usher in our transformation in the way that is most appropriate for our spiritual evolution, no matter how easy or tough it seems. I fondly say, "The angels clap and rejoice when each match is made."

Some people might not be so interested in how someone directly makes them feel. Instead they are more concerned with how others view them based on the physicality or other facts about their mates, such as their mate's jobs, hobbies, or who they know and associate with. This is clearly an attempt to embrace the illusion that someone else can validate who we are. For example, someone may also say, "I want others to see me with a man or woman who looks this certain way. He or she must wear a suit to work and carry a briefcase too!" This is how we look to others to give us a sense of self. So many people end up with empty suits! The suited man or woman of whom they fantasize does not exist. The briefcase may be full of scripts of their old stories and bills to be paid. The bills are the spiritual practices and soul work that must be completed. Some people demand rings, saying, "If you love me, you'll put a ring on my finger." The ring may provide the illusion of specialness, much to the little ego's delight.

Regardless of how the relationship came about, its nature will take on the corresponding pattern of the consciousness of the people involved in it. We must also understand that all relationships, whether they are within one's family, workplace, or briefly with a total stranger, are designed to usher in our spiritual evolution through the lessons they provide. However, the people with whom we are closest often provide the most challenging lessons.

The Creativity of Relationships

In *The Power of Intention*, Wayne Dyer wrote that creativity is one of the faces of intention (2004). This means that in order to intend, there must be creativity to create what is intended. Looking at the vicissitudes and triumphs of mankind since biblical times, we can see a deliberate and creative creator at work. Events took place in an orderly manner, each ushering in the next. Whether we look at Adam and Eve; Job and his wife; Shadrach, Meshach, and Abednego in relation to furious King Nebuchadnezzar, Daniel in the lion's den, with the angels appearing to shut the lions' mouths; Naomi and Ruth, Jesus with his disciples or the cruel mob; or the Holy Spirit within us, we find relationships. If we take a bird's-eye view of the purpose of these relationships, we see that they all signified God's ultimate goal of redemption and transformation! Great relationships often allow an atmosphere where value is placed on unconditional love and compassion. When this is modeled in the world it becomes bedrock for transformation; this is our sacred goal.

The truth that God works for me through me is the same as God working through me for our universe; **God is intentional**. Our wise creator knows that there can be no greater arrangement through which we can be transformed. **One of the most significant aspects of a relationship is that it provides the stage upon which we act. We have the opportunity to observe how we relate to others and how we show up in this world. From this stage of relating to others, we can get a glimpse of any of our shadow parts. These are the aspects of our personalities that we may hide, repress, deny, and doubt, or embrace to heal. These may trigger shame, guilt, fears, anger, hatred, projections, feelings of being better than or less than, etc. For these reasons and more relationships do have challenges, and we can grow through them if we focus on our own stuff rather than on someone else's.**

We must take notice of how these shadow parts specifically show up in our lives. Some people who are plagued by feelings of shame can be burdened by perfectionism. For example, a person who was sexually abused can feel that people can tell just by looking at him or her. This person tries to be perfect in every way possible with the intention that people will see him or her as a perfect person. This type of behavior often also manifests in areas of employment, romantic relationships, the way one behaves, etc. It can also lead to excessive control of one's body, as the person seeks to control the body he or she could not previously protect. This can show up as excessive bathing, washing, anxiety, depression, anorexia, bulimia, or other self-harming behavior.

Some people often have the need to be right; this can stem from having domineering adults in their lives while they were growing up. Also children who were fed with a false sense of self, such as "You are better than other children," can experience the need to be right in their relationships, at work, and wherever they go. It is not unusual to hear someone say, "Oh, my spouse was a spoiled kid, and I always have to give in to him or her." It can become more complicated if the spouse was spoiled because of some guilt on his or her parents' part.

People who take care of others more than they do themselves, or people who neglect themselves soon find that they can be plagued by resentment, anger, bitterness, the need to blame, or feelings of helplessness. People who talked about not feeling validated might try to over accomplish, always seeking validation. In relationships, these people can be seen as boastful, proud, or demanding and may complain when they do not feel validated. If the experience of not being validated caused self-doubt, they might have difficulty moving forward or reaching significant goals in life. They might be misjudged as unintelligent or lazy. They might also procrastinate because of fear of failure or fear of success.

Our wounds also play out in dysfunctional and codependent relationships, while each one attracts the person who will set up the opportunity for them to heal. Let us look at an example of a relationship to understand how we can affect one another.

Susan and John (an example)

Susan, age sixty-two, is married to John, age sixty-one. Susan has issues with low self-esteem and feelings of dissatisfaction with how she performs at work. She works very hard to please her boss, whom she says reminds her of her father. She believes he scrutinizes her, but this is not the truth. She assumes a childlike tone of voice when speaking to him. She is in her second marriage. Her first husband was physically and verbally abusive; they had two children together—a son age thirty-eight, and a daughter age thirty-six. Her second marriage produced a son named Steve, age twenty-seven. Her current husband John is an alcoholic; he is gainfully employed and works during the day. Every night he drinks alcohol all by himself. He can be physically and verbally aggressive when drunk, although this happens very rarely.

Truth (Susan and John)

Susan grew up in a home with both parents. Her father was an abusive alcoholic. His verbal and physical abuse became worse as she grew older and as he sank deeper into alcoholism. Happier times occurred when she was younger, of course, when she had her natural girlish voice.

Now she is an adult, and her boss is kind, respectful, and always patient with her. She projects her father's scrutiny upon her boss and believes he is scrutinizing her. She speaks to her boss in a girlish voice because she believes it will appease him like it did her dad when she was a child. Of course, there is no need to appease him. She produces excellent work, and he has great respect and appreciation for her and her work.

At home, Susan does all she can to please her husband. She buys beer for him each time she shops for groceries. He shows gratitude by thanking her and telling her she is a smart woman who knows his needs and that she is a great wife. This makes her feel good, although she would also love to hear her boss say she is a good worker. When John is intoxicated, he sleeps for several hours at a time. This often provides time for Susan to have for herself and not be subjected to any abuse.

Susan's husband, John, was raised by both parents; they were not alcoholics. His dad was strict, domineering, and hard working. He did not show much physical affection, but John could feel that his dad loved him as a child and as an adult. At first John was easygoing like his mother, who took very good care of each family member. When he started working at age twenty, he began drinking socially with friends. He said drinking helped him cope with his domineering father and helped him feel freer around him. He became an alcoholic, unlike his parents, and can be domineering and verbally or physically aggressive when drunk, although not frequently.

Co-Dependence

Often when a relationship such as the one between John and Susan continues to exist, both parties are getting some form of benefit. This also satisfies deep unconscious needs that might not be readily evident. Each person in the relationship depends on the other for the fulfillment of this need, regardless of whether robs him or her of his or her dignity or well-being. At times someone can tell of another person's past experiences based on how their current needs are expressed and fulfilled. People often seek to recreate whatever is familiar. The result to one's personal growth and spiritual evolution is stagnation. "How cans this happen?" one might ask. The fact is that many of us subconsciously carry around our wounds, and we learn to act and expect things from the premise of those wounds. People in general have a way of feeling more comfortable with the familiar even if it causes pain or looks pretty horrible to someone on the outside looking in. When situations look unfamiliar, we rush to recreate the familiar. Relationships often become codependent as each person involved helps and validates the other. We all want to be validated! We repeat the actions that help us receive validation.

As we look closely at this relationship, we see that John and Susan depend on each other. They have a codependent relationship. Susan receives compliments from John for being a smart woman and a great wife. Although she did not receive compliments from her dad or her boss, this provides her some satisfaction. In an unconscious attempt to recreate her family dynamics, Susan got married twice to men who had challenges with alcohol consumption. Susan also benefits from having some time for herself whenever John is drunk. However, she has set up a cycle of guilt (which punishes) by supplying beers, enabling him to him get drunk and ruining his health. She therefore feeds the need to be punished. She also creates a false sense of power when she quiets him by enabling him to become intoxicated.

Although John did not like his dad's domineering ways, he can become domineering and abusive when drunk. In his sober state, he is not domineering like his dad. Just realize how John created the very situation. Part of him dislikes being domineering, so being drunk dulls his experience of being domineering. His wife, Susan, takes care of the family just as his mother did. In essence, John has become Susan's alcoholic father, while Susan has become John's easygoing mother. People often recreate the pathological issues of their parents, guardians, and significant others. Notice how creative people can be, whether we are creating good or bad. Just think of how brilliantly, positively, or powerfully we can create when we create through our Christ consciousness!

However, the universe has a way of helping us, even though we create and recreate situations that cause us pain. Grace steps in as our wisdom to correct the beliefs, feelings, and agreements that fostered these dysfunctional situations. This is the grace of God working on our behalf. The universal purpose of a relationship also serves to expose our shadow

parts. People may try to hide them, but because of the differences between both partners' shadows, there will be upheavals. Our relationships set the stage for us to practice the spiritual laws of love, forgiveness, faith, thanksgiving; and so on. Relationship supports us by presenting opportunities for the work, at each next appropriate step of our spiritual evolution and transformation.

Whether a relationship is romantic, platonic, familial, or work-related; a brief acquaintance; or a brief interaction with a stranger, two people broadcast to each other what they specifically must heal in order to spiritually transform.

Healing Relationships

Mankind was created to form relationships, family units and to procreate. When Adam was created, the Lord God said, "It is not good that man should be alone: I will make him a helper comparable to him." Gen 2:18. We were also created to Love one another. The various faiths embrace and teach that we must love one another. The Christ also said, "A new commandment I give to you, that you love one another." John 13:34. Christ knew that love creates harmonious relationships. Looking at the big picture, when there is harmony in personal relationships; people are more inclined to act peacefully with others at home and abroad; this supports prosperity and even more harmony.

There must be some willingness in the person seeking to heal a relationship. It is good to begin with a prayer so that he or she asks for and opens their heart to receive guidance.

1. One should pay attention to what others tell them about his or her self. Listen to children as well; they speak from the heart. **One must examine their relationship with themself first. For example, if someone has a challenge with poor self-worth, he or she will most**

likely attract friends or a mate that treats him or her poorly. This seems like a very unfortunate scenario, but it is really God's grace showing up. Through the pain it causes, it provides an opportunity for all involved to spiritually grow while embracing love, forgiveness, courage, and compassion as part of the healing work. God's grace points the way for the "absurd" to be revealed, triggering our innate power, authority, and authenticity; the necessary attributes for healing our relationships with ourselves and others. Through our spiritual work, the illusion of poor self-worth fades into its own nothingness.

2. Scan the periods of life as described in the chapter 7 on Forgiveness. Follow any necessary steps.

3. You must practice showing love to yourself and others. See chapter 6 on Love and follow all steps. Each person has his or her own personal relationship story. One thing that remains constant is our need to pray for guidance before we begin to work on any relationship.

In this example of John and Susan's case, after prayer affirmation etc. they must go about forgiving and loving themselves and each other. They can face their wounds and heal them. They must admit their dysfunction, hold each other accountable then work to support each other's healing. In order to heal, they must cease their codependence and embrace a new healthy and harmonious relationship in which only good can be exchanged between them. They both need to work on forgiving themselves and their parents (See Chapter 8). They need to work on building their self-esteem. John joining Alcoholic Anonymous and Susan joining a group for affected family members is a perfect option. **Phone directories, websites, and public libraries have an abundance of listings of these resources for children and adults, as well as resources for many other types of issues.**

Whenever there is conflict in any relationship, each person involved must endeavor to make the first move to see the other person as a creation of God, realizing that the Spirit of God dwells within them. Each must change any negative view of the other party and embrace understanding and compassion. Instead of trying to change the other person, each one must change themselves. The age-old practice of people coming together to solve problems is always vital. Whether we see the format as peer mediation, conflict resolution, or problem solving, this is a blessed act of coming together in brotherhood.

We must come together to celebrate the joys of friendship as well. We must honor our relationships and be grateful for them. We must be grateful for all the lessons learned. Some might ask the question, "Why are some relationships so peaceful while some are not?" We must remember that as unique individuals, we have different lessons to learn; our histories, our experiences, our ways of handling joys or difficulties differ based on many varying factors. Some experiences are more intense than others. When someone has learned his or her lesson well, there is no need for them to relearn it. Naturally because each soul has their own growth to complete, each relationship and the lesson it brings is unique. **We are programmed to grow and expand beyond our self-imposed limitations; our relationships often provide the stage on which this happens.**

Supporting Relationships

(Repeat each as often as you feel led to. Change words to suit your situation)

Prayer

Our Heavenly Father, I praise your wisdom. You created each person with a beautiful capacity to love. You created relationships and I stand with a desire for a wonderful relationship. I ask through the Christ in me who showed us how to love, that you look into every crevice of my mind and heal any place where unconditional love does not exist. It is my desire to be a conduit of unconditional love. Please help me to change in any way that is pleasing to you, so that my relationships old and new change according to your will. I ask for and open myself to receive your guidance, so that I will attract the friendship that genuinely honor my essence and which can evolve into romantic love that upholds our dignity and uniqueness. Lord, I thank you that in this moment and as I pray you have heard and answered me. I am willing and open to all that your spirit in me directs. Speak to me Lord, I am listening to you in obedience and with a grateful heart every step of the way. Amen.

Affirmation for a New Relationship

Today, I embrace the newness of this relationship, and I allow myself to be love in it. I accept the love and lessons it brings, as I move gracefully through its many facets.

I bless this relationship with love and true friendship. No unloving situation can flourish in it. I prepare a place of love and friendship within myself. I allow Almighty God to love through me.

Denial

I refuse to continue to believe in any worn out idea that does not support healthy relationships. I have no enemies; I am a friend to myself and a friend to others. People are friendly towards me and I am grateful.

Affirmation for Ending a Relationship

I end this relationship in peace. I leave behind all bitterness and regrets. I move forward in love, joy, and peace and I desire this for all concerned. All is well with all people involved and I say "Thank you Lord"

Affirmation for Leaving an Organization

As I leave this organization/department, I offer everyone here blessings of wholeness. I am surrounded by peace. Everyone is surrounded by peace. I leave in peace and gratefully move forward in peace to new and wonderful vistas, all is well!

Treatment for a Family Relationship

I realize that each member of this family is ruled by the harmony of God. The Spirit of God within us reenergizes us with its love. Love is at the center of our beings, and we are its instrument, doing its work. We see each other with spiritual eyes, and all the stress and illusion of disharmony disappears. We love, support, respect, and uphold each other. For these blessings, I am grateful.

The Holy Relationship

There is a relationship that is already established. It is God's constant and unconditional love for us and our love for God. We must reawaken and maintain our awareness of this love by stilling our minds and bodies and going into the silence often. The following exercise serves a twofold purpose. First, it reminds us of our connection with our source, which is Almighty God. Secondly, it helps us to re-establish the relationship we have with our wonderful selves. Only from a firm spiritual foundation of love can we move forward and create healthy relationships. **In order to grow and evolve spiritually, we must demonstrate mastery in our relationships beginning with our relationships with ourselves.**

A Process for Inviting Love (1)

Sit quietly, take several deep breaths, and relax your body. You may close your eyes if you prefer. Think about the presence of God and earnestly feel that you are deeply loved. Bring to your mind a peaceful scene that truly nourishes your senses. Feel and smell the warmth and fragrance of this environment and the soothing effects on you. Listen to the sounds; it can be sounds of nature or an old familiar church bell; this is the sound of peace. Know that this place or situation was created for you by a benevolent God who truly loves you. Let this knowing inspire you to live with a sense of worthiness. Bask in this peaceful scene with a deep sense of joy and gratitude. Feel deeply that you are your own best friend and that you are a good friend to others. Feel a sense of gratitude because your life is enriched by great and loving friendships. Before peacefully leaving this place of love, take a few deep nourishing breaths knowing and accepting that you are deeply loved by your Heavenly Father, yourself and others. You can recreate this scene whenever you feel inspired to. Know that you are always worthy of love.

Process (2)

At times we block the possibility of a loving relationship or living in prosperity because we may be holding some form of judgment or condemnation against ourselves. We may believe that we are not worthy of or capable of attracting love. This can cause us to send out the corresponding energetic signals. The following is suitable for such situation.

Sit quietly in a quiet place, take several deep breaths and relax your body. Close your eyes and envision a ball of light warmly glowing at the center of your body. This light is the symbol of the Christ's healing presence at the center of your being. Take a slow deep refreshing breath and see this light radiating and cleansing your mind and your entire body. Remember that Jesus said "Suffer (let) the little children to come unto me" Remember him telling the Samaritan woman that the man she was intimate with was not her husband and how he rebuked others from cruelly stoning to death this woman that had sinned. He forgave them and he heals and forgives you. Take a deep breath. Begin to intentionally release every negative assumption or judgment that you have against yourself now. Realize and hold the truth that the same mind that was in Christ Jesus is now in you. Whether the issue began in childhood or later, Jesus covered it all. As a way of being, practice the processes from the previous chapter on love.

Process (3)

The following can be used to support processes one and two. Change words to suit your situation and repeat as often as led to.

Treatments

I see myself as a worthy child of God. I deserve to be loved unconditionally. I deserve to be treated with respect and dignity. I deserve to be forgiven by myself and others. I deserve to prosper, find favor with God and mankind and to enjoy wonderful, loving relationships. These are facets of my Spiritual birthright; I open my mind and heart as I receive all of them now. Desiring the same for everyone, I say "thank you Almighty Father."

I am so grateful that Divine love surrounds and fills me. I accept myself and others without judgment. I live with the experience of perfect balance in my life. My mind is filled with compassion and love; this I offer to my fellowmen. I live a life of opulence and wholeness and I allow these blessings to be the vehicle through which I offer loving service in this world. I am the Love I desire. I gratefully receive the love I desire. I let this be so and so it is now and forevermore. All is well.

Chapter 12

Addictions

A s we have seen in the previous chapter, relationships create the climate in the home, workplace, and wherever people assemble. These places are microcosms of the universe. As we focus on our transformation, it would be a great error not to a great error not to address conditions that can greatly alter the functioning of the mind, and hence our actions and quality of our relationships. We have realized that there are social issues generated according to the states of our relationships with ourselves and others. Several may be constant such as poverty, despair, hopelessness, inability to trust, abuse, self-esteem issues and addictions to various things. Each one of these circumstance can feed into the other. I choose to discuss addictions in this chapter because as a counselor I realize it is becoming a bigger challenge, especially with some people in our adolescent population worldwide, who may believe that illegal drug use is a quick fix for life's challenges.

An addiction can be as unique as its first trigger. Normally when it is said that someone has an addiction, we think of a harmful substance. People are not always addicted to harmful substances. For example, food serves to keep us healthy, alive, and to bring us pleasure. Sexual intercourse serves the purpose of procreation and pleasure. Food and sex are good, yet if they are constantly and uncontrollably indulged in, they can become addictive. The focus in this chapter is on substances such as illegal drugs, tobacco, alcohol, prescription pills, and other substances. However, in working with the principles in this book, anyone may substitute a substance or behavior that is problematic or is addictive for them or someone else.

So many people can tell of times they have felt judged, ridiculed, or shamed by peers or significant others. If we are raised in homes where this is common, we are most likely to experience it there first. Schools, playgrounds, organizational functions, and other places where people congregate are some of the most common places where people have these experiences. Our children are more emotionally susceptible at the adolescent stage their lives, and these experiences can send them looking for ways to cope. Unfortunately, some use substances with the belief that it will help them deal with the particular situation.

Some people admitted that they tried illegal drugs to experience the pleasure they heard that it provides. By making this decision, they chose to dishonor self-love for a false sense of self preservation. Statistics have shown that children who have poor self-esteem are more likely to fall prey to addiction. This poor self-esteem might have developed because the child felt he or she was not good enough, good looking enough, or smart enough, was abused or neglected, copied from relatives or acquaintances or other reason.

When lacking a sense of self, people can easier succumb to peer pressure. This pressure might be to engage in all sorts of risky behaviors, which can immediately include or eventually lead to the use of illegal drugs. The addiction can also begin as a person tries to mask unpleasant emotions by using substances that can alter mood and feelings. (This may be described as "numbing out.") Perhaps there was simply physical pain or some ailment, and prescribed medication became addictive.

The truth is that drug addictions create a cycle of self-harm. An addicted person might engage in dangerous behaviors in order to obtain the drug. For example they might become sexually promiscuous, which can be self-harmful in many ways. As a person progresses with drug addiction, the brain is affected, and its function of producing endorphins (the hormone that produces the feeling of well-being) is negatively affected. Subsequently, more drugs are required to keep the person in an unrepressed mood. Eventually, as more of the drug is required and used, its effectiveness wears off again. The drug becomes relatively ineffective. Addicts often beg, lie, and steal to afford the drugs. There are legal and health issues, and there is shame, guilt, and overdose, which often leads to death. The cycle of judging self or others goes into high gear.

Regardless of the magnitude of addiction, healing will require love and lots of it from self and others. Addicts must love themselves enough in order to want to heal. Those assisting in the healing must act from the basis of love, patience, compassion, and mercy. Parents, guardians and the caring persons in the lives of those experiencing the difficulty, must never underestimate the power of their prayer. Often parents, guardians, loved ones and friends may feel intense anger towards the addicted person. They are asked not to take this person's behavior personally. This person is reacting to their own pain. The memory of any unfortunate experience may be triggering emotional hurt, their lack of control can cause pain; guilt causes pain, withdrawal causes pain often triggering more substance abuse. This is a viscous cycle.

Parent's Prayer for a Child with Challenging Behavior

Wonderful Jehovah, I am grateful that you created [*say child's name*] as a fully divine being who is capable of thinking with your mind. As a praying parent, I embrace the truth that all is well in our lives. In this time of sadness and disappointment, I surrender any feelings to seek revenge by shaming, blaming, or withholding love and kindness from my child. I see my child lovingly protected and safe. The angels have charge over her/him. I humbly ask for and receive the wisdom to lovingly and effectively parent this child without judging or condemning myself or others. Please help my child to be receptive to my prayer and your blessing. Help this child to practice self-love and share that love according to your will. I dismantle any mental construct, generational pattern, need for drama, or dysfunctional family pattern from my experience. I rest in you as our source of guidance and peace. These blessings I ask in Jesus's name. I am grateful to you, Almighty Father, I am so grateful.

Affirmation

I give thanks that the freedom and peace of God now permeates our lives and that all is well.

Acts of Healing—Addiction

Whether you are an adolescent, younger or much older, please realize that your healing and wholeness are gifts from God. You ought to return to your wholesome state, and through grace, you can. Grace is unmerited favor from God. It is free and always sufficient for you. You have to stretch out your physical and spiritual hands in order to receive it. Choose to be well again. Choose love, compassion, and truth for yourself. Truth will support you in accepting that you have engaged in a behavior that has caused you self-harm and harm to others as well (if true for you). Examine yourself to find out what emotions are in your experience. Many people with addictions are filled with anger, fear, hate, envy, anxiety, and depression. Any tendencies to lie, blame, steal, hurt, and manipulate others must to be healed as well.

If you are seeking healing, there must be some willingness on your part! Once you are willing and ready, you must embrace the truth so that your healing can be complete. The truth helps you become aware of the aspects of yourself that you might hide, deny, repress or ignore. You must admit that a problem exists as this is the first step in healing. Also, in this way you can have a clear goal to reach through the healing process. Decide to be determined because determination can help you move through pain and also to redirect unproductive patterns of thought and behavior. The following healing processes are offered as ways to support those who choose to be healed.

Healing Process

Before you begin, be sure to read the section on the silence Chapter 2. Then get into the silence and ask Almighty God, Jesus Christ, or the Holy Spirit (whichever feels more natural to you) for divine guidance and a miracle of healing. Jesus said that we should seek the Kingdom first and everything we desire, including healing, can be added. Cast your burdens on the Lord. Listen for guidance and be receptive. Upon receiving guidance, leave the silence in gratitude. **Develop within yourself the feeling** of having already received what you prayed for. Follow the divine guidance you receive.

Key Steps to Healing

The first step to healing is to admit and accept that there is an addiction and an experience of powerlessness over it. Prayer and meditation are powerful practices that can open one's awareness. Fortunately, the adult as well as the adolescent population when taught, has shown some appreciation and acceptance for meditation. Mediation is focused prayer, so it is of paramount value in helping one to really feel and become aware of the depth of the story that supported the creation of the addiction. This quietude creates ample space for any old wounds to open up to the light and for negative beliefs and conclusions to surface. With this information, one becomes empowered not only to receive treatment for the addiction but to heal the underlying cause as well. One may choose to join a group that provides support for helping each member to end their addiction. Many people are successful following groups that embrace the twelve step principles.

Prayer for Help with Addictions

The following prayer is for help with addictions or other behaviors that are not wholesome. This prayer can be said when one begins to feel at peace and settled in the silence in a still, receptive state of mind.

Prayer

Wonderful Counselor and Divine Healer, you know all things. You created me in your Spiritual image and likeness. You know everything about me, and you know that this addiction is a great burden in my life. You said in your words that before we call you will answer us and that while we are still speaking you will hear us. Dear God, I believe that in this holy moment, you are hearing me. I ask that you help me to overcome this addiction, as well as its deeply rooted cause. I allow your divine presence to strengthen me as I experience any harsh feelings of withdrawal. To you, almighty healer, I surrender any self-hatred, procrastination, fears of the pains of withdrawal and, any unwillingness to heal as I embark on this path to health. I ask for my daily bread of your loving support so that I can surrender any thought or behavior that supports this addiction and do the work that I must do. With faith Loving Father, I know that my complete healing is now governed by your love and power. I ask and receive courage and healing in the name of the Christ who by his sacrifice secured my healing; Christ healed so many, and still heals today. I am holding on to Christ's garment of mercy and I accept healing now. Thank you

Almighty God for hearing and answering me now and always. All is well.

Treatments

The following exercises will help one to stay present and stable and strengthen resolve to withstand the urge to succumb to the addictive behavior. These treatments are useful for helping with healing: **Say slowly and mindfully....**

- Today in my receptive state of mind, I allow a current of divine healing to gently flow through my mind. I allow the Spirit of God within me to harmonize the circuit of life and health in my body. Every organ and function in my body works with the perfection of God. My healthy mind holds only thoughts that support wholeness in my body and affairs. As I heal, I am obedient to the guidance of the Spirit of God within me. I consistently treat myself with love and respect. I see my healing from this addiction as sure and complete. I rejoice in gratitude as I let it be so. So it is.

- **In** this moment, there is only God's presence sustaining me. God is one with me everywhere and in every moment. I am grateful for my breath. As I breathe in the peace of God, it soothes my emotions. In this holy moment, I focus on the powerful presence of God in me. I let all unhappy, anxious, agitated, fearful, doubtful, distressing, or depressing thoughts float away now. I realize that my all-powerful God is now supporting me in this dark night of my soul. My hands are in God's hands. I am stable, I am stable, I am stable. I let the feeling of stability hold me up, and I feel so stable. I allow it to be so, and so it is. [*Take a deep breath. Now calmly feel strength and stability embrace you in a powerful and loving way. Hold thoughts of gratitude to God in your thoughts.*]

Process for surrendering addictions

Envision yourself sitting with God, Jesus Christ, or the Holy Spirit. You are sitting facing each other. He looks at you with gentle eyes and assures you of his unconditional love for you. Now feel relaxed, comfortable, and peaceful. Know in your heart that you are truly supported with unconditional love in this moment. If you are in grief, distress, crisis, etc., you may envision that you are lovingly embraced. Feel joy throughout your body.

If you are buying, selling, using, or acquiring illegal harmful substances, overeating, etc. envision giving this addictive substance into the hands of the healing God or Jesus Christ or the Holy Spirit, to whichever you feel led. As you willingly place the substance in his hands, see yourself calmly saying, *"There is peace in this moment. There is peace in this moment. I am grateful for the peace in this moment."* See yourself feeling peaceful, loved, and happy while rejoicing because you have forever given up this substance. **(You may use the vision of handing over a package labeled with a behavior e.g. stealing, voyeurism or whatever the behavior may be)**

Denials

The following denials can keep the mind from negativity

- Nothing blocks my healing. I claim my healing now. I accept my healing now.
- No one and nothing can hinder my healing. I stand firm in my choice for complete healing. I receive my healing now.
- I am not afraid to choose healing. I will always be divinely supported. The universe supports me now. I am so grateful.

Affirmations

The following affirmations must be said with a firm feeling that what you are affirming is indeed already accomplished:

- With joy and thanksgiving, I recognize that my peaceful thoughts now create a day that is calm, peaceful, and successful for me.
- This is a day the Lord has made. I use it fully in support of God's will of love, strength, and integrity for me.
- Only good thoughts, words, and actions go from me. Only good comes back to me. Through the Christ's Spirit within me, I attract people who encourage and support my healing. I let go of thoughts of negativity and fear. There is nothing in me that is negative or afraid. I cooperate with my healing now; I surrender all, knowing that with Almighty God all things are possible.

Additional Exercises

- Complete a forgiveness exercise; be sure to forgive yourself for both abusing your body and all harm done to yourself and others. (See the chapter 7 on forgiveness.)
- Take periods to breathe slowly and deeply.
- Slowly jog or take moderately paced walks. This provides time for exercise and reflection as well as stress and anxiety reduction.
- Take time out to meditate. (This can also be done while walking or breathing.)
- Read inspirational books.
- Develop a sense of humor.
- Habitually reflect on your words, thoughts, and actions. Listen for divine guidance and follow it readily. This obedience creates the space for you to be guided often.

- Spend time in nature; observe its beauty, peace and orderliness. Let this invigorate your spirit and soothe your emotions.
- Journal daily; each time write about a few things for which you are thankful.
- Cultivate a steady stream of thoughts that genuinely bless and uplift yourself and all others.
- Pray for yourself and others daily.
- Take the steps that keep long-range goals alive. For example, if you are a student, try your best to complete your education. If you have to take a brief break for treatment or recovery from your addiction, please resume classes at the earliest opportunity that it is wise for you to do so. Your education supports you in gaining knowledge, power, wisdom, direction, courage and self-respect. Having those qualities mentioned can in turn strengthen your resolve not to harm yourself or others. If you work and had to take temporary leave, you must make sure that you resume working as soon as it is appropriate. These steps can support a healthy recovery with fewer opportunities for slippage.

You are worth all the good that is suitable for and available to you. You were created by Almighty God, who is a wise, loving creator who makes no mistakes. You are truly welcome in this world and you deserve to be here. We pray that you become whole and free. Your gifts and talents are necessary for everyone's transformation. Please complete any professionally prescribed treatment. You are the beloved! We love you!

Chapter 13

Parenting

As we look at relationships and their innate nature to support spiritual evolution, the parent-child relationship becomes inescapably vital. A great deal of lessons learned in these relationships, begin even before the child's birth. Most times it is joyful birth, and at times it is not. What happens during these times often dictate, at least partially, the parent-child relationship. A struggling parent(s) might decide to abandon or give up his or her child (ren) for adoption. At the other end of the spectrum, a parent(s) who may have had no difficulty might raise his or her child to adulthood. Some parents can adopt children and have those experiences as well.

The role of parenting does not usually escape the interferences of the little ego. One can argue that this is a good thing, since it sets up opportunities for the parent-child relationship to be played out on a stage where spiritual evolution happens gradually. A common subject of discussion is that parents mellow with age and become the best grandparents! They become as their grandparents were and even as their parents were as they mellowed with age. Parents at times complain that their children are not like they (the parents) were at a particular age. They go on to describe just how obedient they were compared to the children of today.

Roles as Parents

It's very helpful to understand that everyone belongs to God including our children. Each child is as unique as the snowflakes are. There are differences in siblings, even when raised under the same conditions by the same parents or guardians and with the same advantages and disadvantages. Our magnificent and Omniscient God expresses through each of us differently! Despite these differences, the role of raising our children is ultimately to teach them to follow Gods spiritual laws so that they can venture out on their own with this roadmap, creating productive lives and being transformed as well!.

As parents, we often become our children's first teachers. We teach them through our words and actions. If we teach them to behave in certain ways while we act differently, we help create in them anger, ambivalence, and mistrust; this can lead to their disrespect for us and/or authority. We can help them feel emotionally secure by being consistent and by our confident, loving presence and support. We must understand that our children, beginning in the first stage of their lives and as they mature, have similar experiences as we had. They can feel fear, courage, mistrust, trust, anger, joy etc. just as we did.

In adolescence, hormonal changes and fluctuations can cause changes such as mood swings, feelings of joy, sadness, anxiety, obsessions, depression and happiness; this can occur all in one day! Responses can range from love to hate, acceptance and narcissism to rejection. They may feel confident that they know it all or may have self-doubts. Their experiences ultimately can teach them about themselves, while those raising and supporting them can also learn about themselves, about patience and grow in wisdom. Parents must understand that often children's acts of defiance, rejection or narcissism can be a cry for help in finding their own courage, confidence, and independence. It is not productive to impulsively make up stories about what your children's behavior may mean. For example, a child who refuses to go to school may be far from being lazy or non-ambitious. Such child may be the victim of bullying or have other fears that trigger the refusal to go to school.

A parent who felt "not heard" as a child may tend to judge in this instance, that their child is not listening and that she (parent) is not being heard (again). When parenting we must be observant to become aware of what triggers us. In this way we can face our shadows, heal our own childhood wounds and become more fulfilled and effective parents. For example, Jennifer age 40 has a long standing resentment towards a few of her classmates that began when they were all 13 years old. She felt that she got the least time and attention from everyone else in the group. At times they unfairly left her out of some recreational activities. Today she feels the same way; that her three teenage children a girl and two boys do not give her their time and attention. As long as Jennifer continues to hold the resentment against her peers, she will most likely be presented with similar situations until she heals the past issues. Those closest to us such as family members, are usually the ones revealing our shadows and triggering us so that we can do our healing work. When healing is completed the situation most often dissipates.

The simple approach of letting someone know that they are heard without judgment works well for adults as well as children. This can create more harmony; therefore it would be most productive to convey this to the child. Of course parents want to know that they are heard and understood without judgment. Far too often a parent may neglect to discipline a child for fear of being compared to the other parent who may not be the parent that disciplines the child, and at times may be the one who is not engaged in the financial and heart and soul of raising the child. That parent is in many instances becomes the glorified parent. Time and wisdom, however reveals the truth, so be courageous and know that you loving yourself, and God loving and guiding you as you discipline is of paramount value and importance as you parent with a holy boldness.

In handling these experiences, parents ought to remember that quieting their own minds through prayer can foster much needed wisdom and patience. The results can be that the parent learns just how much autonomy each child can be given and when. Parents must be aware enough so that they do not provoke their children to anger or despair. They must be flexible while at the same time, not relinquishing their rights to safe control and constructive discipline; discipline can determine destiny. A child, who is not disciplined and has no safe set boundaries, can become fearful and mistrusting of the world. Such child may feel unprotected and unsafe, even in their parent's presence. Love, safe boundaries, constructive criticism and the fulfillment of health care and concrete needs are vital to the nurturing of our children.

One of the main challenges is that technological advances have supported a change in culture; this same technology can be used for positive or negative purposes. Young and older adolescents are growing up (socially) quickly and many are pressured to live up to the images they see through the media. Incidences of eating disorders, illegal drug use and death from drug overdose have increased. Violent acts committed by both males and females have also increased. Some of these youngsters are so desensitized that they (although rare) have electronically recorded and displayed vicious attacks on each other. Fortunately, the greater majority of our children practice and kindness respect, and are more accepting of each other's differences; this is a very good sign of the evolving human consciousness.

The Ego and Parenting

Many parents tend to parent according to the dictates of the little ego which seeks to **E**dge **G**od **O**ut and to parent without prayer.

This sometimes means as an example, that the parent can encourage the child to engage in a certain sport or career that he or she (the parent) admires, failed to engage in, or failed to excel at or for one reason or another. Parents might attempt to live out their dreams through their children. These actions can rob children of their own sense of self and their ability and privilege to choose. If a child does not comply, he or she might become filled with guilt while the parent becomes filled with disappointment, anger, shame, and a tendency to criticize the child. However, parents are supposed to encourage their children to succeed. God ordained them as parents to nurture people who will live according to his will. For this reason, parents must pray unceasingly about their roles.

Some parents for example, may try to control their children's choice of friends for various reasons. This can lead to frustration and resentment in the parents as well as the children. The social norm is gradually including more openness to cross racial associations, acceptance of various ways to express sexuality, family arrangements and ways of dressing etc. Our children are learning differently from the way we did. According to scientists, the new technology our children are being taught with is causing new pathways to develop in their brains.

Whenever there is a struggle between ideas, the more evolved idea wins. This is because the spiritual nature of the universe is change, growth, abundance, expansion, and evolution. By evolving, I am not talking about apes becoming men. I am discussing the changing human consciousness or habitual thoughts.

There are two faces to every coin. One side of this coin might be that none of the above relates to parenting in your home. Perhaps your home is in harmony most of the time. Maybe your children are obedient most or all of the time. On the other side of the coin there may be challenges because your child is uncooperative, breaks the rules at school and home or vice versa. Maybe your child refuses to go to school or, if applicable, refuses to get a job or engages in behaviors that can harm him- or herself or others. The challenges that surface in parenting are often as unique as each child is. Children are often reacting to the emotional climate of their home, family relationships, or other issue. Regardless of what is happening there are always lessons for all involved to learn.

The self-esteem movement dictates that we must praise and encourage our children. However, we must also lovingly and firmly correct them whenever it becomes necessary. We must use discipline as a way to correct and not to punish. Confidently tell them the truth in support of their social and emotional growth, despite the fact that they may rebel. Failing to guide and correct them feeds the little ego and can build in them a sense of entitlement and a "better than or a self-righteous attitude." This can also cause these children to have problems with relationships and authority figures that can last through various stages of their lives. Parents should never feel obligated to adorn their children with every fashion that comes on the scene; unless and absolutely if it is something that will help their development into healthy and productive persons.

Take Action

What can we do as parents?

- The first step must be to pray and follow guidance received.
- We can admit that somewhere along our journey through life we might have lost our own sense of wholeness.
- We can examine our intentions to see if we are looking outside ourselves and maybe through our children's achievements to recapture a sense of our own self-worth. We can never find it there because it resides in us.
- Parents can scan their life experiences to find out what caused them emotional pain and how and when it happened. (See chapter 7 on forgiveness and complete any exercise necessary). Remember to breathe through any ill feelings. See them for what they are. They are

illusions; just let them go. With practice, this can be achieved. **Forgive yourself for not freeing yourself sooner. You did the best you knew how to, based on your experiences and the condition of your consciousness.**

As parents, after you have faced and healed any shadow or self-limiting constructs, you will be able to live from a wholesome, expansive, and free state of being. Priorities will shift, and the real self will shine through. When parents' emotional wounds are not dealt with, their children and significant others often present issues that stir up in the parents, the old feelings caused by those old wounds that must be healed. **When parents do the work that supports their healing, they empower themselves to discipline, and to accept and embrace the uniqueness of their children and their children's choices. They also develop the capacity to understand and forgive themselves and their children for any error.** They no longer identify with the false self. They no longer need to hide behind the strength of others or their children's performances. Parents will realize that they as well as their children each have a unique self. They will have opened themselves to receive the wisdom and power to parent with loving authority and success.

It has become vitally important that parents understand how to navigate new technology. We must keep abreast with how and what our children are learning, in order to adequately understand and help them. Libraries and other institutions offer classes for learning how to use different forms of technology. Once we pray we have to cooperate with God and do the work that expands our knowledge. We must also teach our children by our words and actions how to have faith and to practice love, patience, kindness, respect, humility and forgiveness.

No parent should feel that they have to parent without divine guidance. Our Almighty God who ordained us to become parents is compassionate and invites us to seek his guidance and favor in all things. God wants you to succeed in caring for his creation!

The following practices are offered to be used in support of parenting. Please modify to make this more personal. For example you can say children instead of child or him instead of her.

Prayer

Heavenly Father of us all, you are strong enough to save. In you I seek and find my strength and wisdom to parent. You promised "if I seek you first, all things will be added unto me." Today I come in the name of Jesus seeking you with an open and receptive mind, so that my words of prayers shall not return to me void. I ask for and open myself to receive your gift of wisdom and patience. I humbly ask your blessings on my children or any child that I nurture or have charge over. Fill them with the thirst to truly know you. My desire is that they also serve and glorify you. I ask that you fill them with the awareness of your Love, wisdom, courage and joy within themselves. Please protect them from harm or from harming themselves or others. I pray that they honor you with their lives. My Lord, I surrender them to you and allow you to have your way in their lives. I believe your promise in Isaiah 44:3 that said, ***"I would pour my Spirit on your descendants, and my blessing on your offspring."*** Glory goes to your name, Wonderful Counselor! All is well and I am forever grateful.

Affirmation

The Spirit of God fills my child (name) she/he is now safe, surrounded by peace, filled with wisdom and confidence and blessed with perfect health. I am grateful.

Denial

No ill can befall my child. He/she is always divinely protected. We follow Divine guidance and take all necessary steps concerning the wellbeing of my child (name)

Treatment

My children are creations of God. I agree with God and see them as strong, happy and loved unconditionally. I bless them with the consciousness of truth, order, wisdom, authenticity and the willingness to serve according to their Divine purpose. As I pray for them daily, I see them evolving from glory unto glory. This must be so and it cannot be otherwise, because they belong to our Almighty God. I commit them into the loving arms of Christ, the worker of miracles. For this privilege to do so and for answered prayers, I am eternally grateful.

Understanding Developmental Issues

An important step anyone can undertake in any situation in order to find the adequate solution is to understand the situation's cause. The following information can shed much-needed light on how humans have come to think and act the way we do.

The work of psychologist Erik Erikson helps us understand how our experiences play a role in dictating how we see ourselves, how we relate to others, and why we behave in certain ways. We can also examine why harm and disruption at a certain time of development manifest as specific symptoms. We can also understand how lack of achievement or fulfillment of expectations impacts us.

As we care for our children, and relate to the world, it can be useful to refer to the following information. We must keep in mind that as individuals we are unique. One person's consciousness or degree of resiliency, when different from another person's, can dictate different effects under the same circumstances and even if the wound or cause of it is the same.

In the following section, the word **wound** is used to describe any disruption to the growth phase of one's development. Wounds can be physical, such as hitting, not providing adequate health care, starvation, and various other types of abuse. Emotional wounds can occur to people who lived in chaotic conditions, witnessed parents or significant others being abused, or have been in constant fear, perhaps placed in foster care and not knowing when or if they would be sent to a different home, etc. Also when we do things for a child that should be done by the child—or "spoil" him or her, as we say—we create wounds. A child's experiences provide practice and a sense of accomplishment, but when we do things for him or her; we take that opportunity away or, we at least hamper the development of the particular skill.

Stages of Human Development

Stage 1—Infancy (Birth to Eighteen Months)—Trust vs. Mistrust

At this stage, trust or mistrust is developed. The child depends on caregivers to provide feedings, care, affection, and safety. When the child is neglected or abused at this stage (wounded), the symptoms this person will most likely exhibit in life are issues related to safety, survival, material possessions, victimization, lack of trust, problems in intimate relationships, and denying of feelings.

Stage 2—Early Childhood (Two to Three Years Old)—Autonomy vs. Shame and Doubt

At this stage, autonomy is developed. This stage centers around skills such as potty training, and the child strives to have control. Children begin to say no a lot. Developing autonomy is important, as they learn to demonstrate faith in their abilities in whatever they can do. Being disrupted at this stage by things such as physical abuse and /or punishing them for saying "no" fosters shame, doubt and the lack of a sense of self. When a healthy sense of autonomy is not developed, a person can experience difficulties in standing on his or her own, working alone, choosing appropriate situation or partners, and people pleasing. They can also experience a fear of making mistakes, doubts that they can do things right and low self-esteem.

Stage 3—Pre-School (Three to Five Years Old)—Initiative vs. Guilt

At this stage, the ability to have initiative begins to be developed. The child explores his or her environment and at times his or her genital. Wounds at this stage, such as negative reactions from significant others, can cause guilt. Parents at times misinterpret this exploratory behavior and may punish or criticize a child. This is the stage when children exclaim, "Look at me! Watch me climb up! Watch what I can do!" They want to be noticed, and even at this tender age they are looking for approval. When children are wounded at this stage, they may later have difficulty making purposeful decisions; have dependency on other adults; fear of disapproval, which causes them to seek approval often and to lack initiative.

Stage 4—School Age (Six to Eleven Years Old)—Industry vs. Inferiority

At this stage, school environment has much impact on a child's development of a sense of industry. Feelings of success at school lead to competence, while failure leads to a sense of inferiority. At this stage children develop a sense of worth. They acquire a love of learning and enjoy experimenting with new skills and abilities. When their performance is mixed or they fail to receive success, feelings of worthlessness result. Later in life, these people may have problems with procrastination as they use it to avoid tasks that trigger feelings of incompetence. They may engage in fighting with peers, inappropriate sexual activities, learned helplessness, low academic achievement, and anxiety.

Stage 5—Adolescence (Twelve to Eighteen Years Old)—Identity vs. Role Confusion

At this stage, an adolescent is dealing not only with social relationships, but he or she is also experiencing hormonal changes in his or her body as it matures and changes. Teens are now learning to build their self-esteem and sense of self. When a wound occurs at this stage, such as different forms of abuse at home or abroad, bullying, ostracism, etc., the effects can create deep mental scars. This person may not like his or her body size or facial features or some other aspect of his or her life; as a result, the adolescent can develop a weak sense of self. Resulting challenges can be role confusion, lack of assertiveness, feelings of being less than or not good enough, problems with substance abuse, and other self-destructive behaviors. We tend to believe that adolescents are impacted only by their peers at this stage. However, what the significant adults in their lives say to them or how these adults view them matters a great deal to these adolescents. This fortunately can provide some degree of a buffer, and provide hope for them when the adult's message to them is positive. Wounds at previous stages can impact this stage as well.

Stage 6—Young Adulthood (nineteen to forty years old)—Intimacy vs. Isolation

The forming of relationships, especially with peers, has the biggest impact at this stage. Wounds such as physical abuse, social challenges, and issues with sexuality at this time may cause failure to form and/or maintain good relationships. When a fear of intimacy is developed, it can lead to loneliness, isolation, and sabotage of good relationships. Work with this person must involve support that helps him or her to have love for self, honest self-awareness, and the courage to share his or her feelings while remaining true to who he or she is. A counselor must be mindful of physical contact, as this may be a negative trigger based on this person's experience. I believe difficulties at stages two and three can further complicate issues at this stage as well.

Stage 7—Middle Adulthood (forty to sixty-five years old)— Generation vs. Stagnation

The salient events at this stage are work (employment) and parenthood. Adults experience the need to create and nurture things that outlast them. This can often be accomplished by having children and creating and nurturing institutions. Achieving these things leads to feelings of success. Failure to accomplish this can lead to shallow involvement with the world or feelings of stagnation and mid-life crisis. Working and having children are not sufficient to achieve a sense of success at this stage. The individual must enjoy his or her work and family (if living with others). Issues at earlier stages can also affect progress at this stage. Work with such individual should include helping him or her create a vision of what he or she wants to achieve as well as providing support and guidance for the necessary steps.

Stage 8—Maturity (Sixty-Five Years Old to Death)—Ego-Integrity vs. Despair

At this stage older adults need to feel a sense of accomplishment about their lives. When this is true for them, they will most likely have feelings of wisdom and satisfaction. Failure to do so leads to regret and bitterness. It is not uncommon to see grandparents who successfully raised their own children later struggling to care for their grandchildren because of challenges in their children's lives. Circumstances at this time can be complicated, especially when older adults begin to physically and mentally decline. The ego's chatter may strongly echo, "There is dysfunction in your family" or "Your children are dysfunctional" or "You are a failure." The voice of love, however, should echo to these valuable seniors, "Look how successful you are. You raised your own children and now you are helping your grandchildren!"

In working with elders who need assistance, they must be offered support that acknowledges them for who they are and the dignity within themselves. They need to be spoken to with respect and reminded of their precious essence. Many societies respect the truth that our seniors are a blessing to society. We must acknowledge that our societies are built on the "backs" of those who came before us. People of the younger generations ought to sit with them and learn! Whether one is a parent, therapist, minister, or anyone else helping this age group, this information is vital for adequate intervention.

Strengthening and Healing the Parent Child relationship

How can one deal with the child who lives in a harmonious home and yet has difficulties? This parent must change his or her own consciousness first. This means that no matter what the child does, the situation must be handled with love, compassion, and understanding. This of course does not mean that the parent relinquishes the opportunity to discipline the child. The parent must pray for guidance and then accept it. The parent should ensure the child gets counseling or rehabilitation for substance abuse, if applicable; mental health services; spiritual teaching; academic services; and social skills training; whatever is necessary.

Parents, you are ordained to be your child's or children's parents and raise them according to scripturally and morally sound dictates. They, of course, will make their own choices. However, parents must lay the firm foundation. Jesus the Christ performed his first miracle when his mother told him to. He told her that it wasn't his time and she wasted no time arguing with him. She turned to the servants at the wedding feast and told them to do whatever Jesus said to do. Jesus then asked them to fill pots with water. He miraculously turned this water into the best tasting wine. **Mary courageously put her feminine creative energy to use. She called forth his miracle working power that was innate in him. We too must call forth the innate good that is in our children and never underestimate the power of a praying parent!**

Parents Prayer

Almighty creator, you have called me to parent. You have placed your Spirit within me; therefore, I am blessed with a spirit of love and courage and a sound mind. Your Spirit also dwells within my children. I ask in the name of Jesus Christ that you help me understand and accept that my children came into the world through my body and that they are yours; I surrender them to you. Please help me realize that through grace I am sufficient as an individual. Help me realize that every parent has his or her unique calling and that mine is defined only by you. Help me see not what I believe is lacking in me but what you and I know is beautiful in me. In this holy moment, I take dominion over my life, and I allow you to lovingly guide me as I guide my children. It is my intention to guide them according to your will. I thank you loving Father, for guiding me and for answering my prayers here and now. Amen.

Affirmation

Today I step out of the box of limitation. I transcended the dictates of the little ego and truly feel a new freedom. I guide my children with a holy boldness, courage, love, and compassion. Together we express ourselves in unity, love, and respect. All is well.

Denial

No habit of worrying, anger, self-doubt, or frustration can hinder me. I know who I am; I am the essence of peace. All is well with my family and me, and I am thankful.

Treatment

I am grateful for the wonderful opportunity to parent. I know that my Child/ children are gifts from God. As I parent, I allow the spirit of God to guide and befriend me. I choose to be the best of myself in all I think, say and do. I model ways that are of love, kind, forgiving and responsible for my children to follow. I desire the best for them and for the children of this world. I cooperate with God and I am ready to recognize and accept my success in parenting. I am deeply grateful as I watch love, harmony, respect and cooperation bloom in our relationship.

Please feel free to make more of your own so that they are more personal to you. For example instead of the word children you may say the name of a child etc. The prayers of parents are powerful. Remember that Jehovah blessed you with the child/ children. Our God who makes no mistakes desires that you succeed. Always remember that our children will by their attitudes, show us what we must correct or strengthen in ourselves as well as how we can best help them.

Parenting the Special Needs Child

While the general discussion addresses children without special needs, we must recognize the fact that we continue to see a significant increase in babies being born with special needs. Boys almost double the rate of girls being born with autism and other cognitive and developmental disabilities. As debates continue, there is no definitive answer to the question of why there is such a significant increase in incidences of autism and other disorders. There are challenges with other developmental disabilities such as Asperger's syndrome, attention deficit, learning disabilities, multiple handicap, as well as conduct and mood disorders etc. These result in struggles with health and social, behavioral and, academic functioning.

These situations often become challenges for many parents, who may at first react with denial, anger, shame, sadness, depression, hopelessness, guilt, frustration and blaming. When the disability is assumed to be caused by an act of a parent such as with fetal alcohol syndrome, low birth weight, premature birth, organ issues etc. there can be heavy guilt, grief, blaming and regret. On the other hand when the parent did all that was deemed right and yet there is an issue with their baby, there can be anger, blaming or despair. There are other unpredictable emotions that can surface. This may be difficult to comprehend, however hold fast to the truth that God has a Divine plan for your child's life. **Begin the whole process with affirmative prayer as this will center you** and eventually bring about peace and lull the "what if" and "why" chattering in your mind. Because the incidences of babies with disabilities increase, there has been a corresponding increase in research and resources to help in addressing these issues. The following are be steps that can create order when embraced.

Parents' Prayer

Almighty Heavenly Father of wisdom, creator of all. You see and know that I have given birth to our child. There are issues with development which are challenging. I feel as though I am groping in the dark. Nonetheless you are a God of Grace. I ask that you enlighten our family members through the Christ light that guides our way. I know that through your grace, our child achieves the development that you have ordained. I know that we will change for the better because of this child and that others too will change for the better. At times I have doubts that any good can result, however, I humbly ask for and open myself to receive the gift of faith, patience and unconditional love for this child. Help me to accept that in the days ahead I may have to adjust how I expected our child to develop. I join with you Almighty God, in knowing that only good can come out of this situation. I let it be so as I remove the little doubting self out of the way and so it is. Loving Father, I thank you in the name of Jesus Christ.

The following process can be helpful. This may not be appropriate for everyone since our lives and experiences are so unique. Please feel free to adjust these to suit your own circumstance. Commit to the process that matches your needs.

Pray for guidance, surrendering the issue to Almighty God.

If your action caused this issue, Commit to a forgiveness exercise, addressing the wound caused on all involved. (see chp.8)

If necessary, take a stretch. Commit to changing the behavior that caused the issue e.g. smoking, taking alcohol or illegal drug, poor nutrition, or too much caffeine etc. Honor yourself for taking this bold step.

For all parents, relatives and guardians, release the negative emotions such as anger, feelings of shame, guilt, hopelessness and frustration. You may have done all that is necessary to ensure a healthy baby and now you could be grappling to understand why this did not happen as expected.

Reach out to parents who are going through the same difficulty and band together becoming a force for good. Support each other. Everyone including the child has a lesson to learn and some may become clearer of what their calling is. See Chap. 5 for principles in forming a group.

Cooperate with those that are helping you with the child's needs; such as teachers, the health care, behavior and mental health teams.

Exercise

At this time one can begin with a prayer, meditation or simply envision a peaceful scene.

Get into a quiet, peaceful and comfortable spot. Light a tea light and place it in a transparent glass jar and out of the reach of children or adults who have a developmental disability. Begin your practice whether it's prayer etc.; communicate with God. Listen for answers laid on your heart. Observe the brilliance of the light as it peacefully burns. Observe the dance of the flame. Take this as a symbol of the Divinity of your child who is also filled with the Christ light that can never be extinguished. At the end of the session, you must offer praise and thanksgiving to God, for this moment of grace.

Whenever you feel hopeless, frustrated or any other negative emotion, remember the brilliance of this light that symbolized the divinity of your child. Choose to let this realization comfort you.

Note. Please put out the tea light as soon as this practice is completed. Never leave it unattended, never burn near flammable objects. Light attracts light; we do not want the child we just prayed about to go reaching for the light!

Exercise for stress reduction (3-5 Minutes)

Take a deep breath in – hold the thought that you are breathing in peace, joy, hope, wisdom and love. Hold for three seconds. For three seconds breathe out, while holding the thought that you are breathing out anger, disappointment, sadness, frustration, bitterness or other toxic emotion. **You can choose to breathe in and out one item at a time from the corresponding lists. E.g. breathe in peace and breathe out anger.**

Make a deliberate attempt to stay positive. Repeat this exercise as the need arises. Remember as the child matures its needs will change. There is the phase of puberty and young adulthood

and stages of later years. Each stage brings its own challenges; therefore these practices are not intended for a one time use. Spiritual practices must become a way of life.

What do we truly know?

Once, Jesus healed a child that was blind. The onlookers asked Jesus if the child's parents had sinned and caused the blindness. Jesus replied that no one sinned but that the child was born that way so that God can be glorified. In other words, the prayers, research, healings, finding cures, cooperation, charity work that result when we are faced with challenges, all attest to the wisdom and goodness of God through mankind. God did not promise that we would not have challenges; he promised that he will take us through them. We glorify him for inspiring us to take appropriate and successful actions.

It is very beneficial to learn of the latest research efforts and other trends. Social stories are short precise narratives with pictures and may contain words as well. These help children with autism and other cognitive disabilities to understand ideas and language by visual means. The iPod and other communication devices are also being used to teach these children as well. **Just googling the words** *social story*; **one can access books of social stories through the internet. There are magazines, and much more resources dedicated to families of children with special needs. The library and directories provide additional listing for services.**

Many schools provide the appropriate education for this population, from academics to Social Skills. There are camps scheduled for vacation time and these offer the experiences that also help with Social development. It is my prayer, that the stigmas against persons with disabilities are eradicated. This frees up much needed energy for compassionate work and for the understanding which allows the challenges faced by this population to be effectively dealt with.

Chapter 14

Teachers

Since ancient times, it has been recognized that people who disseminate knowledge have a deep and significant role to play in shaping our universe.

This is not only limited to teachers of academia but also to persons teaching religion, the arts, social/emotional skills, spirituality, etc. Anyone who teaches in these capacities has the power to build up or corrupt a nation. It is the little seeds of thought planted in the learners' minds that can germinate into significant acts for evil or good. This explains the saying "the hand that rocks the cradle rules the world."

I believe the person who fulfills their desire and teaches with gratitude and humility for the joy, satisfaction, and fulfillment they and their students receive is following a divine calling. Such a person is a vessel for transformation of the human consciousness. For this reason it is imperative to include teachers in a discussion on transformation.

We say that when the student is ready, the teacher appears. Make no mistake; when the teacher is ready, the student appears as well. In this holy relationship, neither is more important than the other. I believe this is always a divine arrangement. The age of the student never determines how significant the assignment of teaching is. All things being equal, it is as equally challenging to teach a preschooler as it is to teach someone with a postgraduate degree, even though their ages and needs are vastly different.

Because of my profession, I know teachers change their grade level placement throughout their careers. On the surface it can appear that someone assigned to teach at a lower grade level than they previously taught has been "demoted." Nothing could be further from the truth. These changes provide fertile soil for self-growth. With these experiences, teachers become well rounded and open to new levels and vistas for creativity. Teaching financially wealthy children is no more exalted than teaching underprivileged children. Each situation provides the stimulus for the teachers to reach inside themselves for great things; whether it is compassion, respect, courage, or integrity. Make no mistake; it will be whatever the teacher or student needs for his or her spiritual transformation. Yes, children are spiritually transforming too.

The master teacher, Jesus Christ, demonstrated unconditional and timeless love as well as compassion for children. In one instance, the mothers of Salem brought their children to the place where Jesus was so he could touch them and pray. The disciples rebuked them, but Jesus said, "Let the little children come to me ..." (Matt. 19:14). He then laid his hands on them. **Christ wasted no time intentionally demonstrating that children must be a priority.**

Challenges in Teaching

Teaching can be challenging. Teachers can become disillusioned when students, parents, or significant others become antagonistic. In any relationship, understanding and flexibility are vital to harmony. I urge every teacher to acquire knowledge in cultural competency and to always expect the best in student performance and the teacher-student relationship.

The Holy Encounter

I believe that on a deep level the teacher and student are placed together for evolutionary purposes. Both show up with their "must-be-completed lists." This is their holy encounter. At times, the assignment to be completed together may be brief (e.g., when the student transfers out quickly or the teacher had the role of substitute teacher). Regardless of if the relationship is brief or longstanding, children need adults in their lives who are strong patient, kind, consistent, and reliable. They also need adults who respect them, believe in them, and facilitate their learning with enthusiasm. This relationship is certainly not all about the student. The teacher deserves to be supported and respected in every way. Administrators can be more successful when all staff members are supported through respect, support, compassion, and gratitude.

The universe conspires to help the teacher-student relationship in unique ways. Let's look a few examples. In our first example, a teacher realizes a student refuses to listen to directions. Upon closer examination, this teacher discovers the same pattern in his own personal relationships; his children, spouse, acquaintances, or significant other do not follow his directions or are antagonistic. The student's behavior has shined a light on the cause of the symptom this teacher needs to heal. In this case, the symptom could be feelings of powerlessness, unworthiness, self-doubt, etc. This teacher broadcasts the energy of self-doubt etc. and attracts like responses from others, who do not feel confident or at least willing to follow his directions. As this teacher develops the areas needing growth, he will experience through others' responses the great benefits of peace, cooperation and joy in his work.

Another scenario is a child who lies to a teacher. This teacher, who is disappointed, needs to look at herself and then ask the question, "So do I lie to myself by for example, saying or thinking that I will go the gym or get adequate rest and then refuse to follow through? Do I keep saying yes to others' demands when I really want to say no?" Beloveds, this is an example of telling untruths to oneself. This student's action formed a vibrational match to that of the teacher. With this new awareness, the teacher can self-correct and be grateful for this insight and the grace through which this healing opportunity showed up.

This is not to say that everything reflected through a student's action is happening in the teacher's life. It is, however, a reflection that an issue of the same principle may be screaming for attention. At times when an issue shows up at school, such as a child being sad or angry, falling asleep, not completing homework, etc., this can be a symptom of the need for family intervention for the student. The teacher can be the angel who becomes the catalyst for this family's intervention. Ultimately, both teacher and student are born to evolve to higher heights. They are the vehicles for each other's transformation.

We must never underestimate the value of our Teaching Assistants, Teacher's Aides, Lunch room Aides, or Playground and Hall monitors etc. They are teachers who often work with students when they are in more relaxed frames of mind. Being more relaxed or removed from a formal classroom setting boosts students' courage to reveal issues that warrant some sort of intervention. It is beneficial to know that these priceless staff members are assigned to support teachers and students for the same purpose: transformation! It is beneficial for teachers to realize that each experience offers the opportunity to expand wisdom, knowledge, and understanding for both student and teacher. This positive change can only come when the teaching experience is conducted with the intention of equality and good for all concerned.

Teachers, like parents, ought to take care of their well-being and follow the airline safety rule that says, "Put the oxygen mask on you first!" In order for a teacher to be effective, he or she must attend to his or her own needs first. This includes spiritual, physical, mental, and emotional needs. It should in no way be a one-time deal; it should consist of regular and consistent acts of love and care for oneself.

Each teacher and student brings his or her own baggage to the table. A new group of students in a teacher's class can bring a new challenge or a new calm that lasts throughout the school year. The key is not to take anything personally. However, this may be difficult, especially when a particular situation triggers an emotional response. In these times, it would be wise for the teacher to know that his or her work is indeed an offering to God each time it is done with unconditional love.

A teacher can benefit by gaining clarity while paying attention to the following questions and their answers. The answers will obviously be unique to each individual. I encourage anyone seeking clarity to add his or her own questions if need be, since challenges also are unique to each person. **See the following sample questions:**

- How do I see this student or their family members?
- Do I negatively judge or condemn parents or guardians? How do I see myself in relation to them?
- What do I expect from students?
- Do I negatively or positively judge a particular student? Why?
- Does this student trigger a positive or negative emotional response in me?
- Do I like this student? Why or why not?
- Do I favor this student over others? Why?
- Am I taking on responsibilities for things I should not? What happens if I don't?
- Am I doing my best for all my students?
- What are my students showing me? How can we all grow?
- How do I relate to my peers, teaching assistants, other staff members, and administrators? How do they relate to me?
- Do I need to forgive myself or others for anything?
- What do I need to congratulate/acknowledge myself for?

- Am I working as a member of a team, offering and receiving support?
- Do I feel satisfaction, joy, and a sense of accomplishment? Why or why not?
- Do I have the trust and courage to ask for help with a student? Why or why not?
- Do I acknowledge and honor myself for my efforts?
- Do I practice radical self-care?

The answer to those questions can reveal the areas where the little ego is allowed to be in charge. Remember that it is this little ego (thought form) that says, "You're not good enough!" It likes to judge us and others and enjoys wearing the victim's hat. It loves to create situations where it can be the perpetual victim and enjoys being the center of attention. It is unfair, has the burning need to be always right and holds grudges. The little ego must be dethroned voluntarily or it can take personal crises, forcing one to surrender involuntarily. This can appear as loss of control of what is happening in one's life. There are practices included throughout the chapters in this book that are offered as tools for healing and transformation. Of course, everyone has the right to choose just how they want to deal with their own life experiences. Acknowledge yourself for those aspects of your life where the Spiritual ego is in charge. Build on this and keep up the good works!

Practices in Relation to Any Issue

Once clarity is gained in relation to any issue, the following model of prayers and practices are invaluable. Please adjust them according to your unique situation. **Always remember to use present tense. Again I caution that using the future tense creates the expectation that the peace, wisdom, etc., you seek will come in the future and never in the now.** There is also no need to have an issue before you embrace affirmative prayer. We are called to pray without ceasing (i.e., pray daily).

Affirmations

- The Almighty God at the center of my mind now guides my interaction with each of my students. (or, use a name if you have a particular child in mind).
- I praise my awareness of underlying issues crying out to be healed. I gratefully acknowledge and receive it. I diligently take all necessary steps and allow the Spirit of God within me to guide me. [If students trigger a thought of anger or joy or a memory of a childhood situation, this can be an appropriate affirmation.]
- **As** I embrace every one of my students with unconditional love, my classroom is filled with the radiant light of peace, harmony, and joy. I rejoice! [Make sure you hold love in your consciousness.]
- I bless my students with divine intelligence.

Treatment

There is a divine awareness within me that always comes to my aid. It readily flows through me as the guidance I need in the moment. I guard my thoughts with love, creating in my mind easy access for this awareness to fully flow. I fulfill my goals for myself and my students, knowing that I am always divinely guided.

Denials

If there is any issue at hand that is not favorable or if there is a challenge with students, work, etc., denials may be more assuring to some, the same way that affirmations or treatments are to others. The following denials can be useful:

- There is no tension in this place. There is no strife in this place. I see the peace of Christ penetrating the hearts and minds of everyone here, including me. I simply know this to be the truth; I rejoice and give thanks!

- **N**o fear or doubt can hinder my effectiveness. Completing all tasks at hand, I work with poise, efficiency, and success.

Affirmative Prayer

Wonderful counselor, you have called me to do the work of imparting knowledge to your children. My desire is to work in the way that is pleasing in your sight, so I seek your guidance now. I allow you to move through me and teach through me. Let me be aware of your presence as I plan and carry out my duties. You believe in the Divinity in each student and in me; I join you in believing in the Divinity in each student and in myself. Touch the mind of each student and make clear and easy his or her task of learning. Bless each family represented in my classroom so that together, parents, guardians, and I support the students in the best way possible. I ask this in the name of our way-shower, Jesus Christ, who always made time for children. I thank you for hearing me and answering me, even while I speak. All is well.

Teachers Celebrate!

In quiet contemplation, the following truth came into my awareness. Teachers have the right and privilege to celebrate each time they support a student in making a breakthrough. For example, a particular student was having much difficulty asking for help. This student often ended the school day with unanswered questions. His teacher continually encouraged him to participate and held him accountable for his assignments. The teacher also lovingly held in her mind that the student was capable and willing. Then one day the dam of fear broke, and the student began to ask questions courageously. Apart from the objective prodding of the teacher, something greater was happening. The energy of love and truth which the teacher held in her mind began to broadcast itself toward the student. The only possibility left was for the student to respond with a vibrational match. This works the same for a child or adult student. Teachers with this fertile frame of mind can call forth wisdom that is inherent in students. Teachers ought to celebrate this!

Administrators

We cannot address the very important work of teachers without recognizing the major role the administrators play in teachers' success. Administrators are at the helm, and as is the case of teachers, they have much entrusted to them. They can ask themselves the questions above and adjust the words to suit their responsibilities, e.g. substitute staff member instead of student where practical. Principals and Assistant Principals are also entrusted with great responsibilities. The chain of command ends with those who work closest with the students. These are teachers and related service team members such as Social Workers, Speech therapists, OT/PT and Psychologists etc. It is only imperative that these workers are treated with respect by their Administrators and that these workers treat the Administrators with respect as well.

When staff members work with students, they are also dealing with the issues students bring from home. On the part of Administration, there is no place for the little ego in this arrangement; the administrator with the tenacity to support their staff and communicate with them respectfully must be commended. It does not matter where one is on the chain of command, treating others disrespectfully has serious consequences which can manifest as difficulties in their personal life.

We often hear of the good old days when female teaches wore ankle-length skirts and male teachers wore suits, often of the scissor tail style. Regardless of how we view current times, the truth is that we are living in more enlightened days. Enlightenment is always good. We also hear children were very obedient back then.

Today they are as well; however, their points of references are different. They learn differently, and they are dancing to the beat of different drums. They are more in rhythm with what is just and unjust as our human race collectively evolves spiritually. This is true for teachers as well.

It would be very beneficial for administrators to support the ushering in of new learning for all. For example, apart from coordinating workshops in teaching skills, administrators could advocate for workshops that provide all staff members with e.g. Mindfulness training and knowledge of how to *be*, not only how to *do etc.* Staff members on every level would do well to also learn how events like their experiences and family stories at particular stages of their own development, affect how they deal with their students, peers and themselves. They would then be more equipped to deal with specific issues, when helping students and staff to develop academic and emotional intelligence. Everyone is transforming, whether consciously or unconsciously.

Workshops on visioning toward school goals can be very valuable. Major accomplishments are achieved through well-planned goals that are also followed up on. Planning is conducive to order in the mind of every staff member. The intention we bring to our work will always determine results, e.g. whether we grow or not. This work can be daunting at times, however the Administrator and pertinent personnel must diligently guide and support the work and workers on all levels with equal intensity.

I believe that Mindfulness training for teachers and students can be priceless. This can create an atmosphere of cooperation and compassion. The practice of teaching and the task of learning can prosper in an atmosphere where people are less stressed, more focused, calm and emotionally intelligent. This type of workshop and more of its kind can be provided through advocacy of Administrators or other personnel with such leverage.

Affirmative prayer is very valuable when one seeks to release fears, doubts, and uncertainties and embrace divine wisdom. The following prayer is for administrators, but it can be adapted and used by workers everywhere, in any field of work.

Administrator's Prayers

Prayer

Wonderful counselor and Father of all mankind, there is peace and joy in your loving presence. I am so grateful for this work that you have assigned for me to do. I recognize that it is an activity for good. Through me you impact the lives and transformations of so many. Lord, I am willing; I humbly ask in the name of Christ for an awareness of divine guidance, wisdom and joy so that I may lead in a manner that is pleasing to you. It is my intention to serve with unconditional love, fairness, compassion, humility, and courage. Please show me how.

Almighty Father, as I forgive anyone needing forgiveness for any mistakes, please forgive me for any error in thought, word, or deed. I choose to allow your Spirit within me to guide me. I allow your Spirit to be my constant companion. Let me always be aware of your grace as you inspire others to support my efforts for excellence, integrity, and love. I recognize that by myself I cannot do this work; with you all things are possible, so I allow you to help me. I thank you for hearing me now and for hearing me always. Amen.

Affirmations

- Today I allow myself to be divinely guided as I make all decisions.
- I approach life and work with enthusiasm and patience. I value everyone with whom I interact, and they in turn value me.

- I use the qualities of spirit that are mine to use. I give of my best to all I think, say, and do.
- I see the Divinity in everyone with whom I interact and they see the Divinity in me.

Treatment

I have the confidence that as I allow God to work in and through me, my work prospers all concerned. I allow God to be the source of all my ideas. I act with Wisdom and speak as the voice of truth. I am Divine love in action and I create an atmosphere of love and peace wherever I go. I speak with a tone of compassion, understanding, respect, patience and kindness. I *am* a blessing to those with whom I work; all staff, students, parents and guardians. I let the love of God shine through in al that I think, say, and do. For this great privilege, I am grateful.

Our Vocation

There are so many other career paths that are worth specific mention in this book. Every field is a response to the collective consciousness of mankind and are all governed by Spiritual law. We receive benefits through our job as much as we put in physically and by way of consciousness. Our place of work requires the same consideration we give to our homes. We appreciate when visitors treat our homes and the inhabitants with respect. We must allow this respect to thrive at our place of work as well.

A pleasant attitude goes a long way at work. At times someone may go to work despite troubling situations in their lives: the last thing they would want to experience is a leader or peer who is boisterous, unprofessional, and not compassionate or, one who thrives on dictates of the little ego. It requires an overhead cost to employ people. When workers remove as little as a paperclip from their place of work it is not right to do so. In fact, they are broadcasting that they have to fill their need through dishonest means and the Law of attraction will respond accordingly. According to the Law of Attraction honesty is necessary for true prosperity. One must be mindful of time and make up time owed. It is always beneficial to serve with thoughts and actions based on what is fair, ethical, and respectful as well as what is right for all involved. One must forgive mistakes made by self or other and do better while learning from the experience. Attitudes at home often carry over at work and vice versa. This is unfortunate and unfair therefore care must be taken to address situations in one's personal life. Affirmative prayer is very valuable as support for clarity and success in one's work life.

The following are practices to support one's work experience. (Practices from the section on political leaders can be adapted for use in this section) be creative educators!

Affirmations

The Spirit of God within me guides my work. My work is effective and efficient and lifts up all those whom I serve.

My work symbolizes the action of God through me. I choose to work with integrity and positive regard for my fellow workers on every hierarchal level.

Denial

No fear of failure can confound me. I am successful; with God all things are possible.

Spiritual Mind Treatment

I place my work in the hands of God as an offering of love. I choose to offer my gifts and talents as loving service at my place of work. I trust that wherever I go the way is prepared for me; I bloom and flourish wherever I am planted. There is nothing in me that hinder my success. I choose to be identified with compassion, pleasantness, respect, excellence, joy, love, peace and friendship. Only good goes from me and only good comes to me. I am grateful that this is so and cannot be otherwise.

Prayer

Our heavenly Father, I place my trust in you. I am grateful for my employment and the privilege to serve by means of it. Through my work I must fulfill your perfect plan. I ask for daily guidance and am open and receptive to receive it. Dear Father, I allow your ideas to flow in and through me, as I work with order and efficiency in my mind and actions. Help me to understand that true service is always an act of love to you and all creation. I complete my work in a way that is pleasing in your sight so that when others see my work they will glorify you, knowing that it is you who work through me. I ask these blessings in the name of Jesus Christ. Amen.

Our Political Leaders

Being privileged to work in the school setting, I became aware that political systems are macrocosms of the school systems. My belief is that the educational and political systems are major driving forces that shape a nation and affect the world. Since historical times, these institutions have played major roles in the development of the human condition.

For as far back in history as can be recalled, leaders and rulers have been present in the world's organizations. There have been arguments concerning whether it is scriptural or spiritually correct for people of some faiths to become involved in the political aspects of the world. When we look at the teachings of Jesus Christ, we learn that he said we must render to Caesar what is Caesar's. Caesar was the ruler of the land in which Jesus and his disciples were at that time. Jesus was telling them that it was legal and proper to pay their taxes as required by the government. When the Virgin Mary was with child and very close to the time of giving birth to Jesus, she traveled on a donkey with Joseph to Bethlehem. They were going to be registered as required by the census of that city. There have always been world governments as earthly systems to ensure that people are accounted for through census e.g., and afforded lives of justice and dignity.

In reference to the action of God, we read in the scriptures; **He removes Kings and raises up Kings"** Dan 2:21. **By this we understand that God appoints our leaders**. Our leaders have the God given gift of choice which is never revoked. It is their spiritual duty to choose to govern according to the will of God. Everyone has the right to be better off because of our governments. **Our governments are supposed to be run on the basis of truth, love, and justice. This is possible when leaders and rulers do not allow the little ego to dictate how they rule.** When the little ego rules, war and threats of war is often the current state of affairs. In the book of Proverbs we read, "When the righteous are in authority, the people rejoice; But when a wicked man rules, the people groan." Prov 29:2. As inhabitants of the world, we must like Jesus and his family, adhere to the mandates of our governments.

I believe that Jesus was not a political leader because our Heavenly Father did not ordain him to be a politician; it would have been impossible for him to carry out his ministry as it was done. God gives us each a unique career, which means that each career is ordained by God. We do not have to agree with and support ungodly policies of our governments, but we must support what is upright and just. We should work for peace, building up the heavenly kingdom within us and not become enmeshed in the fighting, judging, hatred, cruelty, and dishonesty of this world. Our lives and actions must attest to our obedience to God who is Love.

The human ability however, is limited without God, so we must pray that our leaders and rulers receive divine guidance. The arrangement should not be that we stretch out our hands to receive the government's aid while saying that we have no part in the government. This would be hypocrisy at its best. We must do our share in helping to maintain the infrastructure of our lands and the well-being of each other. As we support our governments in efforts of peace and justice, we are supporting the health, well-being, and transformation of the lives of many, including ourselves. We must also understand that mankind cannot put an end to suffering nor all the ills of crime and poverty we encounter. Only Almighty God has the power to do so. As a matter of truth, Christ said that the poor will always be with us. "For you have the poor with you always" Matt 26:11. We ought to pray for our rulers and leaders worldwide and allow peace to begin within each of us.

Lifting up our Political leaders in prayer

The following prayer can be adapted to suit whatever particular region in which you live. You can also adapt it to reflect if your governmental structure has as its leader a President, King, Queen, Prime Minister, or leader with other designation.

Prayer

Almighty and Intelligent Jehovah, you are ruler of all and everywhere present. In this holy moment your loving and watchful eyes are on us all. I thank you, Lord, that you know the brilliance and beauty of every citizen of this world. You know the worthiness of every person. Our affairs are lovingly on your mind. Lord, I ask your blessing for all political leaders of this world and all those who help them. Grant them an awareness of the resiliency that they possess through grace. Show them how to use it for the benefit for all. Bless our president [say name of president/ruler]. Protect him/her from dangers seen and unseen, known and unknown. Protect her/his family and keep them all under the powerful shadow of your loving arms. Breathe wisdom, peace, and justice into all that he/she does; give him/her daily bread of divine guidance, wisdom and protection.

Help our president to know that infinite spirit surrounds, fills, and directs him/her. Help him/her to decrease and allow you to increase in all the transactions of their office, both locally and abroad. Help our President to be an advocate for the uplifting of the human condition. Help him/her to remember prisoners, the mentally and physically and developmentally challenged, those in war torn areas, the sick, poor, our elderly and those experiencing direct or indirect assaults from disasters.

As I surrender our President to you, I ask in the name of Jesus that he/she becomes aware that you have appointed him/her. Help our President to restore dignity to those lacking it and to support us in maintaining our example as a nation that liberates everyone at home and abroad. Help the people of this nation to respect and obey the laws of the constitution which protects our freedom. Help us to do our share through good citizenship, unconditional love, fairness, kindness, service and compassion.

I thank you, Lord, that in this holy moment of prayer, you are already blessing him/her and their family members with protection. You are now infusing in him/her a sense of courage, justice, integrity, and unconditional love for himself/herself and others. I thank you, God, for helping him/her serve your purpose because your will must be done. I thank you for blessing our president with the thirst for your good works, which he/she will do. Your love for president [say name of president/ruler] is constant, vibrant, and strong. In the name of the Christ, I declare that he/she is divinely inspired, guided, is safe and filled with joy. I declare that this is so in this holy moment of now, and it cannot be otherwise. I am grateful now and always. Amen.

Note: Political leaders can use affirmation, Spiritual Mind Treatments and Denial from the section addressing Teachers, Administrators and Vocation as well as the following.

Prayer

Dear Heavenly father, with gratitude I humbly embrace my holy assignment as leader of your people. I surrender my mind to you and allow you to work mightily in and through me. I ask that you bless me with my daily bread of wisdom and guidance. Strengthen me as I lay aside my personal will and embrace your will. I move forward with zeal doing your will and leading with integrity, fairness, justice and unconditional love for everyone. I believe in your words which promised that angels shall have charge over us. Today I ask for this divine protection for myself, my family and all people of every nation. I intentionally and completely surrender to your activity in my leadership and allow you to be God in every activity. I pray that this world becomes a more loving place because I execute my assignment as leader according to your blessed will. I pray in the name of Jesus Christ who taught us to love unconditionally. Lord, I thank you for this privilege to serve in such a wonderful way and for your hearing and answering of my prayers, even now.

Affirmations

Divine intelligence expresses through me as Love, wisdom, power and authority.

I am divinely supported in the operation of my official duties. Cooperation and clarity rules this day!

Denial

There is no condemnation, hatred or bitterness in me. I am about my heavenly Father's business and it shows in all of my work.

Treatment

I allow Unconditional love to lead me as I work tirelessly for justice for all people in this nation. I believe and know that oneness lies at our core. We are all Almighty God's beloved children. There is so much good in each of us; by my works I stir up the demonstration of this truth.

Chapter 15

Death and Bereavement

Our bodies are indeed wonderfully made! After taking a course in embryology, I had to agree with others that it is miraculous, that so much occurs in the right way as the human body is being formed. Each cell of our body is a center of intelligence! Through our bodies we experience sorrow and joy, illness and health, displeasure and pleasure. We move, become still, sleep, and dream. We awake from our dream both literally and metaphorically. Our bodies change; this change often coincides with our physical growth and our increase in wisdom, knowledge and understanding. Our bodies follow the rhythm of nature as we experience life and physical death.

People are Social beings; we become emotionally attached to each other. Death, although an inevitable process of life, becomes a cause for despair to many. The idea of not seeing a loved one in the physical especially after the social bond had been formed is often extremely difficult for many. Examining different Faith based religious and Spiritual teachings and listening to persons who had near death experiences, we understand that there is a resurrection and that only the physical body dies; Spirit never dies. Most people believe this, while some have questions and feelings of ambivalence concerning a resurrection or life after death. Just as peoples' beliefs vary, so do their responses to losing someone to physical death. The quality of the relationship that existed between the deceased and the one who may be grieving and perhaps other beliefs such as religious or spiritual, often determine the intensity of grief or whether there is any grief or sorrow.

Preparation

Normally there is some knowledge beforehand that someone such as family member, friend or acquaintance is about to die. This can become a great time in which to help this person attend to various issues such as finances and plans for last rites etc. or to help on their behalf. It is natural that at times there may be disagreements between and among people involved. It is always better at this time to make amends and to solve any problem while ensuring a winning solution for all involved. For those involved, whether they are a child, parent, sibling, relative or friend, this can be a challenging time. At times the death is sudden and therefore no preparations were made. Whether expected or sudden, death is a major stressor in the lives of most people dealing with it. There can be anger, blaming, resentment, denial, feelings of guilt, anxiety, sadness, depression devastation, despair, shame or simply peace and acceptance.

As the work of Spiritual transformation continues, this event can be embraced as a time to embrace the principles of love, faith, forgiveness, compassion and gratitude as discussed in previous chapters. One should also keep in mind that self-love and forgiving oneself if necessary, often becomes imperative at this time. This can provide closure and lessens any painful regrets while grieving. Group prayer is often emotionally supportive and priceless. In some cultures there are gatherings of relatives and friends for prayer and feasting. This can occur for several days and even on the anniversaries of the death for several consecutive years!

Pain

The one who may be passing / making their transition / or dying, should be assisted in making amends as well. They must be supported in taking care of any other issues that may be burdensome or of concern to them. The issue of physical pain management if pain exists must take priority. At times someone may be too weak or heavily medicated to indicate that they are feeling pain. Someone shared with me the fact that they had been hospitalized and had no movement in their body, not even to blink nor open an eye. This person felt pain and heard every word that was said around and about her. This person also recalled that two nurses provided bedside care on alternate days. When she would hear the voice of one particular nurse she shuddered inside. She knew that this nurse would clean her breathing tube in a rough manner causing severe pain. She also heard when her children bargained with the Doctor to leave her on life support because she would be healed. She regained movement and evidently lived to give this account and another that was quite humorous! (To be able to chuckle at this in retrospect is very freeing!) We must advocate for pain management when necessary and be careful of what is discussed around sick persons. Hearing and not being able to respond can add to suffering. Unconditional love and regard for one's self and all involved should lead the way during this process. **The little ego should have no place in this process**; it is a major obstruction to grieving in a healthy manner or allowing others to grieve in a healthy manner.

Practices

When children are involved in any way, when possible, care must be taken to ensure that they do not become traumatized. This can happen when the death was sudden, when they have witnessed traumatic events such as drowning, house fire, accidents, wars etc. Not being a witness but being related to the victim is enough to cause trauma as well. Children must be observed for signs of depression, hopelessness, excessive happiness, sudden peace or anger. Please note that there were incidents where children who displayed excessive happiness or sudden peace, (not always because of the death of someone) had planned to end their own lives. The thought of an end to what was causing the trouble for them offered peace and happiness. Unfortunately, some did actually follow through. The following practices are not only useful for children; these are practices that are priceless for adults as well.

Ways to Support our children through the grieving process.

Praying is always a necessary first step. Psalm 30:5 we read "... *Weeping may endure for a night but joy comes in the morning.*" Scriptural passages provide much hope. We must not be afraid to cry; some people are afraid that if they cry they will fall apart. **Jesus wept**, leaving a beautiful example of how we can show our own humanity, support others and relieve our stress.

Once I was working with a child who constantly cried in class and was depressed because his school mate died. Words of comfort and assurance did not seem to comfort him. I realized that a more tangible memory would begin the healing process. We began the writing process and soon in the days that followed, he was back on the playground. Did he remember his friend? Of course! However the difference was that his kind words written to his deceased friend was a catalyst for the beginning of the healing of his own emotions; our words of love, compassion and goodwill towards others return to bless us!

When working with children we must check for trauma as stated before. Check to see if the child is eating and sleeping well, whether they are overly anxious, fearful, withdrawn, depressed etc. Such children should have grief counseling soon. It is effective to work with children in groups (although working with a single child is good too) and to lead conversations that address what they perceive their loved ones would want for them. The aim here is to get them to realize e.g. "Grandma or Grandpa would want me to be happy." This in essence, can give them permission and courage to begin to feel happy.

Hold discussions especially as a group and support these children as they tell stories and give accounts of the good experiences they had with this deceased. There are many books in the library concerning bereavement for children and adults. These can be read to the children. Facilitate discussions about the deceased favorite things, favorite memories, their funny sayings, and their kind deeds; this can help to foster a healthy attachment to the deceased. Talk about the deceased not being able to be sick, sad or feel any more pain; this can provide lessons about life itself. Have the children verbally engage in the entire process. Be careful to ask the child if they regret saying or not saying anything, or doing or not doing something. Writing or drawing exercises can be useful in helping the one grieving to express their intention in this manner. Please carefully supervise children because at this time they can become vulnerable to those who are helping them, whether it is a relative, friend or stranger!

Patience

Whether child or adult, patience must be demonstrated through the helper's words and actions. Once, the acquaintance of a child passed away. This child continued attending school and acted quite normal. Several days later she suddenly began crying uncontrollably and appeared to feel panic. She was taken to a worker who seemed shocked and yelled "get her away from me!" I took the child, worked with her and I was glad that I did. Later in a discussion there was cause for me to explain that the delay between the death and the child's reaction did not mean that she was pretending to be distressed. This delay is normal in both children and adults. When a person is not showing emotions, this does not mean that they don't care, is not sad or is not suffering. I also came to an awareness that this worker was afraid of her own pain due to having had a close loved one pass away. People grieve differently. Some people may be joyful based on how they view death. We must let our words, facial expressions and other actions show that we care!

A very common occurrence is the fact that memories of the deceased can be triggered by an event least expected to do so. Recently my beloved mother who was a cheerleader for this book, made her transition. She resided in a great neighborhood, fairly close to a variety of stores that sell items and food products, meeting the need of people of the various ethnicities. I was always filled with childish excitement when I visited mommy, most often on weekends; she emitted the energy of love and joy. I would shop there then load up my pantry with many of these food items. Recently on a weekend, the time of the week I most often visited, I went into my pantry and saw an unopened box of ginger tea which I bought from the Caribbean market in her neighborhood on one of those visits. I picked up the tea, looked at it and that was enough to switch my state to crying and sadness for a great part of the day. Whether it is a song, a scent, a picture, a memory or any other trigger, we must be mindful that children as well as adults are susceptible to these occurrences. We must be compassionate and allow the one grieving to talk about their feelings and its trigger, if they so choose. Good listening and empathy is a valuable key to wholesome support.

As mentioned earlier, writing is a catharsis for many issues. If the child desires to write a note, poem or letter e.g. they can be assisted with the spelling and in writing what their fears, concerns or wishes are. Discussion, writing or drawing can also address memories that trigger sadness etc. Some children may prefer to draw and not speak or the reverse; that would be great as well. They must be given the choice to keep their work or not. Some children prefer to keep their work. A responsible adult can help them to safely throw it in running (not stagnant) water or to safely burn it for them. The metaphor here is that the messages are borne away by water or carried away in the smoke as they say "this is for you Grandma or Grandpa" etc. The practice of releasing balloons with the deceased's name on it helps adults as well as children.

Support for our adults.

All of the above processes can be used by adults as well. I chose to use children as examples to strengthen our awareness that children also go through the grieving process. The adult must be willing to ask for and accept help and to care for their self. The goal is that the one grieving finds a sense of peace and wholeness despite what is going on. The way one grieves varies from person to person so patience with self and others is invaluable! The first of each holiday, and other significant anniversaries without the deceased can trigger sadness and deep feelings of loss. Later anniversaries may trigger the same emotional response. Adults as well can be vulnerable at these times; they must be careful and aware when making decisions and transactions, especially those dealing with custody or financial issues. There are religious and Spiritual organizations as well as agencies that offer bereavement counseling for individuals, families and groups. For those involved, please seek these out if the need arises. The Telephone operator, telephone directories, internet, libraries etc. usually provide listings of such organizations and agencies. The master key at these times is to pray affirmatively. Do not isolate yourself; help someone who is grieving if you emotionally can. "A burden shared is a burden lightened!" Again, the key is to pray affirmatively with faith. **In the presence of God there is fullness of Joy.**

The following are prayers of comfort

A comforting prayer for one's self

Almighty Father, I am in your presence with feelings of sadness. I feel burdened and weak. I am not sure how I will proceed in the days ahead, so I am asking you to guide me through your spirit in me. I feel as though I am falling apart and I am having a difficult time. I ask that you hold me up until this storm in life is over. I ask for and accept the strength to carry on. Carry me Lord; Carry me now because I trust you. Mother, Father God I know that you hear me now because you promised that you will always hear me. I thank you for hearing and helping me now. Through the Christ Spirit in me, I ask and am grateful.

A Prayer for another

Dear Jehovah, I come in the name of the Christ in us. (Name of person's) Dad has died. He is having a difficult time and has issues that are causing him emotional turmoil. Please help him to remember that you are a loving Heavenly Father who loves and cares for him. Help him to know that there is nothing that can separate your love from him. Lord I am holding the space for Divine guidance, comfort and love for him in my heart. Let him feel the assurance that when Jesus wept, he understood that we will weep too; he understands our sorrows. Under the shadow of your presence Lord, help him to commit all actions that are according to your will. Be his guardian and his guide and hold him up. I surrender this prayer knowing that you my God, is sufficient in all things. With humble gratitude, I say thank you. All is well; I let it be so and so it is, now and always.

Group Prayer

Wonderful Creator and God of compassion, your spirit in us is a comforter and your grace will always be our sufficiency. Sadness and grief cloud our feelings and we ask, "Why?" We know that death comes to all and yet we ask "why do our loved ones die, why?" Dear God we seek your comfort today. You promised the resurrection and eternal life, yet in this difficult time we want to feel your comfort. Help us to let go of any anger, regrets, resentment or bitterness. This may take time but we trust that you will complete this in us. Show us the signs of redemption; we are as children who need something to hold on to. Our hearts feel broken, yet we know that with your love you are binding them up with comfort and in unity with each other. We ask for and open ourselves to receive understanding, peace and healing now. Through the Christ in us, we expect and accept your peace which surpasses all human understanding. We know you promised that as we believe, our words of prayer will not return to us void; they will prosper in the thing we ask for. With this knowing we accept your comfort and humbly say, "Thank You Father, thank you Father, Thank you Father. All is well now and forever more."

Epilogue

A credit card company in promoting the necessity of its card, used advertisement with the following words, **"You can't leave home without it!"** I chuckled; some commercials have this effect on me because I love the play of words, which feeds into my joy of musing. I then mused, while thinking that affirmative prayer practice is indispensable and that **"We can't live well without it!"** In referring to Spiritual Law, Jesus said "If you know these things, blessed are you if you do them" (JN 13:17). This book was intentionally written to provide knowledge and instill wisdom of spiritual laws. When we are finished praying, we must be prepared to remain aligned with our source God, through our thoughts, words, and actions. We must be prepared to maintain our spiritual practice and to co-create with almighty God our provider. Doing these things keeps us spiritually informed and well fitted in our new wineskin of wisdom.

It is very vital to come to the understanding that our bodies are temples through which God acts. In reverence and gratitude, we ought to care for our physical, emotional, mental and spiritual selves, creating in our being, the condition of our spiritual fitness at these various levels. In this atmosphere of wholeness, our heavenly Father's will can be done in and through us, unhindered. (See chapter on fortifying ourselves). It is absolutely necessary that we do any spiritual work needed to bring healing to ourselves for any mental, physical or emotional trauma, which we may have experienced. Such healing creates a clear channel through which our prayers are offered and our answers revealed.

We must be "About our fathers business" as Christ was at age twelve. (LK 3:49). This involves learning about and practicing Spiritual Laws. We can begin to teach our children Spiritual Laws, beginning when they are young as well. As we seek and receive spiritual wisdom, we ought to share our knowledge with each other. This is an act of love that supports the transformation of mankind. The effectiveness of our prayers expands exponentially as we abandon ourselves to the embodiment of love for one another. We must practice and embrace the spiritual laws of love, forgiveness, gratitude and faith.

Prosperity is our birthright; however it is only when we obey these Spiritual Laws, that we position ourselves to prosper. These laws work through their power as catalysts for the Law of Attraction. **We must surrender the falsity that we can visualize having our needs met and actually succeed, without first embracing and practicing Spiritual Laws such as love, forgiveness, faith and gratitude.** These laws are immutable; they cannot change to suit our personal desires, regardless of who we are or what we have. God does not play favorites. If these laws are not willingly followed, our acts of visualization, affirmation, treatment, denials or meditation for prosperity, will be futile. Instead, we may attract more negativity, because our inner life determines our outer life.

We must also find ways to be of service in this world and to practice love for ourselves and others. We must practice becoming still and receptive to the still small voice of God's spirit in us. When we become still in the silence, we become revitalized and are more effective when we speak and act.

We must demonstrate faith, patience and courage. View seeming setbacks as entering a period of grace, while seeing the wisdom in Jehovah God's plan. This can be challenging but nonetheless, a time to reevaluate, reorganize, change direction or simply wait. **Life is never against us. In times of conflict, we must allow**

the Spiritual ego or higher self to inform and inspire us. In this way we can choose to accept that peace is the ultimate truth of any troubling situation. We must strive to become the peace we seek and be open to the next most appropriate action. Only truth can be victorious! We must be like water in a stream, taking the path of least resistance; eventually the stumbling rocks in our path become smoother, allowing us to move over and around the drama with grace and ease.

When prayers are offered as a request for physical healing, remember to complete processes that heal the root causes of the illness so that the symptom does not reappear. Be gentle with yourself and know that God is working with you. It is impossible to work on yourself without God's presence working along with you.

We must all celebrate I firmly agree that the present is not a prisoner of the past. Life is new every morning. As we live we accumulate ideas and experiences that often bind us to past experiences. When they are negative in nature, we can become mesmerized by a life of stagnation and mediocrity. We forget all about our divinity, we forget that we are worthy and that our daily bread is already provided. We let doubt and fears rob us of our good. I have moved through fear and claimed the right to celebrate.

It is my earnest desire that as you evolve, you boldly take dominion over your life's circumstances and use your affirmative practices and words to edify and bless yourself and others, always praising Our Heavenly Father. **This book is lovingly offered as a tool for transformation; a handbook for affirmative living.** I trust that you claim and embrace your right to celebrate as you climb each rung of liberation and transformation. I pray that you get the profound understanding that when you do the spiritual work, your mind changes for the best and you become transformed by the renewing of your mind.

I celebrate

In gratitude for what has been, what is, and what is to come, I celebrate.

I celebrate my choice to surrender all to God so that I can be used as an instrument of agape love, doing God's will on earth as in heaven. I lovingly wrote this book as a manifestation of my choice to embrace freedom by surrendering doubts, fear, and resistance, self-sabotage, hiding, and playing small.

I celebrate myself and my willingness to persevere despite the little ego's trickery in trying to reinforce the message that I should not, would not, or could not be heard.

I write in celebration of my continuing spiritual evolution and my choice to allow God to dream through me.

I write in celebration of this glorious privilege of supporting others in experiencing God as God truly is … The great I AM.

I celebrate my choice and privilege to be love in action and to consciously cooperate with God's Spirit in me, as every step is revealed to me.

I celebrate my acceptance that by myself I can do nothing and that with God all things are possible; I can do all things through Christ, who strengthens me.

Beloved, dare to dream big, I pray affirmatively that your reasons to celebrate are immeasurable!

Different forms of prayer have been offered in this book. Pray according to your level of consciousness and as you feel guided to. Communicate with God in simple language, more advanced language, your native language, or foreign language. Pray audibly or inaudibly. Remember to take a statement of truth into prayer then meditate on it with a surrendered mind. For example, for physical healing, a statement can be "God is my health." For relationships, a statement can be "The Spirit of God now expresses through me as harmony." For finance, a statement can be "Abundance is mine and I accept it now." For employment or vocation, a statement can be "God is my source of right work and I am grateful." Believe these statements and listen for guidance as prayer is a two way communication process; listening is crucial! Always remain in a state of openness, love and gratitude. Stay grounded in a life of Affirmative Prayer and service. Affirmative prayer, Affirmations, Spiritual mind treatments and Denials change and renew our minds. Subsequently our life becomes transformed!

Pray affirmatively without ceasing...It Works if You Work It!

About the Author

Grace Ann Reynolds Victor is a mother of four and a grandmother. She received degrees in Science, Psychology and Social Work, at Kingsborough Community College, New York University and Stony Brook University respectively. She completed her Ministerial studies at One Spirit Interfaith seminary and University of Metaphysics, subsequently receiving Ministerial designations from both institutions. She peruses studies in Metaphysics on the Doctoral level.

The author is a Licensed Clinical Social Worker (LCSW-R) who also works in the school system as a Counselor. Licensed in the state of New York, she creates and officiates unique traditional ceremonies for weddings and other celebrations. Her work is based on her love and compassion for others, her recognition of the divinity in all people and that we all share a common bond. Knowing that we are all a part of the great harmonious whole, she embraces and enjoys supporting others to live lives of clarity, service, gratitude, elegance, opulence, peace and joy through workshops, sermons, writing and counseling. She lives in New York with her family.

Glossary

Abba— a term of endearment for the word *father*.

Affirmation—a positive statement of spiritual truth; the "yes action" of the mind.

alpha and omega—the beginning and the end.

authority—rightful power; influence, mastery, dominion.

being—fundamental nature

Bible—the sacred and inspired Scripture of the Christian religion.

bless—to invoke good upon.

consciousness—the sense of awareness or knowing the totality of one's thoughts and feelings.

Christ—Christ is the Divine man. Christ is in everyone as his potential spiritual perfection. Jesus embodied all the divine ideas of God, including the Christ Mind; therefore, he became Jesus Christ. As the only begotten Son of God, he became the Messiah or "anointed one."

compassion—a characteristic of love and mercy prompted by an understanding heart.

conscious cooperation—God creates in the ideal, while man creates in the manifest world what God has idealized.

codependent—psychologically influenced by or needing another.

decree—to command; to ordain.

demonstration—the proving of a truth principle; the manifestation of an ideal through using the creative principle of God.

denial—a relinquishment of an undesired state; the mental process of erasing from our consciousness the false beliefs of the sense of mind; opposite of affirmation.

divine mind—God's mind; the all-knowing mind.

divine order—the first law of the universe; divine arrangement.

dominion—supreme authority, sovereignty.

ego—the self-awareness of the individual; a thought form.

error—that which is untrue; a transgression.

evolution—the development man achieves through working with spiritual law.

faith—the perceiving power of the mind linked with the power to shape substance; a deep inner knowing that that which is sought is already ours for the taking.

forgive—to pardon; the giving up of something.

glory—great honor or fame, great splendor, prosperity (metaphysically—realization of divine unity).

love—devotion; adoration.

God—the Almighty One. God as principal is absolute good expressed in all creation.

gold—spiritual gifts (metaphysically).

grace—goodwill, unmerited favor, disposition to show mercy.

harmony—agreement in action

Heart—love, the affectional consciousness in man. the center from which Divine substance is poured forth.

I AM—the metaphysical name of the spiritual self; the indwelling Lord of life, love, wisdom, and all the internal ideas in divine mind.

Illumination—the light of Christ; spiritual understanding, intuitive knowing.

imagination— the faculty of mind that images and forms.

inspiration— an inflow of divine ideas.

intuition— the natural knowing capacity.

Jehovah—the great I AM; God; the Spiritual Man.

Jesus—Man of Nazareth, son of Mary, son of God, the way-shower.

Kingdom of God— the Christ consciousness.

Kingdom within— the realm in man's consciousness, where he knows and understands God.

law—the faculty of mind that holds every thought and acts strictly to the truth of being.

Law of Attraction—the law that all conditions and circumstances in affairs and body are attracted to us to accord with the thoughts we hold steadily in our consciousness.

mastery—rule; control; expert skill or knowledge.

master teacher—Jesus Christ.

meditation—focused prayer; continuous and contemplative thought; to dwell mentally on anything.

metaphysics—the systemic study of the science of being; that which transcends the physical

Mental Equivalent (Law of)—whatever is truly embodied in mind finds a corresponding objectification.

mind—God (metaphysically); the starting point of every act, thought, or feeling.

name of Jesus—spiritual understanding proves that the name of a great character carries his name potency and that whenever his name is repeated silently or audibly, his attributes become manifest. Jesus knew this, and he commanded his disciples to go forth in his name. The marvelous healing works they did in his name prove the great spiritual power present in his name

Negative---The state of consciousness that repels good and attracts its own likeness.

omnipotence—infinite power. God is infinite power, all powerful, all the power there is.

omnipresence—God is everywhere present. There is no place God is not present.

Omniscience—God is all knowing, all knowledge.

Oneness--- of the same consciousness, mind and principle.

Perfection---A state of consciousness, completely free from the shadow of negation.

prayer—the communion between God and man. Prayer is an affirmation of truth.

Prodigal (two) sons—Two departments of the soul or consciousness.

Resistance—indication of an unyielding personal will; opposition of some force

Silence—A state of consciousness entered into for the purpose of putting man in touch with the Divine mind, so that the soul may listen to The still Small Voice."

Spirit—God as the moving force of the universe.

subconscious mind—the memory mind.

References

Brother Mandus. 1959. *The Grain of Mustard Seed*. London: Fowler & Co.

Dyer, Wayne. 2004. *The Power of Intention*. Carlsbad: Hay House Inc.

Felder, Leonard. 1997. *The Ten Challenges*. New York: Harmony Books.

Ferrini, Paul. 2004. *The Laws of Love*. Greenfield: Heartways Press.

Gawain, Shakti. 1997. *The Four Levels of Healing*. Novato, CA: Nataraj Publishing.

Holliwell, Raymond. 2006. *Working with the Law*. Camarillo: DeVorrs Publications.

Holmes, Ernest, and Raymond Charles Barker. 1953. *Richer Living*. New York: Dodd, Mead and Co.

Ponder, Catherine. 2006. *Dynamic Laws of Prayer*. Camarillo-DeVorrs.

Price, John Randolph. 1987. *Prayer Principles & Power*. Austin Quartus Books.

Seale, Ervin. 1991. *The Great Prayer*. Marina del Rey: DeVorrs & Co.

Tutu, Desmond. 2005. *God Has a Dream*. New York: First Image Books.

Fillmore, Charles. 2000. The Revealing Word. Lees Summit: Unity Books.

Carlson, Nancy. 1998. I Like Me. New York: Puffin books.

Holmes, Ernest. 1991. A Dictionary of New thought terms. Marina del Rey DeVorrs.

Holmes, Ernest.1948. This Thing Called You. New York: Penguin Books.

Emerson, Ralph Waldo. 2000. The Essential writings of Ralph Waldo Emerson. New York: Random House.

Erickson, Erik H. 1997. The lifecycle completed. New York: WW Norton.

Patterson, Dorothy Kelly.1995. The Woman's Study Bible; New King James Version. Nashville: Thomas Nelson Publishers.

Additional Resources for Edification and Spiritual Development

Barker, Raymond Charles. 2005. *The Power of Decision*. Camarillo: DeVorrs.

Beckwith, Dr. Michael Bernard. 2008. *Spiritual Liberation*. New York: Atria.

Butterworth, Eric. 1994. *The Universe Is Calling*. San Francisco: Harper Collins.

Cady, Emily. n.d. *Lessons in Truth*. Unity Books.

Dyer, Wayne. 2001. *There Is a Spiritual Solution to Every Problem*. New York: Harper Collins.

Hay, Louise L. 1988. *Heal Your Body*. Carlsbad: Hay House.

Hay, Louise L. 1991. *The Power is With You*. Carlsbad: Hay House.

Hendricks, Gay and Kathlyn Hendricks. 1992. *Conscious Loving*. New York: Bantam Books.

Holmes, Ernest. 1948. *This Thing Called You*. New York: Penguin Books.

Khalsa, Dharma Singh and Cameron Stauth. 2002. *Meditation as Medicine*. New York: Fireside Books.

Kieves, Tama. 2004. *This Time I Dance! Creating the Work You Love.* New York: Tarcher/Penguin.

Kieves, Tama. 2012. Inspired & Unstoppable. Wildly Succeeding in Your Life's Work! New York: Tarcher/Penguin.

King, Dr. Barbara. 1995. *Transform Your Life.* Marina del Rey: DeVorrs.

Millman, Dan. 1995. *The Laws of Spirit.* Novato: New World Library.

Orloff, Judith. 2004. *Positive Energy.* New York: Harmony Books.

Tolle, Eckhart. 2005. *A New Earth.* New York: Plume Books.

Vanzant, Dr. Ianyla. 1998. One Day My Soul Just Opened Up. New York: Simon & Schuster Inc.

Index